Pinter's
Comic Play

Pinter's Comic Play

Elin Diamond

Lewisburg
Bucknell University Press
London and Toronto: Associated University Presses

© 1985 by Associated University Presses, Inc.

Associated University Presses
440 Forsgate Drive
Cranbury, NJ 08512

Associated University Presses
25 Sicilian Avenue
London WC1A 2QH, England

Associated University Presses
2133 Royal Windsor Drive
Unit 1
Mississauga, Ontario
Canada L5J 1K5

The paper used in this publication meets the minimum requirements of the American National Standard for Permanence of Paper for Printed Library Materials Z39.48-1984.

Library of Congress Cataloging in Publication Data

Diamond, Elin.
    Pinter's comic play.

    Bibliography: p.
    Includes index.
    1. Pinter, Harold, 1930–   —Criticism and
interpretation.   2. Comic, The, in literature.
I. Title
PR6066.I53Z627   1985   822'.914   84-45230
ISBN 0-8387-5068-0 (alk. paper)

Printed in the United States of America

To Elisa B. Diamond and
Philip H. Diamond

Contents

Acknowledgments

To Ruby Cohn I owe profound thanks for her guidance in my research and for her constant generosity and encouragement. I would not be writing these acknowledgments today without her. I am also grateful to Herbert Blau and Allen Dunn for taking time to comment on certain sections of the manuscript. To Wendy Salkind, Carol Neely, Barbara Rugen, Kristin Morrison, Deborah Bloom, Edith Warner, Barbara and Tim Carryer, my deepest gratitude for their steady support and good will during the preparation of this book. My sincere thanks to Thomas Van Laan, Chair of English, Rutgers–New Brunswick, for making departmental resources available to me, to Fred Main and the Rutgers Research Council for their timely and generous aid, and to Larry Qualls for photographic assistance. I am especially grateful to Nancy Miller who patiently, skillfully typed (and retyped) the manuscript. Finally I wish to thank my family who watched the growth and completion of this study with amazement, good humor, and love.

Permission to quote from the following works is also gratefully acknowledged:

From "The Love Song of J. Alfred Prufrock" in *Selected Poems* by T. S. Eliot. Copyright © 1930. Reprinted with permission of Harcourt Brace Jovanovich. I am grateful to *Modern Drama* for permission to borrow material from my articles:

"Pinter's *Betrayal* and the Comedy of Manners," in *Modern Drama* 23, no. 3 (September, 1980). Copyright © 1980 University of Toronto.

"Parody Play in Pinter" in *Modern Drama* 25, no. 4 (December 1982). Copyright © 1983 University of Toronto.

Introduction

> I had a pretty good notion in my earlier plays of what would shut an audience up; not so much what would make them laugh; that I had no ideas about.
>
> Harold Pinter

Exposed to his work and educated by his critics for over two decades, Harold Pinter's audiences leave the theater haunted by their own laughter. As problematic as the unexplained anxieties of Pinter's characters is the comic response such anxiety provokes. Yet Pinter's plays are in dialogue with and are energized by the literary, popular, and theatrical traditions of English comedy. As audiences we may be baffled by the unverifiable, but we respond to wordplay and clown choreography. Although Pinter denies that his characters wear labels, we can identify the nagging wife, the belligerent father, the errant son, the foolish pendant, the wily bum, the roaring cuckold—Greco-Roman types that Pinter inherits from English domestic and manners comedy. On Pinter's stage, vicious battles for dominance may be structured as music-hall routines, tensions heightened by exuberant verbal performance. Yoking metaphysical terror to comic character and action, Pinter affords us access to his plays—even as he revises the conventional uses of comedy.

Pinter's comic writing contains three recognizable, sometimes overlapping elements: the exposure of the imposter (particularly the braggart); verbal game playing; and linguistic and theatrical parody. These elements invoke conventions that the plays themselves challenge. In traditional comedy, stage imposters are unmasked, emancipated from their errors,[1] but Pinter's posers are refused such liberation. Verbal game playing, as in the dueling between wits or the gulling of the fool, usually concludes in scenes

11

of reconciliation and harmony, but Pinter admits no happy endings, and he groups his characters in ambiguous tableaux that leave
his audience in doubt as to who has succeeded and why. Pinter's
parody is also skewed, revealing not only the mocking spirit we
expect but also noncomic tensions we do not expect. If Harold
Pinter's comedy springs from traditional roots, he undercuts our
laughter even as he invites it.

Inviting and undercutting, creating an environment that is simultaneously recognizable and disturbing, this use of comedy
reflects Pinter's early interest in Kafka and Beckett but is consistently implied in his self-reflections. From his earliest speeches and
interviews, Pinter has insisted that his writing is personal, private;
that he does not understand why people go to his plays; and that he
is certainly uninterested in pleasing or amusing his audiences.[2]
One Pinter anecdote describes a letter he received from an irate
woman who wanted to know who his characters were, where they
came from, and whether they were supposed to be normal. Pinter
responded by turning the questions back on her (a maneuver his
characters use), questioning her origins, the status of her behavior.[3]
In his address to the 1962 National Student Drama Festival in
Bristol—a speech that reads like an artist's manifesto— Pinter
rejects the theater of easy communication, the traditional drama of
drawing-room chat, complicated plots, and timely resolutions.[4]
(Acting in the 1950s he knew this theater intimately). He also
rejects the assumption that characters should be straightforward
and "verifiable"—a word that for Pinter has demonic associations.
Desiring verification, an audience seeks to label characters, thus
denying their complexity.[5] Pinter then goes on to challenge the
assumption that "reality" is a "shared common ground" and that
dramatic reality can represent it truthfully. For Pinter, reality is a
"quicksand" of shifting possibilities and unstable truths in which
the present as well as the past becomes unverifiable.[6] However,
unlike Samuel Beckett whom he admires and whose influence he
acknowledges, Pinter has been unwilling to do away with the
signifiers of conventional realism. What Pinter dramatizes from
The Room to *Other Places* is the *impossibility* of verification—the
foiling of the audience's will to verify, to resolve, to label the meanings the play produces.[7] But to foil verification is to allow for the
apparently verifiable; Pinter must give the impression of a stable
reality while positing the suggestion of an unstable quicksand.
Through comedy he achieves this stability. Comic action and

character are Pinter's means of structuring his plays and of controlling audience response to them.

In a typical Pinter situation, a character seems fearful for reasons that are not revealed, yet the character's behavior is recognizably comic: an inflated posturing reminiscent of the self-justifying poser. Though we lack reasons for, say, Rose's obsession with the basement in *The Room,* we perceive her fear through her attempt at concealment. Since that attempt involves her talking incessantly to a silent husband, her fear seems to grow out of a comic situation. Is laughing at Rose or at any Pinter poser the same as assuming the detached attitude posited for the audience of comedy? To the extent that we recognize the nagging, overweening wife in the Rose-Burt interaction, our attitude imitates what laughter theorists call "superiority," a self-aggrandizement obtained at the expense of a character's foolishness.[8] On the other hand, Pinter's characters give us no information—or contradictory information—about themselves, so that we become uneasy with our responses. Stacking character confusion against audience uncertainty, Pinter places unverifiability at the center of our experience of the comic.[9]

The subtle relationship between traditional stage comedy and uneasy audience response, then, is the focus of my analyses; I identify the comic context of the work, then follow play action as we experience it in the theater. My intention is to investigate Pinter's manipulation of traditional comedy as a means of positioning and ultimately destabilizing his audience. To this end, the theories of Henri Bergson and Sigmund Freud offer useful pointers. Specifically Bergson's "mechanical encrusted on the living" accounts for the absentmindedness and rigidity in the language and behavior of Pinter's early characters.[10] Freud's "tendentious" joke, which permits us to economize on inhibition and release aggression, accounts for the pleasure of the "third party"—in this case, the playwright's audience. We delight in the "effortless satisfaction" of our own aggressive tendencies as we witness comic combat on Pinter's stage.[11]

No study of Pinter's humor can ignore the traditional elements in his verbal comedy. As a young man Pinter studied, acted, and wrote about Shakespeare and may have been shaped by Shakespeare's comic word-world—the satire on love rhetoric in *Love's Labor's Lost;* Parolles' verbal posing in *All's Well;* Hal and Falstaff's parodies of court pomp in *Henry IV, Part 1*—as well as by the wordplay that explodes sentimentality in the love comedies and intensifies the dark mood of the tragedies. As an actor Pinter played Iago and no doubt savored the comedy of malice.[12] The Vice's wit, his comic invention in the presence of spectators, may have inspired Pinter's own con artists—Goldberg, Mick, Lenny, and Spooner. Repertory actor before turning playwright, Pinter was well acquainted with stock drawing-room types, and through parody he both mocks and celebrates their diction. Across the canon, Pinter exploits the traditional comic verbal devices of repetition, tautology, and lopsided logic; to these he adds exuberant comic solos as well as parodies of technical jargon and clichés, of music-hall monologues and interrogation routines.

My chapter on "Posers and Losers" opens this study by analyzing Pinter's use of the traditional comic imposter in four early works. "The Parody Plays" treats Pinter's ironic play on the styles and techniques of theater, film, and television, three media for which he writes. "Playing on the Past" explores Pinter's works of the 1970s, as they absorb and extend earlier methods. These categories are not mutually exclusive—posers are a favorite type and parody can be found in nearly all the plays—but they nevertheless isolate specific strategies in Pinter's comedy. Each play analysis contains a consideration of comic language, and a brief discussion of verbal comedy in two plays from *Other Places* closes the study.

By scrutinizing the comic in Pinter's drama, we develop, I think, a new perspective on the familiar Pinterian themes of menacing intrusion, dominance and subservience, sexual and territorial combat. In every play, Pinter sets up situations that involve his characters in power struggles, but he refuses to supply motivations for either the situations or the struggle. Instead, he borrows conventions from traditional comedy that discourage motive hunting. Imposters are conventionally self-deluding and boastful, motivated only to perform their imposture for an audience. Game players are conventionally clever and devious, self-expressive only in game maneuvers.[13] Verifying the motives of a comic character seems gratuitous since comic convention itself supplies the motives. And yet the behavior that gives the lie to motive hunting is deceptive; we are never comfortable with our responses to Pinter's comedy but are forced again and again to revise our perceptions. Identification of the traditionally comic elements in his drama helps to clarify the tense struggles Pinter orchestrates for his characters and the subtle traps he lays for us.

Pinter's
Comic Play

1

Posers and Losers

Questioned in an interview about the double-edged humor in his plays, Harold Pinter replied:

> I'm rarely consciously writing humor, but sometimes I find myself laughing at some particular point which has suddenly struck me as being funny . . . more often than not the speech only seems to be funny—the man is actually fighting a battle for his life.[1]

"Seems to be funny" smacks of after-the-fact criticism, an uncharacteristic position for a writer who concerns himself with the second-by-second experience of his plays—what happens "when the curtain goes up and we are faced with a situation . . . which is just happening at this moment."[2] In the theater an audience does not *seem* to laugh. If the situation strikes us as funny, we, like Pinter, find ourselves laughing. Yet Pinter's comment lends insight into the prickly atmosphere that surrounds our laughter. Incongruously, characters fighting for their lives contribute to comic situations. Incongruously, we laugh though we hear the desperation in their voices and sense their internal struggle.

Written within two years of one another, *The Room, The Birthday Party, A Slight Ache*, and *The Caretaker* are Pinter's "room" plays, in which intruders threaten the security of room dwellers. Why the protagonists need security and why the intruders constitute a threat are motivational details Pinter refuses to supply. Instead, the protagonists' frantic attempts to protect their secure positions (in Davies's case, to gain a secure position) provide the dramatic focus of the plays. As a means of controlling their worlds, Rose, Edward, Stanley, and Davies adopt poses of strength; for each change is fearful, yet change proves inevitable. In a program insert to the first Royal Court production of *The Room* and *The Dumb Waiter*, written after completing the four plays I discuss in this chapter, Pinter commented on the fatalistic direction of the action. "Given a man in a room and he will sooner or later receive a visitor."[3] Confrontations between room dwellers and intruders change and ultimately destroy the security of rooms, yet the process of destruction is comic. Why?

Discussing the action of *The Room,* Pinter pinpoints the terror but also indicates the comedy in Rose's situation:

> This old woman is living in a room which, she is convinced, is the best in the house, and she refuses to know anything about the basement downstairs. She says it's damp and nasty, and the world outside is cold and icy, and that in her warm and comfortable room her security is complete. But, of course, it isn't; an intruder comes to upset the balance of everything, in other words points to the delusion on which she is basing her life.[4]

Oddly, this analysis ignores both Rose's obsession with the basement room and her quasi-mystical attachment to Riley. Instead, Pinter assumes the stance of a traditional comic dramatist who exposes the folly, the "delusion," of an antisocial character.[5] What destroys Rose is not the intruder but rather her voluble and misguided insistence that the security of her room (and, by implication, her life) is complete.

With their aggressive verbalizing, Pinter's posers bear a family resemblance to the traditional comic imposter or *alazon* who intrudes on the feast of the hero by claiming, without merit, a share of the reward.[6] Of all Pinter's early protagonists, only Davies is actually an intruder: Rose, Edward, and Stanley are imposters of a different sort, sufferers of the "delusion" that their worlds are secure. This delusion is represented as an incongruous combination of posturing and terror: that is, their *alazon* behavior consists in what Daniel C. Boughner calls the contrast between "verbal defiance and abject fear . . . in the face of danger."[7] Thus we laugh at Rose's noisy attacks on the blind Riley in *The Room:* "I'm one ahead of people like you"; and at Edward's glib gibes at the speechless Matchseller in *A Slight Ache:* "You must excuse my chatting away like this." Stanley's attempt at verbal defiance in *The Birthday Party* is made ludicrous by Goldberg's menacing exuberance; and Davies of *The Caretaker* reinacts a clownish parody of the braggart soldier, his boasting threats undermined by his feeble knife and his terror at being chased by an electrolux. Unlike their comic predecessors, however, Pinter's posers suffer a grotesque exposure. Rose is blinded, Edward and Stanley are destroyed, and

Davies is pushed toward destruction. In Pinter's revision of traditional comic closure (particularly in drama featuring the *alazon*), posers become abject losers.

Our response to Pinter's tense comedy can be linked to Pinter's own sense of the incongruous. Discussing his first "dramatic image," the event that inspired *The Room,* Pinter recalls:

> I saw two men in a small room. The smaller of the two, a little barefooted man, was carrying on a lively and rather literate conversation, and at the table next to him sat an enormous lorry driver. He had his cap on and never spoke a word. And all the while, as he talked, the little man was feeding the big man—cutting his bread, buttering it and so on. Well, this image would never leave me.[8]

While an immediate result of "this image" would seem to be the silence of Bert in contrast to the garrulity of Rose as she feeds him, another effect is present: the dizzying imbalance in Pinter's experience of the event. A silent big man eats mechanically while a little man, chattering, feeds him. Pinter's description is restrained, but we understand that his own perspective created the incongruity; he found the two men unusual, yet they did not regard themselves as strange. Significantly, Pinter gives neither a past for these two nor verification for his impressions. The image stayed with him because neither was obtainable.

The scene that inspired *The Birthday Party* suggests a similar disjunction. In his interview with Lawrence Bensky, Pinter quotes from a letter he had written to a friend:

> I have filthy insane digs, a great bulging scrag of a woman with breasts rolling at her belly, an obscene household, cats, dogs, filth, teastrainers, mess, oh bullocks, talk, chat rubbish shit scratch dung poison, infantility, deficient order in the upper fretwork, fucking roll on. . . . [He goes on] Now the thing about this is *that* was *The Birthday Party*— I was in those digs, and this woman was Meg in the play, and there was a fellow staying there in Eastbourne, on the coast. The whole thing remained with me, and three years later I wrote the play.[9]

Again, incongruity forms Pinter's impressions—the messy bawd of a landlady and her boarder, and the playwright in their reality but acutely outside of it.

These incongruous collisions become dramatic problems that Pinter works out through his poser-protagonists. All suffer, to varying degrees, from perceptual conflicts. Rose fears the "black dark" because it cannot be reconciled with her warm, lighted room. The

Matchseller's incomprehensible presence at the back gate shakes
Edward's well-insulated existence; Stanley's mind crumbles at his
Kafkaesque birthday party where his attackers befriend his protectors; and the precarious, shifting alliances between Mick, Davies,
and Aston confuse all parties, for no individual reality is reconcil-
able with another. Identities also blur: Rose and Edward confront
cipherlike characters with whom they partially merge, and antago-
nisms in *The Birthday Party* and *The Caretaker* are confused by
similarities between the antagonists.[10] Such existential incongruities subvert the traditional comic catharsis in which audience
and characters learn or "see" the truth—blindness, emotional and/
or physical, works thematically throughout all four plays. In Pinter's words, reality becomes unstable ground, "like a quicksand,"[11]
and by the final curtain, his posers are profoundly displaced persons.

For the audience Pinter's comic situation is a "structuring moment,"[12] recognizable and identifiable. But as reality becomes distorted for the characters, our vision also suffers. We see them
alternately as victims and victimizers, now the butt of a joke, now
the perpetrator. Pinter's comedy, then, is inseparable from audience discomfort. Wanting us to experience the perceptual incongruities that he himself felt when he walked into a room and found
a little man feeding a big man, Pinter provides no past history to
explain the tensions we encounter in present time. Scanty biographical information arrives in disconnected fragments and is always unverifiable; yet since we meet tensions *in medias res,* and
since we almost immediately witness extravagant comic posturing
in response to those tensions, we assume that a critical problem
exists, unresolved, in the past. Playing on that assumption, Pinter
invites us to laugh as his poser-protagonists but never to boast of
our superiority. Their comic struggles to maintain the status quo
supply our only information about the status quo. As the comic
mood darkens, our awareness of the characters deepens but not
our understanding of their gnawing terrors. Courting our laughter
in spite of and because of the characters' fear, Pinter makes us
accomplices in their destruction and victims of the discontinuities
that bring about their destruction.

THE ROOM

Describing the manner in which he was first signed by an agent,
Pinter recalled that he and a friend read *The Room* aloud and that

the agent "laughed a good deal and two days later wrote to me suggesting that he represent me."[13] Whatever else the agent saw in *The Room*, he appreciated its comedy. Pinter's critics on the other hand have emphasized Rose's pathos,[14] the room-womb symbolism,[15] the play's seemingly deliberate mystification, and Pinter's genius for creating an atmosphere of growing menace.[16] Rose herself provokes contradictory responses. Esslin finds her "motherly, sentimental";[17] Gordon calls her "over-protective" and "castrating";[18] for Quigley "she is ambivalent about her role and life in 'the room.'"[19] In Esslin's view Rose is a victim, in Gordon's a victimizer; in Quigley's view she suffers an existential crisis. In fact, Rose Hudd encompasses all three views. She is increasingly plagued by perceptual discontinuities and is forced to accept her contingent status in a world she wants to believe is secure. But while the play moves suggestively toward the final catastrophe, Pinter detours us into comic forays in which Rose alternates between victim and victimizer; Pinter encourages our laughter even as he weaves a pattern of fear.

One detour begins with the main character whose rambling monologue opens *The Room*. It is Pinter's method initially to diminish the importance of Rose's feelings by diminishing Rose herself. Talking to—and at—a silent Bert, Rose is branded a comic type, the nagging wife; his nose buried in a magazine, Bert acts the necessary supporting role of henpecked husband. Ionesco uses the same image in the opening scene of *The Bald Soprano* but relieves the oddity of Mrs. Smith's nonnaturalistic monologue with Mr. Smith's tongue clicking and, finally, his interruption. Pinter's comedy provokes greater tension: Bert never speaks, though Pinter designates pauses where he *might* respond. What strikes us as incongruous is that Rose talks on about Bert's illness, Bert's food, and Bert's driving, but never about Bert's silence. Instead her speech accommodates his silence:

> Anyway, I haven't been out. I haven't been so well. I didn't feel up to it. Still, I'm much better today. I don't know whether you ought to go out. I mean, you shouldn't, straight after you've been laid up. Still. Don't worry, Bert. You go. You won't be long.[20]

> (p. 102)

Rose's "anyway" bridges the gap between bits of unrelated matter; her "still" indicates a transition, allowing her to converse with herself.

In this monologue, Pinter lays the groundwork for his comic

strategy: Rose's hermetic and incoherent speech style establishes a
familiar comic situation—marital apathy at the breakfast table—
but the content reveals a peculiarity, namely, her obsession with
security. Rose's first line, "Here you are. This'll keep the cold out"
(p. 101), creates an immediate tension between the warm interior
(including the "hereness" of Bert) and the cold exterior (the foreign
"thereness" of the world outside). The tension is extended in the
contrast between two rooms: Rose's cozy, warm, lighted room and
the cold, dark, forbidding basement. Pinter offers no explanation
for Rose's fear of the basement but clearly establishes its symbolic
power. The fact that someone might live there ("I think someone
else has gone in now" [p. 102]) defies the logic of her world, for the
walls "were running" (p. 102) and "the ceiling right on top of you"
(p. 105) the last time she looked in. With ludicrous bravado she
tells Bert, "You've got a chance in a place like this" (p. 105), suggesting a threatening aspect to the basement room where, she
implies, they would not have a chance. In contrast to Bert's silence, Rose's harangue exemplifies what Henri Bergson in *Laughter (Le Rire)* called "absentmindedness";[21] her repetitious verbal
gestures are as mechanical as the action of pouring Bert's tea or
buttering his toast.

    With Mr. Kidd's arrival, comedy broadens and Rose's perceptual
problems begin.

> *A knock at the door. She [ROSE] stands.*
> ROSE: Who is it?
> *Pause.*
>   Hello!
> *Knock repeated.*
>   Come in then.
> *Knock repeated.*
>   Who is it—
> *Pause. The door opens and* MR. KIDD *comes in.*
> MR. KIDD: I knocked.
> ROSE: I heard you.
> MR. KIDD: Eh?
>
>   (p. 105)

After an entrance like this, it would be difficult to take Mr. Kidd
seriously. In everyday life we suppress the urge to laugh at
deafness or senility, but in the theater such handicaps are grist for
gags. Feydeau uses speech impediments to concoct misunder-
standings, and Joe Orton's grisly farces mock a variety of physical

ills, from old age to gunshot wounds. Pinter's Mr. Kidd, however, is as much the jokester as the butt. Responding to Rose's question about the cleaning woman, Mr. Kidd refers slyly to the "woman round the corner" (p. 106). He remembers his sister and her lovely boudoir but coyly refuses to state the cause of her death.

Mr. Kidd's "memories" also loosen Rose's grip on past and present, time and space. Cheerfully he misremembers which chair belongs to Rose, but he recalls that her room was once his bedroom. He mystifies the spatial configuration of the building, claiming not to know how many floors it contains. At one point he implies that the house is empty; later he says it is "packed out" (p. 109). Mr. Kidd's banter suggests an other-dimensionality that tilts toward absurdity, but the comedy is double-edged. Blocked communication tends to isolate Rose, and her unanswered queries create an atmosphere of anxiety and tension.

Bert leaves. Alone in the room, Rose nervously fetches a bin, opens the door—two strangers on the landing stare back at her. Rose's shocked "Oh!" illustrates Pinter's "Hitchcock alertness,"[22] but he may have been inspired by a scene closer to his own experience. As a repertory actor, Pinter played in Agatha Christie's *Love from a Stranger*[23] in which a woman, learning that her husband is a murderer, takes advantage of his leaving: she *"snatches her coat from the banisters and runs wildly across to the front door and opens it. [Her husband] is standing there."*[24] Rose's shock titillates us all the more because she is not running wildly but performing a mundane action. We recall the gothic storm scene in *Wuthering Heights* when Lockwood reaches out to latch a window and feels a small, chilly hand grasp his; or, in a slapstick setting, when Abbott and Costello roam through a house of gadgety horrors and discover a corpse behind revolving bookshelves. "The world," says Pinter, "is full of surprises."[25] In this case the aftereffects are benign. Instead of splitting Rose's skull with a hatchet, Mrs. Sands merely says: "So sorry, we didn't mean to be standing here, like. Didn't mean to give you a fright" (p. 111). For Rose, however, being surprised is the antithesis of being in control. Despite Mrs. Sands's assurances, Pinter has now altered our perspective on the room. It protects Rose from an icy exterior but leaves her vulnerable to intruders.

The other-dimensionality of the Sandses' discourse extends the comedy of the previous scene. As Mr. Kidd's memory about the chairs conflicts with Rose's, the Sandses' landlord is someone other than Rose's Mr. Kidd. As Mr. Kidd's ludicrous reveries confuse and exclude Rose, Mr. and Mrs. Sands' bickering about whether or not he sat down, whether or not she saw a star, relegates Rose to the periphery of the action. Gradually the couple take over Rose's room, and their total disregard for her feelings is as incongruous as their disputes. Like Mr. Kidd, the Sandses are appropriately named, for they transform the "shared common ground" of Rose's reality into a "quicksand" of uncertainty.[26]

More than Mr. Kidd, the Sandses call attention to Rose's ignorance of the house and by implication her isolation in the room.

MR. SANDS:	He [the landlord] lives here, does he?
ROSE:	Of course he lives here.
MR. SANDS:	And you say he's the landlord, is he?
ROSE:	Of course he is.
MR. SANDS:	Well, say I wanted to get hold of him, where would I find him?
ROSE:	Well—I'm not sure.
MR. SANDS:	He lives here, does he?
ROSE:	Yes, but I don't know—
MR. SANDS:	You don't know exactly where he hangs out?
ROSE:	No, not exactly.
MR. SANDS:	But he does live here, doesn't he?
	Pause.

(pp. 114–15)

Mr. Sands's arch insistent repetitions of "does he?" and "is he?" exacerbates the uncertainty Rose tries to conceal. This dialogue is the prototype of the notorious Pinter interrogation, the issue being not whether Rose knows the landlord but whether Mr. Sands can bully her into silence. Ironically, it is Mrs. Sands who shatters Rose's calm:

Yes, I felt a bit of damp when we were in the basement just now.

(p. 115)

At this point—the basement mentioned—Pinter fully exploits the comic potential of conflicting perspectives.[27] On the one hand, we are familiar with Rose's obsessions and know that her terror will grow with this chatty revelation. On the other hand, Pinter draws attention to the Sandses' history; returning to an issue from *their* first moments on stage, the couple argue about Mr. Sands's refusal to sit down. The two perspectives converge in consecutive lines of dialogue:

MR. SANDS: Yes, there was a bloke down there, all right.
                He perches on the table.
MRS. SANDS: You're sitting down!

The argument continues:

MR. SANDS *(jumping up):* Who is?
MRS. SANDS: You were.
MR. SANDS: Don't be silly. I perched.
MRS. SANDS: I saw you sit down.
MR. SANDS: You did not see me sit down because I did not sit bloody
              well down. I perched.

                                               (p. 116)

Who was the man in the basement? Did Mr. Sands sit or perch?

Through the rapid change in subject, Pinter forces the audience to give the questions equal weight. Of course they are not equal: the first bears heavily on Rose's psychic unease because it confirms her worst suspicions, and the second seems too ludicrous to consider. For Mr. and Mrs. Sands, however, sitting or perching is part of a series of moves in a game of dominance. Since Mr. Sands's method of playing is simply to insist on his point of view ("I'm telling you you didn't see a star" [p. 114]), Mrs. Sands must score points when she can; she must catch him sitting after he said he would stand. The ironic result of their quarrel is that Rose must interrupt to ask about that which frightens her most: "You say you saw a man downstairs, in the basement?" (p. 116).

Almost immediately the two parties reverse positions. After Mrs. Sands's highly graphic speech describing the circumstances of the strange man behind the partition, Rose suddenly turns our focus to a discrepancy in Mrs. Sands's account and tries to pinpoint the couple, as she did Mr. Kidd, in time and space:

ROSE: You said you were going up?
MRS. SANDS: What?
ROSE: You said you were going up before.
MRS. SANDS: No, we were coming down.
ROSE: You didn't say that before.

                                 (pp. 117–18)

This is true, though neither reader nor spectator will remember. Pinter now places us at the vortex of the confusion. *Our* memories of the past are insufficient to corroborate or deny the characters' opinions. Moreover, our superior sense of Rose's discomfort during Mrs. Sands's narration is canceled by Rose herself. Her fears were not gratuitous; there is someone in the basement and, according to Mr. Sands, he is prepared to rent out her room. With this revelation, past actions, including a simple question of logistics (were the couple going up or coming down?) take on a nightmarish fluidity. The present, the reality of the room itself, is divested of its tranquillity. After a perfunctory knock, Mr. Kidd rushes in without waiting to be asked.

At his entrance, Pinter employs the comic device of cross-purpose dialogue, thus reinforcing the pattern of conflicting perspectives. Mr. Kidd sputters about a future meeting while Rose insists on clarifying the past. Their disjunction undermines the strong posture Rose assumed seconds earlier: we see her struggling to make herself understood, and that struggle, perversely, involves her in a comic routine. When they finally agree on the topic of conversation, Rose takes a position that is decidedly laughable:

MR. KIDD: Shall I tell him it's all right?
ROSE: That what's all right?
MR. KIDD: That you'll see him.
ROSE: See him? I beg your pardon, Mr. Kidd. I don't know him. Why should I see him?
MR. KIDD: You won't see him?
ROSE: Do you expect me to see someone I don't know? With my husband not here too?

                                                                    (p. 120)

Her married woman's propriety impugned, Rose now joins the ranks of stock comic wives from Lady Fidget to Lady Bracknell, whose social poses protect against scandal.

The sexual allusion to Riley contrasts comically with his appearance when he enters, seconds later, blind and ragged. Pinter himself would have preferred less mystification: "I don't think there's anything radically wrong with the character in himself, but he behaves too differently from the other characters: if I were writing the play now, I'd make him sit down, have a cup of tea."[28] This retrospective view sounds disingenuous. Would Rose have offered him a cup of tea? Precursor of the hysterical Davies (*The Caretaker*), Rose excoriates Riley for ruining her evening, slandering her, and "stink[ing] the place out" (p. 123). Her hectoring invective directed at a blind motionless man is, in the Freudian sense, comically incongruous, a ludicrous overexpenditure of emotion and energy; yet her language attests to the enormity of her panic.

The ensuing dialogue between Rose and Riley, impossible to justify rationally, nevertheless culminates Pinter's strategy in *The Room*. We have noted how other perspectives, introduced by each visitor, erode Rose's security—Mr. Kidd by his vagueness, Mr. and Mrs. Sands by their disturbing mixture of narrative, argument, and attack. Riley now alters irrevocably Rose's points of reference: he replaces "room" with "home," replaces Rose's former reality with the "here" and "now" of their interaction, replaces Rose with another entity whom he calls Sal. Their dialogue sounds like an intimate code:

ROSE: I've been here.
RILEY: Yes.
ROSE: Long.
RILEY: Yes.
ROSE: The day is a hump. I never go out.
RILEY: No.
ROSE: I've been here.
RILEY: Come home now, Sal.

(p. 125)

The present perfect in Rose's lines suggests a relinquishing of the recent past, a preparation for departure. Instead of the formless circumlocutions she directs at Bert, the nervous evasions she uses with Mr. Kidd and the Sandses, and in contrast to the vulgarisms she first screams at Riley, Rose brings to this dialogue complete reciprocity of diction and emotional register. Exposing Rose as an imposter, Riley verbally "touches" Sal, and Rose/Sal concretizes their rapport by caressing his eyes and head.

Bert's fast entrance transforms the scene into ludicrous farce— the cuckold's discovery of wife and lover. But the surreal mood prevails, for when Bert announces, "I got back all right" (p. 125), the audience wonders where he has got back to. After Rose's verbal intimacy with Riley, the room seems more shadow than substance, and she is suspended in time. In reaction Bert concentrates on images of space; with violent action verbs, he retraces his movements from departure to return, attempting to impose *his* perspective on the events taking place:

BERT: I caned her [his van] along. She was good. Then I got back. I could see the road all right. There was no cars. One there was.

> He wouldn't move. I bumped him. I got my road . . . I go where
> I go. She took me. she brought me back. [ellipses mine]
>
> (p. 126)

But he is too late. Kicking Riley's head against the stove, Bert merely intensifies Rose's absorption in Riley's world; through blindness she takes on his identity and symbolically follows him "home."

Rose's sudden blinding is, of course, Pinter's ultimate shock technique, as startling as the Sandses' appearance on the landing but much more potent. In one sense, the logic of the blinding is irresistible. Rose's pose of strength, based on the insistence that she is secure in her room, is a form of self-deception that she "sees" (through the agency of Riley) only by going blind. Because she refuses to accept her contingent status in the world, Rose is brought to this final incapacitation. However, such a conclusion assumes a strict fatality to the action and ignores Pinter's *comic* logic in the play. Throughout *The Room*, Pinter has continually toyed with our perceptions, not only by disseminating slowly and suspensefully fragments of information about the basement, but by disseminating that information through comic situations that alternately mock and corroborate Rose.

Image patterns in *The Room* further complicate our perspective. Ironically, the characters who challenge Rose's security in the room also verify the perception on which that security rests: the warm, lighted room versus the cold, dark world. Mr. Sands, the least sympathic toward Rose, attests to the danger outside: "It'd be a bit dodgy driving tonight" (p. 114), and Mr. Kidd at his second entrance seems as obsessed with the "black dark" as Rose herself. Mrs. Sands (her name, Clarissa, suggests brightness) affirms that Rose's room offered "the first bit of light" (p. 113). However, the dichotomy between warm/light and cold/dark eventually collapses; the comedy in *The Room* arises from the fact that no character consistently verifies the perceptions of another.

The ludicrous argument about whether Mr. Sands sat or perched and Mr. Sands's rude emphasis on "perceive" raises the question of how we label our perceptions of others and how we ourselves are labeled. Pinter will explore this issue in later plays (see, for example, *Old Times*); in the poser-loser plays he explores the unverifiability of the labels with which we establish our primary relationship to the world: our names. When Mrs. Sands remarks that her parents "gave" her her name, she draws attention to the arbitrariness of social labels, and when Mr. Sands repeatedly forgets Rose's name, he implies that she may be an imposter. Rose herself refuses to believe that a blind black man could be named Riley, but her own name offers no guarantee of security or credibility. When Riley renames her "Sal," she is dislodged from her temporal and spatial moorings; moreover, the behavior of "Sal" provokes Bert to violence and condemns Rose to permanent blindness in the darkness she fears.

Finally the issue of labeling perception confronts the audience. While we respond to Rose's comic posing and understand that her noisy self-delusions isolate her from the world, we are unable to lay claim to a wider field of perception. The comic process of destabilizing Rose has made it impossible for us to assume a stable position for ourselves. Pinter reminds us of our bafflement at the close of *The Room:* after his protagonist's sudden blinding, he calls for a "*sudden blackout,*" creating a "black dark" that links us symbolically to Rose.

A SLIGHT ACHE

In Rose's meager enclosure, menace lurks not only in the "black dark" but in seemingly mundane encounters with strangers who disorient her in space and time. Edward, at the outset of *A Slight Ache,* appears to be better insulated. With a book-filled study, ample garden, and attentive wife, Edward epitomizes the gentleman scholar dwelling in privileged privacy on his country estate. Yet in spite of—or because of—these trappings, Edward falls from his secure position, and Pinter choreographs the fall with an artful use of comic devices. Edward's pomposity recalls the "learned scholar" type (derived from the *alazon,* or imposter) whose self-flattering pose begs for comic exposure. More to the point, Pinter gives Edward scholarly mastery of "the dimensionality and continuity of space . . . and time," even as the play dramatizes his psychic disorientation in space and time. Put in terms of the comic character's traditional flaw, Edward's attainment of abstruse knowledge disguises his lack of self-knowledge. The Matchseller, Edward's antagonist in *A Slight Ache,* initiates comic tension. Speechless, nameless, nearly motionless, the Matchseller is more obscure even than Riley, for he claims no hold on Edward, no knowledge of his past. Nonexistent in the original radio version of the play, the Matchseller serves a comic function in the theater as an emblem of poverty in contrast to Edward's wealth. By lengthening the distance between Edward and the Matchseller, Pinter exploits the structure of comic inversion—the beggar changes places with the rich man. An unlikely participant in a mock adultery, the ragged Matchseller upsets Edward's mental equilibrium and usurps his position in marriage and home.

The reason for Edward's obsession with the Matchseller is unknown and unknowable, but Pinter supplies clues that might form the plot of a more realistic play. Edward's wife Flora reveals that she was raped by a red-bearded poacher and immediately connects the Matchseller with that man. In his turn, Edward remembers the flaming red hair of Fanny, the squire's daughter, and later asserts that the Matchseller disgusts him as forcibly as this same Fanny. But Fanny is also a "flower" (p. 183),[29] and Edward's wife Flora used to have "flaming red hair" (p. 184). Is the Matchseller the very man or perhaps the symbol of the shared memory that has haunted Edward and Flora throughout their marriage?

Since Pinter ridicules Edward and Flora's marriage, the melodramatic tone of such questions clashes with the mood of *A Slight Ache*. References to "red hair" and "red beard" resemble references to Rose's home with Riley in *The Room*—fragments of plot that raise dramatic tension but themselves lead nowhere. More crucial to Pinter is the conflict between a protagonist who is "unreliable, elusive, evasive"[30] and a silent antagonist.

Two of Pinter's short prose pieces, "The Examination" (1965) and "Problem" (1976),[31] rehearse the issues of *A Slight Ache*; both contain narrator-monologuists whose self-assured bravura gives way to controlled panic as they confront and are ultimately replaced by a silent other.[32] Unable to follow "the courses" of Kullus's silence, the examiner of the first story ends by being examined; his room becomes Kullus's room. The narrator of "Problem" meets an anonymous telephone caller silence for silence until the telephone itself stops functioning. Forced to leave his home (symbolically ceding territory), he calls and finds his number engaged. Drily he concludes: "Someone is trying to do me in." In *Monologue* (1973), the stage image comments on the situation in the short stories. Protesting too much his physical and intellectual prowess, Man speaks to an empty chair, symbol of an absent rival who has replaced him in the affections of a woman they both loved. In the two stories and the short drama, the audience is persuaded to view the situations ironically. Behind the inflated, muscular language we sense palpitations, inferiority incipient in claims of superiority.

Against their will, these minor Pinter protagonists resemble Rose inasmuch as they became identified with their silent antagonists. Calling home from a phone booth, the narrator of "Problem" not only renounces his position, he assumes the behavior and perspective of his antagonist. The narrator of "The Examination" errs similarly: certain of Kullus's "participation," the examiner grants intervals of silence that he takes to be distinct from the natural lapses of interrogation. But Kullus deliberately "deepen[s] the intensity" of these intervals, "taking courses" impossible for the examiner to follow, and "when I could no longer follow him . . . I was no longer his dominant." Gradually Kullus extends the silences outside the examination to those silent lapses within it. Pursuing Kullus "from silence to silence," the examiner is forced to enter Kullus's perspective ("Kullus" contains "skull"), thus abdicating his own. Concurrently, the room reverts to Kullus's control, and he rearranges curtains, stool, and blackboard. With morose insight, Man of *Monologue* sums up these situations: "The ones that keep silent are best off."

Edward, like these Pinter protagonists, considers himself "naturally dominant"; unlike them, his loss of dominance is played out comically in duologues with the Matchseller and Flora. Fearing silence, Edward compensates with noisy, self-aggrandizing attacks and a ludicrous pose of condescension so that we experience the quality of silence Pinter describes in "Writing for the Theatre": that silence covered by "a torrent of language, the violent, sly, anguished or mocking smoke screen" that gives "an indication of that which we don't hear."[33] In this former radio play, language structures action with a rare intensity, charting a one-act journey through comedy to catastrophe.

The play's opening locates the audience on the familiar territory of English drawing-room comedy. "EDWARD *and* FLORA *are discovered sitting at the breakfast table*," like countless couples from Sheridan to Coward. He buries his nose in the newspaper, while she chirps about the garden and lovely weather, and pours out the tea. As Flora discusses the honeysuckle, convolvulus, and japonica, Edward responds with a ludicrous comic petulance:

I don't see why I should be expected to distinguish between these plants. It's not my job.

(p. 170)

Stalking the wasp, he assumes another comic posture, that of the
self-absorbed happy eccentric and Flora is left with the straight-
man role.

EDWARD: Cover the marmalade.
FLORA: What?
EDWARD: Cover the pot. There's a wasp. *(He puts the paper down on
          the table.)* Don't move. Keep still. What are you doing?
FLORA: Covering the pot.
EDWARD: Don't move. Leave it. Keep still.
          (Pause.)
          Give me the "Telegraph."
FLORA: Don't hit it. It'll bite.
EDWARD: Bite? What do you mean, bite? Keep still.
          (Pause).
          It's landing.
FLORA: It's going in the pot.
EDWARD: Give me the lid.
FLORA: It's in.
EDWARD: Give me the lid.
FLORA: I'll do it.
EDWARD: Give it to me! Now . . . slowly . . .
FLORA: What are you doing?
EDWARD: Be quiet. Slowly . . . carefully . . . on . . . the . . . pot! Ha-ha-
          ha. Very good.
              He sits on a chair to the right of the table.
FLORA: Now he's in the marmalade.
EDWARD: Precisely.

                                                              (p. 171)

"Precisely"—that is, Edward, changes plans midway and neglects
to inform Flora, who mistakes his meaning, not through ignorance,
but because she proceeds according to a different logic: the wasp,
Edward implied, should be kept out of the marmalade.

Edward's genteel sadism—scalding and "blinding" the wasp,
then smashing it with a spoon—establishes his personality as a
comic poser. Politeness conceals cruelty; actions belie stated intentions. Apparently there will be no connection between what Edward says and what he feels. Needing to control, Edward will use
language to create the illusion that he does control. Comic in itself,
the wasp-killing episode contains darker elements. Drawing our
attention to the marmalade jar (the wasp trapped and buzzing
inside), Pinter suddenly alters our focus. Flora asks: "Have you got
something in your eyes?" (p. 172). Edward's "slight ache" has no

apparent cause and the phrase itself is maddeningly unspecific. But we are unable to probe further; the wasp tries to crawl out the spoon-hole and the "killing" resumes. Edward's slight ache nevertheless raises the possibility of potential incapacity as his comic behavior conceals—or, as Freud would say, displaces—aggressive tendencies.[34]

The wasp dead, the focus shifts to another annoying creature, the Matchseller, and three changes occur immediately: Edward's pose of strength shows signs of faltering; the gap widens between Edward and Flora's perception of events; and the tranquillity of the present is invaded by considerations of a past event—the exact time of the old man's arrival at the back gate. In one short speech Edward presents us with a new perspective on his existence:

> It *used* to give me great pleasure, such pleasure, to stroll along through the long grass, out through the back gate, pass into the lane. That pleasure is *now* denied me. It's my own house, isn't it? It's my own gate. [emphasis mine]
>
> (pp. 175–76)

Assonance in the line "stroll along through the long grass" underscores Edward's "great pleasure" in space and nature, now "denied" him by the Matchseller's presence. Momentarily Edward replaces the clipped, mannered speech of the drawing room, where his authority is assured, with a plaintive expressiveness. Flora's speech, however, remains prosaic. That she has trouble "understanding" Edward is consistent with her straight-man role during the wasp killing; she supplies responses that conform realistically to the logic of the situation: an old man should not prevent egress from the garden; old men are "harmless" (p. 176).

Seen next rummaging for notes in the scullery, Edward reveals his professional interest in the "dimensionality and continuity of space . . . and time." At this point the audience may equate Edward's pedantry with a comic pose that will soon be punctured, but Pinter also uses the phrase to comment reflexively on the action. In *A Slight Ache*, more explicitly than in *The Room*, the problem of space and time penetrates the characters' thinking, blocks out the action, and gives rise to many of the play's comic situations. For example, space dominates the first exchanges and reinforces the personality differences between Edward and Flora: she knows the exact location of the flowers, while he plays ignorant; he, on the other hand, choreographs the movements of the wasp into the

marmalade and finds the exact angle at which to pour hot water
down the spoon-hole. Flora and Edward's references to time are
few but revealing:

> FLORA: Do you know what today is?
> EDWARD: Saturday.
> FLORA: It's the longest day of the year.
> EDWARD: Really?
> FLORA: It's the height of summer today.
> EDWARD: Cover the marmalade.
>
> (pp. 170–71)

Intuitively Flora merges time and space. Playing on the words
"longest" and "height," she gives Saturday spatial *and* temporal
emphasis. Edward refuses her expansiveness by forcing the focus
down to the wasp's movements along the rim of the jar. The quick
change in subject is surprising and funny. It also reveals the nar-
rowness of Edward's perspective; his focus on the wasp excludes
not only the garden but the day as well.

Nevertheless, the wasp provokes Edward's first reference to
time: "Curious, but I don't remember seeing any wasps at all, all
summer, until now." He kills the wasp, removing all ambiguity.
With the Matchseller, however, Edward feels temporally and spatially confined:

> For two months he's been standing on that spot, do you realize that?
> Two months. I haven't been able to step outside the back gate.
>
> (p. 175)

Like Rose, in her monomaniacal sensitivity to the basement, Edward worries about the simultaneity of situations. While Rose lives
in her safe, warm room, a silent other lives in the cold dark; while
Edward pursues a comfortable existence, the Matchseller stands
out in a storm, unmoving, though it "raged about him" (p. 181). As
Rose vilified Riley in order to maintian control of her room, Edward sets up a series of self-flattering oppositions to distinguish
himself from the Matchseller. The latter is "false," a "bullock," his
presence at the back gate "absurd," and the situation a "farce,"
whereas Edward, pronouncing these judgments, asserts his au-
thenticity, his social and sexual superiority, and his intellectual
intolerance of aberrant or ludicrous behavior. Significantly, Edward labels the Matchseller "an imposter," the comic type whose
unmasking we have associated with Edward, but Edward himself

takes the role of truth seeker who will "get to the bottom of it."
With the entrance of the Matchseller, however, Edward's attempt
at an oppositional relationship becomes itself a ridiculous pose,
whose exposure means the collapse of all opposition and which
leads Edward to identify with and become replaced by his antagonist.

EDWARD *(cheerfully):* Here I am. Where are you?

(p. 182)

Answering that question is Edward's entire purpose in his first
interview with the Matchseller. Attempting to control the spatial
and, by extension, the psychological logistics between the "I" and
the "you," Edward makes a grandiose effort to get the man to sit
down. Faced with an adversary whose weapons are silence and
immobility, Edward explodes with a torrent of historical tidbits,
autobiographical and geographical references. His loquaciousness
is comic illustration of Pinter's "smoke screen," for camouflaged in
the torrent are four repeated requests:

Sit down, old man.
Sit yourself down, old chap.
Now, now, you mustn't . . . stand about like that. Take a seat.
Sit down.

(pp. 182–83)

Positioning the Matchseller is Edward's means of controlling the
situation, of literally putting the intruder in his place. Failing that,
Edward enlarges himself, giving his "I" global proportions. Beginning with his private property ("my canopy," "my table" [p. 184]),
he moves on to absorb the village (where, though not a squire, he
is looked on "with some regard" [p. 182]). He then extends himself
to Asia Minor (where he "wouldn't mind making a trip" [p. 184])
and to Africa (which he calls a "country" [p. 183]). Listing the
contents of his liquor cabinet, he whirls through England, Scot-
land, Spain, Germany, and France. Edward's arcane questions are
designed to intimidate, but verbal pyrotechnics provoke laughter:[35]

Do you by any chance know the Membunza Mountains?

(p. 183)

What do you say to a straightforward Piesporter
Goldtropfschen Feine Auslese (Reichsgraf von Kesselstaff)?

(p. 185)

Equally laughable (and revealing) is the suggestion that Edward
and the Matchseller share the same perspective:

> I was in commerce, too. *(With a chuckle.)* Oh yes I know what it's
> like—the weather, the rain, beaten from pillar to post, up hill and
> down dale . . . Let me advise you. Get a good woman to stick by you.
> Never mind what the world says. Keep at it. Keep your shoulder to the
> wheel. It'll pay dividends. [ellipses mine]
>
> (p. 184)

As with Goldberg's cant (see *The Birthday Party*), the sense of
Edward's language lies buried in clichés. With his geographical
expertise he enlarges himself, and mouthing clichés he generalizes
himself. If Edward appears to be "dominant" at this point, it is only
because he makes more noise.

Acquainted with Edward in the first scene, we are predisposed
to laugh at his manner of "getting to the bottom of it." Though the
Matchseller stands silent and unmoving, Edward, like Rose in *The
Room,* erects a verbal wall of protection, and for both the effort
backfires. Creating responses for the Matchseller, Edward slips
into revelations: his attitude toward his "good woman" is already
suspect; he then stops abruptly after mentioning Flora's "flaming
red hair," a clue linking her to the squire's daughter. However,
such revelations are incomplete and indeterminate. What Edward's verbosity actually reveals to the audience is his comic unawareness of being verbose.

Obsessed with positioning the Matchseller, Edward abandons
his position of authority behind the desk. Curiosity impels him
toward the old man, and, stooping over to retrieve his matches,
Edward assumes a subservient position, prefiguring his final
humiliation. When he orders the Matchseller into the corner
("Back. Backward . . . Get back!" [p. 186]), Edward is obeyed, but
the order (as though to a bullock) also admits defeat. He cannot
"get down to brass tacks" while the Matchseller stands before him.
Finally he tries a direct approach—

> I want to ask you a question. Why do you stand outside my back gate,
> from dawn till dusk, why do you pretend to sell matches, why. . . ?—
>
> (p. 187)

which pushes the Matchseller to near-collapse, letting Edward
maneuver him into a chair. The old man seated, a significant
change occurs in Edward. He relaxes his oppositional pose and for

the first time gropes toward identifying himself with the Matchseller.

> Aaah! You're sat. At last. What a relief. You must be tired. *(Slight pause)*. Chair comfortable? I bought it in a sale . . . When I was a young man. You, too, perhaps. You, too, perhaps.
> *(Pause.)*
> At the same time, perhaps—[ellipsis mine].
>
> (p. 187)

While it is improbable that the Matchseller knows the value of Chateauneuf-du-Pape, it is possible that two young men crossed paths at a time when their social positions were not so markedly distant. One has succeeded, the other failed. (Pinter revives this image in *No Man's Land*.) However, if the idea attracts Edward, it also disturbs him, for he soon takes a defensive tone to Flora: "I could not possibly find myself in his place" (p. 188).

What is the Matchseller's place? From the beginning of the play Edward denied that the old man was there to sell matches. Leaving the study, he asks Flora to take him out to the garden where, surrounded by "our trees," Edward attempts an appraisal:

> He's a little . . . reticent. Somewhat withdrawn.
> . . . .
> He's had various trades, that's certain.
> His place of residence is unsure. He's . . .
> he's not a drinking man.
>
> (p. 188)

Ready-made phrases of description are funny for their inadequacy, but this is the language of conventional discourse that Flora uses and expects. Edward has learned nothing about the Matchseller and he resists understanding that confronting the Matchseller means confronting himself. Rebounding off the old man, Edward's chatter hangs in the air, accusing him, ridiculing him. Desperately trying to explain the Matchseller's presence, Edward attributes to him a past—his own. He knows no other. His reasoning seems to be that if the Matchseller were like him, if he, too, had traveled, wanted to get ahead, Edward might be able to know him, talk to him, eventually get rid of him. The inverse possibility—that the Matchseller bears no resemblance to him, but that he resembles the Matchseller, is an imposter like the Matchseller—is too horrifying to consider.

Typically, Pinter shifts our focus from the mystifying effects of
the Matchseller's presence to droll conflicts between Edward and
Flora. This transitional scene retrieves the comic spirit of the first
scenes and displays the widening distance between their points of
view. Flora promises that the Matchseller will "move on," that
"he's not here through any design" (p. 189). Edward insists that she
is "deluded," that the Matchseller's "cunning" escapes her notice.
Our sense of Edward's desperation dissipates with the introduction
of Flora's salutary attitude and her affirmation that the old man is
merely "weak in the head." Borrowing Edward's phrases, Flora
proposes to "get to the bottom of it" (p. 189), and when Edward
accuses her of "plotting," she coolly extricates herself, pronouncing
"with dignity" an exit speech:

> You should trust your wife more, Edward. You should trust her judg-
> ment, and have greater insight into her capabilities. A woman . . . a
> woman will often succeed, you know, where a man must invariably fail.
>
> (p. 190)

Such sententiousness (concealing a mild sexual innuendo) recalls
Lady Bracknell's best retorts. Flora identifies herself with that
category of politely defiant women installed in the drawing rooms
of Wilde, Coward, and Maugham.

However, Flora's "judgment" of the Matchseller introduces a
comic reversal not unlike the moment in *The Room* when a dis-
credited Rose suddenly corrects her interlocuters. In her interaction with the Matchseller, Flora suddenly restructures the
Edward-Matchseller opposition into a parody of the conventional
comic triangle.

> FLORA   (*intimately*): Tell me, have you a woman? Do you like women?
>   Do you ever . . . think about women?
>   (*Pause.*)
>   Have you ever . . . stopped a woman? . . . Sex, I suppose,
>   means nothing to you. Does it ever occur to you that sex is a
>   very vital experience for other people?
>   (*Seductively.*) Tell me all about love. Speak to me about love.
>   [ellipses mine]
>
> (pp. 191–92)

The "farce" to which Edward alluded is now being played out as
Flora cuddles the Matchseller behind a closed door while Edward,
the cuckold, sits in full view of the audience. Flora has promised to

"wave from the window" when she is ready to admit Edward—a signal endemic to farce plots—and we recall Edward's two references to Flora's "plotting." As a final touch, Edward bursts in (Flora calls through the door: "Don't come in" [p. 193]) and finds the Matchseller partially undressed. Repeatedly Edward has called the old man a "bullock" (the suggestion of castration is now fully ironic); after interrupting Flora's tête-à-tête, he hisses: "You lying slut. Get back to your trough!" (p. 193). His accusations are harsh, yet animality accords well with the sexual emphasis in farce. Wearing the cuckold's horns, Edward completes the triangle—a menagerie à trois.

For Ronald Hayman, Flora's behavior is motivated only by Pinter's "prediliction for spotting the tart in the lady."[36] For Alrene Sykes, Flora's behavior is psychologically motivated, reflecting a need for "the husband and child she has apparently been denied."[37] At opposite poles, these two points of view tend to correct one another. No mere pawn, Flora is nevertheless used by the playwright to support the situation developed in the Edward-Matchseller interviews: by reacting emotionally to the Matchseller, Flora confirms his intimidating influence. Formerly in the straight-man role, rational mate to an irrational, obsessive partner, Flora suddenly reveals a sexual hunger that belies her role of matron of the drawing room.

As the wasp killing was comic because of Edward and Flora's different attitudes toward the task, so the Matchseller's presence highlights their innate separateness. Edward guesses at the Matchseller's motives, but Flora gives him a reason for standing at the back gate:

It's me you were waiting for, wasn't it? You've been standing waiting for me. You've seen me in the woods, picking daisies, in my apron, my pretty daisy apron, and you came and stood, poor creature, at my gate, till death do us part.

(pp. 192–93)

A pastoral voyeur, a devoted husband, the Matchseller even becomes a saint in Flora's array of fantasy admirers. While Edward tries to make him sit down, Flora touches him, proposes to bathe him, and finally takes possession by naming him ("I'm going to keep you. I'm going to keep you, you dreadful chap, and call you Barnabus" [p. 192]). Edward stoops to pick up the matchboxes, but Flora (having bestowed a saint's name) *kneels at his feet.* Edward tries to make the Matchseller talk, but Flora intuits speech ("God knows what you're saying at this very moment" [p. 192]). By inventing a relationship in the past (he was her poacher/rapist) and promising affection in the future, Flora attaches herself to the old man in time. By continually changing her physical posture, she almost seems to make him move. Thus Flora seems to dominate the beggar; she may eventually kill him since she believes he is already dying. However, Pinter undercuts Flora as definitively as he does Edward; the Matchseller responds to neither to them. We laugh at Edward's bullying but Flora's one-sided seduction is equally ridiculous. "The ones that keep silent are best off," said Man in *Monologue*. The dominant character at this point seems to be the Matchseller.

In his second interview, Edward attempts to reclaim authority by insisting on direct dialogue ("Did you say something? . . . Anything?" [p. 194]). But the Matchseller's silence, like Kullus's silence in "The Examination," has become "too deep for echo," and Edward, like the examiner, can "neither suspect nor conclude." He can only create dialogue as he did in the first interview, but with this important difference: he includes the emotional responses of laughter and tears. Dropping his self-flattering pose of the first interview, Edward makes a radical shift into self-objectification: he acts the part of a comic character and three times notes—and creates—the Matchseller's grin or laughter, once his tears. Such hermetic behavior might seem to nullify the Matchseller, but in fact the reverse is true. By anticipating the Matchseller's response, Edward aligns himself with the Matchseller's perspective (the perspective of the silent other), and the result is self-alienation, a confusion of identities, and a loss of authority.

That laughter accompanies Edward's destruction is consistent with the comic movement that opens *A Slight Ache*. We enjoyed the incongruity of Edward's sadism in a drawing-room setting; we laughed at the writer of theological and philosophical essays trying to impress a matchseller with a list of international wine and liquor labels. When Edward laughs at himself in this section of the play, he reveals a disturbing self-consciousness that precludes laughter. Nevertheless, the instances of laughter in these crucial speeches, combined with the closing action of the play, indicate how much Pinter depends on traditional comic structures to decenter the audience and to develop his thematic material.

Edward's first comic cue (the Matchseller's grin) comments on his increasing disorientation in time and space. As he reaches back into the past to confirm his present importance, he discovers, as do we, that past events are not easily recoverable.

God damn it, I'm entitled to know something about you! You're in my blasted house, on my territory, drinking my wine, eating my duck! Now you've had your fill you sit like a hump, a mouldering heap. In my room. My den. I can rem . . .
(*He stops abruptly.*)
(*Pause.*)
You find that funny? Are you grinning?

(pp. 194–95)

Edward's joke is a bitter one. The Matchseller grins at the thought of Edward's memory, and, indeed, the past about which Edward is so certain seems to blur with his inability to separate himself from the Matchseller. The distant past dovetails into the recent past, for among Edward's memories is the time when "I could pour hot water down the spoon-hole." Having witnessed that event, we become implicated in Edward's recall of history; our memories can be lined up with his. While we confirm that he did in fact pour hot water down the spoon-hole, we might note that the "den" was formerly a study and the planned lunch was to be goose, not duck. Through Edward's mental refractions we experience directly Pinter's theory of time past, time present:

> Apart from any other consideration, we are faced with the immense difficulty, if not the impossibility, of verifying the past. I don't mean merely years ago, but yesterday, this morning. What took place, what was the nature of what took place, what happened? If one can speak of the difficulty of knowing what in fact took place yesterday, one can I think treat the present in the same way. What's happening now? We won't know until tomorrow or in six months' time, and we won't know then, we'll have forgotten, or our imagination will have attributed quite false characteristics to today. A moment is sucked away and distorted, often even at the time of its birth.[38]

A moment "sucked away" is neither present nor past but a terrifying amalgam of the two. To the extent that our memories contradict Edward's, we understand the full measure of his uneasiness. We, too, are infected with it for the three-masted schooner he refers to is unfamiliar to us, and unverifiable. Did he view it this morning? Six months ago? Deepening the obscurity is the stage reality Edward himself has created. Blinds pulled, curtains drawn, the room assumes a shapelessness that correlates with the lack of temporal definitions.

The second instance of laughter in the interview focuses specifically on Edward. Ironically the self-alienating laughter that

he musters now seems to complete the movement we associate
with the traditional exposure of comic pretense. It is after Edward's nostalgic reverie in which he affirms his importance and
vigor despite "all kinds of usurpers, disreputables, lists, literally
lists of people anxious to do me down" that he breaks off and
concedes, "Yes, yes, you're quite right, it is funny" (p. 196). He
seems to acknowledge the blindness of his self-importance; in
Henri Bergson's terms, he has been properly "humiliated" into
correcting a too-rigid faith in himself. Edward now becomes freer
with the Matchseller, joining him in self-mockery ("Yes! You're
laughing with me, I'm laughing with you, we're laughing together!") and insisting on a former relationship ("My oldest acquaintance . . . my kith and kin" [p. 196]). With his mime of
looking through a telescope, his reference to the Matchseller
"without a head—I mean without a hat," Edward recalls the self-
ignorant captain in Conrad's "The Secret Sharer" who upon first
viewing his "double" thinks he is headless and at the end of the
story provides him with a hat. Is the Matchseller Edward's secret
sharer? The redemptive end of the Conrad echoes the end of romantic comedy in which unhappiness is transformed into secure
happiness, ignorance erased through self-knowledge.

Edward's next speech undermines this traditional comic structuring for it reveals not recognition but obsession, and the language of obsession revives Edward's comic habit of enlarging the
scope of his actions: "I viewed you . . . through the bars of the
scullery window, or from the roof . . . or from the bottom of the
drive . . . or from the roof again" [ellipses mine] [p. 197]) until
Edward dramatizes himself in a bit of farcical comedy—jumping up
and down on a hot roof. This time the laugher he invokes at his own
expense changes to tears; the degenerative move from pompous
intellectual to hopping clown provokes not corrective humiliation
but humiliating collapse. Nevertheless, Edward continues to distance himself from emotion: it is the Matchseller, he claims, who
weeps. He tells the old man to blow his nose and then blows his
own nose, explaining that he has "caught a cold. A germ. In my
eyes" (p. 198). (Is it possible that his germ, his "slight ache" during
the breakfast dialogue, was nothing more than a terrible urge to
weep and that "the airs pertaining between me and my object and
the eternal quivering" [p. 198] refer not only to his inability to see
the world and himself clearly but to the fact that tears are welling
up in his eyes?)

In the densely lyrical reverie that follows, Pinter amplifies Edward's comic self-ignorance with images of human suffering. Ed-

ward reintroduces the problem of the "dimensionality and continuity of space . . . and time" and now the ellipses in the phrase prove significant. Typically Edward is unable to meld the two; typically he adapts better to a spatial dimension. He describes a womblike space, a nook, where he was sheltered from eternal quivering. No sounds reached him—"I no longer heard the wind"—and he had no sense of time—" or saw the sun" (p. 198) Like Leopold Bloom he lies on his side in fetal position, but like Molly Bloom he contacts all the gardens of the earth and his "earth-flowers" transcend and subsume the smaller categories of japonica, convolvulus, and honeysuckle. Edward's deathlike passivity is accompanied by a soothing absence of self-consciousness:

> . . . But it is only afterwards I say the foliage was dark, the petals flaking, then I said nothing, I remarked nothing, things happened upon me, then in my times of shelter, the shades, the petals, carried themselves, carried their bodies upon me, and nothing entered my nook, nothing left it.
>
> (p. 198)

What destroys his nook is not self-consciousness, however, but aging.

> But then, the time came. I saw the wind. I saw the wind, swirling, and the dust at my back gate, lifting, and the long grass, scything together.
>
> (p. 199)

The familiar long grass through which he strolls has become a metaphor for death and decay. But the Matchseller's response to Edward's nostalgia for the womb and his anxiety about mortality is "shaking . . . rocking . . . heaving" laughter. The movements themselves may express Edward's own internal suffering, perhaps his memory of birth into a world of pain, but, ironically, Edward's inspired rehearsal of human anguish merely affirms his status as a comic character, one who (for the third time) makes his audience laugh. As he shrieks, "You're laughing at me!" the Matchseller rises, acknowledging at last the veracity of one of Edward's statements.

Pinter charges Flora with the task of transforming Edward into a Matchseller and of closing the play with a shocking reprise of the adultery motif she introduced earlier. It is tempting to rationalize Flora's behavior as a sexual allegory analogous to Edward's allegorical suffering. Prototype of the wife/whore whom we meet in Stella (*The Collection*), Sarah (*The Lover*), and Ruth (*The Homecoming*),

Flora is more powerful than the others because her adultery is less antisocial than asocial. Resilient like the earth (her name an earth symbol), Flora survives rape and floods; in her changing alliances, she is as unpredictable as the weather. Rather than fear time, she makes time serve her, announcing that "summer is coming," thus denying that Saturday is the longest day of the year, the start of the waning of summer. Unlike Edward, Flora views time as continuous, an ever-changing, cyclic process that triumphs over linear, mortal time.

However, allegorical as well as psychological explanations must be suspect in Pinter because they can not be fully defended. The logic of Flora's behavior lies not in the motivational connections we impose between the character's words and actions but rather in how two traditional comic structures—the adulterous triangle and the exposure of the poser/imposter—exist in deliberate disharmony. It is impossible to argue on evidence from the play that Flora's adultery results from Edward's exposure or that the reverse is true. Rather it seems more likely that Pinter uses Flora's plainly ludicrous seduction of the old Matchseller to counterpoint Edward's disastrous capitulation to him. In the last moments of the play Flora's mock adultery collides with Edward's passionate anguish of the previous scene, jarring our perception of all these characters. Edward's plaintive comment to the Matchseller— "Even now you look different. Very different"—[p. 197] characterizes our reactions throughout the play. At the opening we responded to a modified drawing-room comedy in the style of Wilde or Coward. With Flora's seduction of the Matchseller the scenery changes; her pornographic sensuality recalls Joe Orton's bestial farces. Then in Edward's interviews we move from stilted drawing-room diction to incantatory rhetoric, as he moves from a standing to a prone position. If we pity Edward at the end, it is because we have been made to suffer his malady. Again and again we are forced to revise our reactions to the characters until we are divested of our superiority over them. With Edward's last words to the Matchseller. "Who are you?" (p. 199), we may understand that "I" and "you" have become interchangeable. Yet the question teases like a riddle. Who in the audience can reply?

THE BIRTHDAY PARTY

Pinter's first three-act play, *The Birthday Party*, written between *The Room* and *A Slight Ache*, greatly extends his comic territory.

The situations in all three plays are ostensibly similar: an individual preternaturally attached to the security of his home is, in the course of the action, routed from it. However, the subtle psychical unbalancing of Rose and Edward differs from the assault on Stanley Webber. We first meet Stanley in his boardinghouse where he is mothered to distraction by his landlady Meg Boles, tolerated by her husband Petey, and teased by Lulu, a young woman in the neighborhood. In the early scenes, Stanley seems depressed and frightened; at the end, he's a drooling vegetable, stripped of his seedy individuality, corseted in a business suit, being led out the door. If the change in Stanley, stretched over three acts, strikes us as more horrific than Rose's sudden blinding or Edward's collapse, the reason lies not with the victim but with the victimizers. Stanley's disintegration is played out within and dominated by the farcical antics of a unique pair in the Pinter canon: Goldberg and McCann.

Attempting to explain their nonnaturalistic behavior and the "Organization" they are presumed to represent, critics discuss Goldberg and McCann as symbols of Judeo-Christian morality,[39] of bourgeois conformity-conscious society,[40] even of death. Martin Esslin calls *The Birthday Party* a "kind of modern *Everyman*" in which Goldberg and McCann play death's emissaries come to summon Stanley in a hearselike black limousine.[41] What Esslin seems to be responding to is the pressure of fatality that we sense from Stanley himself. Even before confronting Goldberg and McCann, Stanley acts like a victim, and his fear "heightens our respect for these as yet unseen powers."[42] Because they break Stanley so thoroughly, it is tempting to view Goldberg and McCann as "powers," personifications of society, religion, or death.

Symbolism, however, does not explain the special blend of comedy and malevolence with which Goldberg and McCann manipulate others and entertain us. Death in *Everyman* merely arrives, but Goldberg and McCann *work;* they come to Meg's boardinghouse with a "job" to do. How they do their job, not why, is Pinter's dramatic concern, for as usual he is niggardly with information that might be molded into motives. To justify the pair's scheming, their clowning, their destructiveness, and their power, we have to look at another figure in the morality play tradition, not in *Everyman*,[43] but so popular and influential that Shakespeare and his contemporaries knew and used him: the trickster, tempter, and malicious humorist—the Vice.

Born in a Christian homiletic tradition, the Vice of the fifteenth- and sixteenth-century morality plays was pitted against forces of good for possession of man's soul. According to Bernard Spivack, this confrontation, an allegorical debate or battle in nondramatic literature, was altered by the exigencies of the theater.

> . . . the pageantry of the military Psychomachia became transformed on the stage into a plot of intrigue. Such a plot, the persistent structural feature of the whole morality drama, required the services of a single intriguer, a voluble and cunning schemer, an artist in duplicity, a deft manipulator of human emotions. . . . The Vice was the dramatic star of the play on the side of evil.[44]

As star, the Vice not only moves the action of the moralities, he explains what he is doing in comic, self-aggrandizing monologues. His rapport with the audience makes him a kind of master of ceremonies, a character larger than life—larger, that is, than the life of his victims who are restricted to the stage world in action and speech. The Vice's role as commentator in no way diminishes his energy within the play. "The heart of his role," says Spivack, "is an act of seduction": he "manipulates[s] the hero out of . . . virtue . . . and insinuate[s] himself into his victim's bosom."[45] To work his stratagem, the Vice employs deceit, which translates most often as a "virtuous alias under which he conceals his name and dissembles his nature."[46] L. W. Cushman notes:

> Mischief in *Mankind* represents himself temporarily as a farm laborer . . . Hypocrisy in the *Lusty Juvenatus,* as a butcher, Ambidexter [*Cambises*] as a gentleman, a lawyer, a student."[47]

The Vice never plots mischief for revenge; vengeance is a perverse but human emotion. The Vice plots mischief to demonstrate how easily it can be done. His raucous pleasure in executing schemes is directly proportional to his freedom from human morality and responsibility: "if one monosyllable can be said to be more frequent than any other . . . it is the interminable 'ha ha ha' of the Vice's laughter."[48] Inevitably his laughter is reciprocated by the audience who are his confidants in the "sport" of deceit.[49] Yet this laughter creates an uncertain mood, for if the Vice is impervious to human suffering, his victims are not; the audience's laughter inevitably backfires by ironically revealing their need of the message dramatized in the morality.

Along with other critics, Spivack contends that the tradition of the Vice was so popular, so entrenched in the life of fifteenth- and sixteenth-century drama, that he survived almost intact in plays that bore no relation to allegory or morality.[50] Though he was naturalized into human semblance, with the accents and attributes of his fellow mortals, we can nevertheless recognize him in characters as diverse as Diccon, "the bedlam," of Mr. S.'s *Gammer Gurton's Needle*, Iago of Shakespeare's *Othello*, and Goldberg in Pinter's *The Birthday Party*. All three exhibit the Vice's clever scheming, his dissembling, his gulling of simple characters, his boastful monologuing, his merriment, his energy, and, most of all, his motiveless malice. This latter attribute receives a different emphasis in each of the plays.

In *Gammer Gurton's Needle*, creating mischief is Diccon's primary purpose. He opens the play with a swaggering monologue in which he reports, as an outsider, the "howling and scowling," "sighing and sobbing" at Gammer's house.[51] Not knowing the cause (obviously not caring), he profits by the confusion to steal bacon as barter for ale. We next see him tipsily applauding the interlude singers: "And let us drink and swill till our bellies burst!" When Hodge, the Gammer's man, arrives and explains the loss of the needle, Diccon draws a "magic circle," pretending to conjure the devil for help.

> DICCON: Come hether then, and stir thee not
> One inch out of this circle plot,
> But stand as I thee teach.
>
> (2.1.89–91)

Terrified, Hodge shits on himself and runs off, leaving Diccon to plot and boast of further confusion.

> I will give ye leave to cut my throat
> If I make not good sport.
>
> (2.1.17–18)

The sport proves to be a wild wrestling match between old Gammer Gurton and her neighbor Dame Chat—Diccon having convinced Gammer that Chat has stolen her needle and enflamed Chat with the "rumor" that she (Chat) has stolen Gammer's cock. Diccon next gulls the priest, Dr. Rat, earning him a beating by Dame Chat (punning on the French *chat* or cat). When arbitration and punishment are about to be levied, Diccon unwittingly proves the hero of the village by kicking Hodge in the backside and disclosing the presence of the needle.

In *Othello*, the mischievous Vice turns villain. While Iago re-

sembles Diccon in his mirth and monologuing, his victims are not
village rustics nor do his stratagems result in an episodic series of
clownish drubbings. Presenting the tragic fall of a hero, Shakespeare focuses on the process of disintegration, emphasizing the
Vice's talent for wheedling insinuation. Iago's stratagems offend
morality at the deepest level of human existence. He destroys the
bond between husband and wife, between general and loyal fol-
lowers; he murders and causes murder to be carried out. Why does
he do it? Spivack argues that Iago's stated motives "come crowding
in frivolous profusion and jostle each other off to oblivion." In other
words, their number and frequency parody human emotion rather
than give expression to it.

> A figure out of another world is being naturalized into the drama of the
> Renaissance, and part of the process is to array him in new garments of
> the prevailing cut. Iago's resentments and jealousies are, in fact, just
> such motives as a dramatist might employ to refashion in tragic natu-
> ralism a stock figure out of an archaic dramatic convention that had no
> use for the conventional incitements of human life.[52]

If we accept this argument, Iago's motives, along with the rest of
his behavior, can be seen as a facet of the Vice's dissembling. In his
unpitying coldness, in his final "Demand me nothing. What you
know you know,"[53] Iago embodies a divine malignity, as Diccon,
hovering behind haystacks, knotting the plot, embodies uncon-
trollable misrule.

Pinter's *The Birthday Party* falls between Mr. S.'s farce and
Shakespeare's tragedy, combining the comic energy of the one, the
unchecked destructiveness of the other. True to his forbears, Goldberg has vague motives. He and his assistant McCann have a job to
do, but Goldberg approaches the task with an eagerness and gusto
that exceed the requirements for its execution. Not satisfied to gull
Meg and intimidate Stanley, Goldberg engineers a birthday party
for no other reason than to demonstrate and enjoy his cleverness.
Typical of the Vice, Goldberg juggles identities and plays roles. His
chief role is the criminal—but a comic criminal, or as A. P. Rossiter
puts it, a "savage comedian."[54] In his music-hall-like interrogations,
Goldberg displays both Diccon's aptitude for mischief and Iago's
for evil. (Pinter knew Iago well, having played the role in repertory.)[55] The comic situations created by Pinter's Vice fracture and
finally destroy what Stanley believes to be a secure environment.

What constitutes security in *The Birthday Party?*—or, rather,
who are the Vice's victims? It is useful to recall a fundamental

principle of the moralities: evil is a primordial condition to which
all mankind is susceptible; the Vice merely catalyzes its appearance.[56] Meg, Lulu, and, to some extent, Petey, are deceived by
Goldberg because their lives are based on petty self-deceptions,
the worst of which (in Pinter's world) is the belief that present
conditions of security guarantee its continuation. Pinter provides
Goldberg and McCann with a slim past connection to Stanley just
as Shakespeare provides Iago with "resentments and jealousies."
Under the aegis of the "Organization," they destroy Stanley and
simultaneously expose the deceptions by which his protectors live.

Structurally, *The Birthday Party* unfolds as a traditional morality
play:

> . . . the Vice enters, as a rule, after the first principal act, that is, after
> the scene between man and the Good. His appearance on the scene is
> an important event in the plot of the play.[57]

Indeed, Goldberg and McCann *are* the plot; their "appearance on
the scene" marks the first major event of *The Birthday Party*. Yet
Pinter deviates from the formulaic morality. Though the Vice represents an implacable evil, the Vice-victim relationship in *The
Birthday Party* is charged with ambiguity. Though Meg and the
boardinghouse protect Stanley from the outside world, the "good"
they represent is a ridiculous comedy of the quotidian, which
Pinter exposes in the first scene of the play.

The opening exchange of *The Birthday Party* establishes the
nature of domestic life at the Boles home and introduces Meg
Boles, one of Pinter's best developed comic characters.

> PETEY *enters from the door on the left with a paper and sits at the
> table. He begins to read.* MEG's *voice comes through the kitchen hatch.*
> MEG: Is that you, Petey?
> *Pause.*
> Petey, is that you?
> *Pause.*
> Petey?
> PETEY: What?
> MEG: Is that you?
> PETEY: Yes, it's me.
> MEG: What? *(Her face appears at the hatch.)* Are you back?
> PETEY: Yes.
> MEG: I've got your cornflakes ready. *(She disappears and reappears.)*
> Here's your cornflakes.[58]

(p. 19)

Listening to Meg's disembodied voice, we are prepared to find her foolish. Like Rose in *The Room,* she speaks to someone who does not answer; but, thicker-skinned than Rose, she ignores the response when it is given. Popping in and out of view like a Bergsonian toy, Meg asks the same question three times, even when Petey's "What?" invalidates the need for another "Is that you?" or for the "Are you back?" that follows. Her bovine insouciance and gullibility are unique in the Pinter canon and will serve as a comic counterpoint to both Stanley's tensions and Goldberg's mischief. We watch her bound upstairs to fetch Stanley and return *"panting,"* oblivious to the absurdity of her flirtation.

Meg's verbal behavior exhibits typical Bergsonian "absentmindedness":[59] When she asks Petey, who is reading his newspaper, "You got your paper?" (p. 19), the question, we assume, is not posed literally but rather forms part of the breakfast ritual that she and Petey enact every morning. Thus Petey answers "Yes" not so much to her question as to confirm his presence in the dialogue. In some exchanges, Meg and Petey speak a phatic sublanguage whose arrangement of sounds claims equal importance with its content.

MEG: Is it good?
PETEY: Not bad.
MEG: What does it say?
PETEY: Nothing much.

(p. 20)

The meter of Meg's lines might depend on an actress's inflection, but Petey's lines are inescapably two-beat phrases of see-saw rhythm. In other exchanges, language acts reflexively, foregrounding the banality of their discourse with parodic permutations of simple ideas:

MEG: Is Stanley up yet?
PETEY: I don't know. Is he?
MEG: I don't know. I haven't seen him down yet.
PETEY: Well then, he can't be up.
MEG: Haven't you seen him down?
PETEY: I've only just come in.

(p. 20)

"Up," "down," and "in," adverbs of direction, become meaningless pointers heard despite their colloquial context. To laugh at this dialogue is to acknowledge that Petey and Meg no longer listen to what they say. Speech has become habit, like morning tea.[60]

Verbal and gestural repetitions instill a quality of sameness. Meg's typical question, "Is it nice?" cues laughter, but equally significant is the fact that out of forty lines of dialogue (counting single words set off by pauses), thirty are questions, and each question earns a monosyllabic response. Furthermore, twice before Stanley's arrival and once afterwards, Petey rises to pick up a plate from the kitchen hatch, returns to his seat, and reburies his nose in the newspaper. Repetition of sound and movement create an ambience of constancy, a bland surface on which later arrivals will make their mark.

Stanley's mark is felt immediately. Unlike Petey, he criticizes Meg's "lovely flakes," the stale milk, and the gravylike tea; sensing that these criticisms are just, we accept Stanley's perspective at the expense of Meg's. Stanley introduces a new vocabulary— "succulent" (p. 27), the first three-syllable adjective to be heard— and Meg's misunderstanding of the word is a joke we share with him. Moreover, seen through Stanley's eyes, Meg's self-deception becomes apparent. For Meg, Stanley is both little boy and ardent lover during morning and afternoon tea. From Stanley's rebuffs, we know this intimacy is one-sided (although his actual participation at "tea" remains ambiguous).

Meg's lack of discernment creates comedy even as Pinter plants suspense. Meg tells Stanley about "the two gentlemen" (p. 29), and immediately their perspectives bifurcate, Meg remaining ignorantly in present time while Stanley falls back into the past. Melodramatic gestures (he *"grinds his cigarette," "paces the room"*) and a rather trite account of a sabotaged concert are the trappings of a cinematic fugitive, but Meg construes his distress to be physical: "Did you pay a visit this morning?" (p. 33). This misconnection recalls the comic collisions of *The Room* in which crucial revelations (Stanley's like Mrs. Sands's) are simultaneously underscored and diminished by surrounding comic dialogue.

If Stanley provides a critical perspective on Meg, Lulu, entering next, invites us to scrutinize Stanley:

LULU (*offering him [her] compact*): Do you want to have a look at your face? (STANLEY *withdraws from the table.*) . . . Don't you ever go out?
(*He does not answer.*) I mean, what do you do, just sit around the

house like this all day long? *(Pause.)* Hasn't Mrs. Boles got enough to
do without having you under her feet all day long? [ellipses mine]

(p. 35)

Lulu proposes a picnic. Stanley, evasive, asks her to "go away" with
him, though there is "nowhere to go." Because it isolates him from
his familiar world, Stanley's reaction heightens our interest. Witnessing the preceding scenes, we are aware (as Lulu cannot be) of
Stanley's agitation about "the two gentlemen." Stanley stimulates
our sense of expectation, and Pinter does not prolong the suspense.

Enter Goldberg and McCann, without knocking. A slight
nuance, yet this gestural omission fractures the realistic pattern of
the opening scenes. Visitors like Lulu knock, but the Vice arranges
his own entrances and exits. According to Cushman, the Vice's first
entrance "is equivalent to the introduction of new life and spirit,
and is generally characterized by noise and bluster."[61] New life and
spirit are evident in the Kafkaesque gangster appearance of Goldberg and McCann and in their comically rhythmic opening lines:[62]

MCCANN: Is this it?
GOLDBERG: This is it.
MCCANN: Are you sure?
GOLDBERG: Sure I'm sure.
            Pause.
MCCANN: What now?

(p. 37)

Goldberg's answer provides a curious blend of noise and bluster.
Telling McCann to relax, he exchanges gangster diction for the
droll, sentimental, bombast of an after-dinner speech maker. The
Jewish inflection is unmistakable:

Breathe in, breathe out, take a chance, let yourself go, what can you
lose?

(p. 37)

Goldberg launches into a detailed account of his Uncle Barney,
another stereotype: the "cultured" wealthy man with a house "just
outside Basingstoke" (a town, for most Londoners, synonymous
with commuter routes and anonymity). Like his gangster language,
Goldberg's images have a familiar ring, yet the effect disorients us.
Within moments of his arrival in a strange house, Goldberg is

"*settling in the armchair,*" breezily reminiscing. Unsolicited autobiography is always puzzling. Add an apparent unconsciousness of
a new environment (even McCann asks: "What about this, Nat?
Isn't it about time someone came in?" [p. 38]), and Goldberg becomes impossible to define in a naturalistic context.

Who, then, is Nat Goldberg? Primarily he is a talker. After the
minimal language in the scenes with Stanley, Meg, Petey, and
Lulu, Goldberg's verbosity becomes as gestural and amusing as
Meg's repetitious questions. For Goldberg, language means
power, but unlike Lenny in *The Homecoming*, whose verbal
strength derives from distinct, lurid images, Goldberg fills a room
with noise, a splatter of clichés, and autobiographical detail that
intimidates by its very lack of clarity. "Don't talk to me about
culture" (p. 38), says Goldberg, employing a typically Jewish turn
of speech. But the line resonates: one does not talk *to* Goldberg at
all. His speech making parodies Pinter's own notion of language as
a necessary smoke screen, for no one challenges Goldberg; he
fabricates his own "necessity."

Pinter's early dramaturgy does not admit the soliloquy, yet Goldberg's speeches are near-monologues that divert dialogue into
comic reverie. Unlike Iago's soliloquies, Goldberg's speeches contain no plotting, but they testify to other Vice attributes. For example, the traditional Vice speaks nonsense, a clutter of "irrelevant
matters."[63] All of Goldberg's five major speeches are remarkable for
their utter irrelevance. In act 3, after formally meeting Stanley,
Goldberg spins off into a typically exuberant verbal performance.

> Yes. When I was a youngster, of a Friday, I used to go for a walk down
> the canal with a girl who lived down the road. A beautiful girl. What a
> voice that bird had! A nightingale, my word of honour. Good? Pure?
> She wasn't a Sunday school teacher for nothing. Anyway, I'd leave her
> with a little kiss on the cheek—I never took liberties—we weren't like
> the young men these days in those days. We knew the meaning of
> respect. So I'd give her a peck and I'd bowl back home. Humming
> away I'd be, past the children's playground. I'd tip my hat to the
> toddlers, I'd give a helping hand to a couple of stray dogs, everything
> came natural. I can see it like yesterday. The sun falling behind the dog
> stadium. Ah! (*He leans back contentedly.*)
>
> (p. 53)

Sentimental style ("When I was a youngster, of a Friday") and
antiquated diction ("*bowl* back home") mingle with hackneyed expressions ("I never took liberties"; "We knew the meaning of re-

spect"; "I can see it like yesterday") and lofty accusations ("We weren't like the young men these days in those days"). In the lines, "What a voice that bird had. A nightingale," Goldberg conflates the English slang for girl ("bird") and the cliché ("sings like a bird"). His bestial images rouse laughter ("I'd give a helping hand to a couple of stray dogs, everything came natural"), as do his skewed clichés (the sun "falling" instead of "setting" behind the dog stadium). His funniest utterance is the final "Ah!"; like the Vice, Goldberg delights in his own verbal agility.

The traditional Vice juggles identities and Goldberg juggles several—Nat, Simey and Benny. He presents himself as a family man and mentions his wife and mother, but he describes them with the same phrases. Did they behave identically? Did they exist? In act 3, when Goldberg gathers Meg into his pantheon of wonderful women ("A good woman. A charming woman. My mother was the same. My wife was identical" [p. 81]), we realize the fruitlessness of attaching meaning to his logorrhea. If Meg's speech is language that talks for itself, Goldberg's is language that runs away with itself. Goldberg, the most autobiographical character in *The Birthday Party*, speaking the most lines, remains the most opaque. This, too, accords with the Vice tradition. We recall Iago's boast to Roderigo: "I am not what I am" (1.1.65).

Manipulating human emotion, the Vice ingratiates himself in order to work his plots; thus Goldberg gulls Meg as a first step toward controlling Stanley's world.

GOLDBERG: Ah, Mrs. Boles?
MEG: Yes?
GOLDBERG: We spoke to your husband last night. Perhaps he mentioned us? We heard that you kindly let rooms for gentlemen. So I brought my friend along with me. We were after a nice place, you understand. So we came to you. I'm Mr. Goldberg and this is Mr. McCann.

                                                                (p. 40)

Goldberg's first "so" underscores the gentlemanly character of Mr. McCann, and the second, the good character of Meg's establishment. Diccon approaches Dame Chat similarly. Since card-playing, ale-drinking Dame Chat considers herself an honest woman, Diccon flatters her discretion by revealing his "secret": "I tell you as my sister. You know what meaneth 'mum'!" (4.2.93). More subtly, Iago skewers Othello by aping the qualities of honesty and loyalty that the soldierly Othello prizes.

Like his predecessors, Pinter creates verbal comedy in the interaction of a clever Vice and his dull-witted gull. When Hodge complains that Gammer Gurton has lost her "neele," Diccon pretends to hear "eel": "Her eel, Hodge? Who fished of late? That was a dainty dish!" (2.1.41). We laugh at Roderigo's confusion as Iago spins fantasies of his future success with Desdemona while urging him: "Put money in thy purse" (1.3.337–38); but wheedling a room from Meg, Goldberg finds himself comically miscommunicating:

GOLDBERG: Well, so what do you say? You can manage to put us up, eh, Mrs. Boles?
MEG: Well, it would have been easier last week.
GOLDBERG: It would, eh?
MEG: Yes.
GOLDBERG: Why? How many have you got here at the moment?
MEG: Just one at the moment.
GOLDBERG: Just one?
MEG: Yes. Just one. Until you came.
GOLDBERG: And your husband, of course?
MEG: Yes, but he sleeps with me.

(p. 41)

Goldberg discusses the number of boarders while Meg has switched topics to the number of beds.

Stanley, more than Meg, stimulates Goldberg's talents. When McCann bodily prevents Stanley from leaving in the opening seconds of act 2, we have no doubt that Goldberg and McCann are his hunters; dissembling, therefore, is meaningless. They are not trying to insinuate evil in Stanley but to accuse him of it. However, with the Vice's enjoyment of sport and wordplay,[64] Goldberg and McCann make a show of breaking down Stanley's defenses. Their names alone are ridiculously emblematic: the Jew and the Irishman, a preamble to a long-winded joke or a parodic comedy team. Pinter invents a rhetoric just for them, a verbal smoke screen behind which individual personalities are indiscernible. Their special entertainment is an interrogation act consisting of questions and accusations fired at Stanley and characterized by comic nonlogic.

GOLDBERG: What have you done with your wife?
MCCANN: He's killed his wife!
GOLDBERG: Why did you kill your wife?
STANLEY (*sitting, his back to the audience*): What wife?

MCCANN: How did he kill her?
GOLDBERG: How did you kill her?
MCCANN: You throttled her?
GOLDBERG: With arsenic.
MCCANN: There's your man!
GOLDBERG: Where's your old mum?
STANLEY: In the sanitorium.
MCCANN: Yes!
GOLDBERG: Why did you never get married?

(p. 59)

Did Stanley leave his wife? The question tantalizes as it might explain his exile in the Boleses' home. On the other hand, Pinter devalues the question by juxtaposing it with blatant absurdities (throttling with arsenic) and contradiction ("Why did you never get married?")!

Removing Stanley's glasses, Goldberg and McCann accuse him of evils beyond family murders. Stanley offends religion ("You stink of sin" [p. 60]), society ("No society would touch you" [p. 61]), even life itself ("What makes you think you exist?" [p. 62]). Though critics note that McCann speaks for "Irish" issues, Goldberg for society and family, no coherent biographical information can be gathered about either inquisitors or victim.[65] Treachery and betrayal seem to be Stanley's crimes, yet no specific crime is verified. However we interpret the pseudo-philosophical inquiry into the possibility or necessity of the number 846, Goldberg's interpretation is most telling: "We're right and you're wrong, Webber, all along the line" (p. 61).

The interrogation routines in acts 2 and 3 provoke verbal and physical gags. Goldberg and McCann improvise new questions to counter Stanley's few replies and even produce a four-line stanza with a two-step beat:

GOLDBERG: You skeddadled from the wedding.
MCCANN: He left her in the lurch.
GOLDBERG: You left her in the pudding club.
MCCANN: She was waiting at the church.

(pp. 59–60)

In the tradition of the Vice-buffoon,[66] Goldberg and McCann become crudely funny bunglers:

GOLDBERG: You'll be integrated.
MCCANN: You'll give orders.

GOLDBERG: You'll make decisions.
MCCANN: You'll be a magnate.
GOLDBERG: A statesman.
MCCANN: You'll own yachts.
GOLDBERG: Animals.
MCCANN: Animals.
GOLDBERG *looks at* MCCANN.
GOLDBERG: I said animals. (*He turns back to* STANLEY.)

(p. 94)

Goldberg's "*look*" gives the audience time to register the error and laugh, but McCann's tendency to err is familiar to us. Alone he seems the classic tough, blocking Stanley with his body, "*hold*[*ing*] *the grip*" when shaking hands. But anger brings out McCann's native buffoonery. After McCann, Goldberg, and Stanley meet, McCann orders Stanley to sit down. Stanley agrees—if McCann will also sit.

MCCANN *slowly sits at the table, left.*
MCCANN: Well?
STANLEY: Right. Now you've both had a rest you can get out!
MCCANN (*rising*): That's a dirty trick! I'll kick the shite out of him!
GOLDBERG (*rising*): No! I have stood up.
MCCANN: Sit down again!
GOLDBERG: Once I'm up I'm up.
STANLEY: Same here.

(pp. 56–57)

Confusedly McCann yells at Stanley *and* Goldberg, and then confronts the stupefying problem of their agreement.

Clever, manipulative, clownish, Pinter's Vice characters are, like their forbears, evil: "rotting, scabrous, the decayed spiders."[67] At the birthday party climaxing act 2, their comic and horrific aspects converge. Playing the tempter, the traditional Vice corrupts mankind with a call to the tavern; Diccon and Iago, postmorality Vices, are no less bibulous. Filled with ale, Diccon applauds the singers between acts (*Gammer Gurton's Needle*, 2.1), and Iago sings and tempts Cassio to drunkenness during the "night of revels." Dispensing enough liquor "to skuttle a liner" (p. 63), Goldberg calls for toasts and music, then, not surprisingly, delivers a speech. Stanley's birthday party becomes a brilliant demonstration of the Vice's finesse. We view the party as Goldberg would have us view it: Meg and Lulu are unsuspicous, Stanley is intimidated, and Goldberg triumphantly plays two roles at once—grandiloquent guest and cruel victimizer, agent of mirth and agent of evil—with the audience's knowledge and with absolute impunity. During Goldberg's cliché-gorged speech, we catch a reference to "tea in Fullers, a library book from Boots" (p. 66), clues linking Goldberg to Stanley's memories of Maidenhead ("There's a Fuller's teashop"; "And a Boot's library" [p. 49]). However, no one on stage verbalizes the link; it is as dubious as Goldberg's pose as "gentleman." What we do acknowledge is Goldberg's high-spirited confidence and his well-executed sport.

Seducing a willing Lulu provides extra sport for Goldberg and accords well with the Vice role of lewd tempter. In the morality play *Like Will to Like*, the Vice, Nichol Newfangle, addresses a woman in the audience:

> How say you, woman, you that stand in the angle
> Were you never acquainted with Nichol Newfangle?[68]

Goldberg's repartee with Lulu reveals the Vice's aptitude for witty sexual dialogue, his ironic understanding of the game they play.

LULU (*to* GOLDGERG): Shall I tell you something?
GOLDBERG: What?
LULU: I trust you.
GOLDBERG (*lifting his glass*): Gesundheit.

(p. 69)

LULU (to GOLDBERG): You're the dead image of the first man I ever loved.
GOLDBERG: It goes without saying.

(p. 71)

The unraveling of their relationship is both typical and untypical. That Lulu faints at the end of a very alcoholic party may not surprise; however, spread-eagled on top of a table, she incongruously evokes a double image of the sacrificial and the sexual. Morning-after recriminations sound both familiar ("You used me for a night. A passing fancy" [p. 90]) and unfamiliar ("He [her first love, Eddie] didn't come into my room at night with a briefcase" [p. 89]). At the party Lulu likens Goldberg to Eddie; later she finds that "Uncle Natey's" games would shame Eddie. Turning all accusations back on her, Goldberg with the help of McCann humiliates Lulu as Iago humiliates the whore Bianca, when he accuses her of conspiring to kill Cassio:

> Look you pale, mistress? . . .
> Behold her well; I pray you look upon her.
> Do you see, gentlemen? Nay, guiltiness will speak,
> Though tongues were out of use. [ellipses mine]
>
> (5.1.105–10)

McCann is more blunt: "Your sort, you spend too much time in bed" (p. 90).

For Meg, our sympathy is greater because her foolishness proceeds from genuine affection. At the birthday party, Goldberg manipulates this affection, wheedling Meg into complicity with his sport: "Now—who's going to propose the toast? Mrs. Boles, it can only be you." McCann extinguishes the overhead light and shines his flashlight at Stanley. Full of emotion, Meg speaks to Stanley's ghoulishly lit face; she concedes that he may have lived elsewhere, but living with Meg "for a long while now . . . he's my Stanley now" (p. 65). Her Stanley, however, no longer exists, if he ever did. The flashlight reminds us of the interrogation (just before Meg's entrance) that left Stanley physically functioning but speechless. The next time Stanley makes contact with Meg, he tries to strangle her.

How are we to react to Stanley? Esslin, in one interpretation, sees Stanley as the "artist whom society claims from a comfortable, bohemian, 'opt-out' existence."[69] If we view Goldberg as an incarnation of the Vice, Stanley becomes even more generalized: an Everyman whose temptation and demise are inevitable. However, if Goldberg is affiliated with the postmorality Vice tradition, we need not think of Stanley as an abstract victim but as an individual with human, even contemptible faults.[70] As with Rose in *The Room*, Pinter undercuts Stanley. When Meg reveals that "two gentlemen" are arriving, Stanley punishes her with a mini-interrogation, creating (or recreating) an image he knows will terrify her: "They're coming today . . . in a van . . . They're looking for someone" (p. 34). At this juncture, Stanley may know that "they" are coming for him, but projecting the horror onto Meg seems a gratuitous cruelty. Earlier in this exchange, Stanley *"lies across the table,"* a gesture of irritation and futility. That this inspires Meg to think of constipation amuses us—another comic miss—but during the party Stanley puts Lulu in the same position, suggesting a twisted vengeance as misplaced as Meg's remark. In the first interrogation scene, Stanley is surprised by Goldberg's questions but soon recovers with "You're on the wrong horse" (p. 58), before proceeding to answer Goldberg in kind:

> GOLDBERG: When did you come to this place?
> STANLEY: Last year.
> GOLDBERG: Where did you come from?
> STANLEY: Somewhere else.
> GOLDBERG: Why did you come here?
> STANLEY: My feet hurt!
> GOLDBERG: Why did you stay?
> STANLEY: I had a headache!
>
> (p. 58)

Stanley soon stumbles, losing the beat, but he has demonstrated a familiarity with the rules of the game. He and his torturers even share a vocabulary: both Goldberg and Stanley use the word "trust" in an effort to win McCann's confidence and both speak of each other as a bad smell.

In the end Goldberg proves too strong for Stanley and the final image of persecution (during the interrogation reprise in act 3) identifies attacker and victim clearly. Still, the text makes it impossible to judge. In his 1964 production of the play, Pinter as director emphasized Stanley's insensitivity to Meg, so perhaps Goldberg is correct in labeling him an imposter: "Webber, you're a fake" (p. 59).[71]

But the accusation resonates. At the end of act 2, Goldberg, an expert in fakery, appears to be omnipotent, but in act 3, after a night of drinking and socializing, Goldberg experiences an uncomfortable slippage. If Stanley suffers by exposure to Goldberg and McCann, the reverse is also true. Pinter's Vice catches the very disease he inflicts. The first symptoms of mutuality are signaled (unwittingly, of course) by Meg:

> *Enter* GOLDBERG. *He halts at the door, as he meets their* [PETEY *and* MEG's] *gaze, then smiles.*
> GOLDBERG: A reception committee!
> MEG: Oh, I thought it was Stanley.
> GOLDBERG: You find a resemblance.
> MEG: Oh no. You look quite different.
> GOLDBERG (*coming into the room*): Different build, of course.
>
> (p. 80)

But alike in other ways? Exploding with quips and retorts in act 2, Goldberg in act 3 stammers like Stanley.

> PETEY: How is he this morning?
> GOLDBERG: Who?

PETEY: Stanley. Is he any better?
GOLDBERG *(a little uncertainly)*: Oh . . . a little better, I think, a little better. (p. 81).

"*A little uncertainly*" signifies, in Goldberg's case, a profound alteration. McCann, too, recedes from his former posture. Once he used his bulk to prevent Stanley's egress; now he is driven out of the room by the latter's "talking." Without realizing it, Goldberg and McCann reverse roles. Alone on stage in act 1, Goldberg asks his nervous partner, "What's the matter with you?" (p. 37). Alone once again in act 3, McCann interrogates:

MCCANN: What's the matter with you today?
GOLDBERG: Questions, questions. Stop asking me so many questions. What do you think I am?

(p. 85)

In the brief silence that follows (while "MCCANN *studies him*"), we have time to comprehend the indirect allusion to Stanley. Finally, completing the parallel, Goldberg tries to strangle McCann, as Stanley did Meg.

As he loses control of himself, Goldberg seems to lose his resemblance to the Vice. He acts as though he, not Stanley, were being victimized and in two long speeches drops his gangster role to review his philosophy of life: "Play up, play up, and play the game" (p. 87). The "game" demands certain rules of conduct dictated by Judeo-Christian morality ("Honour thy father and mother"), by social institutions ("School? Don't talk to be about school. Top in all subjects"), and by cultural fads ("That's why I've reached my position, McCann. Because I've always been as fit as a fiddle"). Clogging the content is Goldberg's gush of hackneyed expressions ("I kept my eye on the ball"), Jewish turns of phrase ("And for why?"), and nonsequiturs ("Don't go near the water"). The sum total of everything sacredly mediocre, Goldberg nevertheless lacks conviction.

Because I believe that the world . . . *(Vacant)* . . .
Because I believe that the world . . . *(Desperate)* . . .
BECAUSE I BELIEVE THAT THE WORLD . . . *(Lost)* . . .

(p. 88)

Goldberg's cluttered "I" is incapable of defining the complex, ever-changing world. Pinter's stage directions point toward melodrama, but in the theater the image is comic. Goldberg's efforts to complete the phrase resemble a motor that refuses to start; his mechanical stereotypes have broken down.

Through family, by doggedly mining *this* myth, Goldberg retrieves his strength. Recounting his father's deathbed speech, he mouths the platitudes of the typical Jewish patriarch: "Do your duty and keep your observations" (p. 88), beware of "schnorrers" and "never forget your family" (p. 88). Then, parodying the long genealogical lists from Genesis (and, perhaps, from Beckett's *Watt*),[72] Goldberg asks McCann: "Who came before your father? His father. And who came before him?" With inspired inanity, he trumpets: "your father's father's mother! Your great gran-granny!" (p. 88). Goldberg is nearly recovered.

Reappraising and replaying his different roles, Goldberg should seem vulnerable; we see him on his knees. Yet he is least "real," least like a coherent personality during these speeches; the stereotypes are too jumbled, too facile. He clouds his identity, calling himself Benny, Nat, Simey—presumably any Jewish male name will do, just as McCann is Dermott or Seamus—any Irish male name. Our acquaintance with these two has not improved our understanding of them; they remain the generalized "Jew and Irishman" we met at the outset. Yet Pinter undercuts stale stereotypes with a line designed to shock:

GOLDBERG: All the same, give me a blow. *(Pause.)* Blow in my mouth.
(p. 89)

The fact that Goldberg begins and ends this long section by presenting his open mouth to McCann makes at least three points: that Pinter wants to emphasize Goldberg's primary physical symbol—his mouth; that Goldberg's sexual perversities alluded to in the scene with Lulu are prefigured here; and that Goldberg's adherence to the Vice tradition is affirmed. The Vice's real identity, his actual place in society, was as obscure as his motives. The suggestion of Goldberg's homosexuality accords poorly with the image of a Jewish patriarch, which accords poorly with the image of a pitiless gangster. Who is Nat Goldberg? Inquiring as to his real nature is like lifting the Vice's mask. Under the grinning mask is another mask that grins.

The Birthday Party is unique in Pinter's early work in underscoring the abuses of language. Not until *Old Times* will Pinter so fully exploit the hollowness of quotidian discourse, or show so clearly the power of language both to define and destroy human relationships. Words transcend their roles as signifiers, becoming gestures as revealing to the themes of the play as Stanley's lying across the breakfast table. Meg and Petey's see-saw question-answer patter is as artfully monotonous an effect as a dripping faucet or the steady hum of an overhead fan. During the interrogation of Stanley, lines serve as slaps or probing needles.

The birthday party, the central event of the play's title, creates a thematic double entendre. Offering Stanley a new birthday is a comically confused but ingenious expression of Meg's affection; in one stroke she nullifies Stanley's past—that shadowy time when he was another person, with another birthday—and offers him a whole new life. Stanley can no more accept a new birthday than he can forget the past. And he is not alone. As in *The Room,* the characters of *The Birthday Party* have uncertain relationships to their familial pasts, paticularly to their fathers. Meg recalls "a very big doctor" father (p. 70); Stanley remembers a father who failed him; even Lulu, after the night spent with Goldberg, worries, "What would my father say if he knew?" (p. 89).

Birthday parties connect people to their pasts, but Pinter uses Stanley's party to demonstrate an inverse image of connectedness. The one who is feted sits silent and alone at center stage while voices around him meld into an eerie chorus of party chat. With Goldberg and Lulu on one side of the stage, McCann and Meg on the other, Pinter tampers with the conventions of stage dialogue. Lines in sequence refer to two separate actions, and characters who seem to be talking to one another are in fact on opposite sides of the room:

GOLDBERG: Lulu, you're a big bouncy girl. Come and sit on my lap.
MCCANN: Why not?
LULU: Do you think I should?
GOLDBERG: Try it.
MEG *(sipping):* Very nice.
LULU: I'll bounce up to the ceiling.
MCCANN: I don't know how you can mix that stuff.
GOLDBERG: Take a chance.
MEG *(to* MCCANN*):* Sit down on this stool.
LULU *sits on* GOLDBERG's *lap.*
MCCANN: This?
GOLDBERG: Comfortable?
LULU: Yes thanks.
MCCANN *(sitting):* It's comfortable.

(p. 68)

The passage is clever but difficult to stage. Actors must listen to
two dialogues while the characters they play respond only to one.
However, if done well, the audience has the uncanny experience of
viewing the world through Stanley's eyes. We share his divided
perceptual frame, forced to turn our heads when he does to absorb
the party chat.

Dividing the focus, forcing the audience to concentrate on several subjects at once, is Pinter's comic strategy throughout *The
Birthday Party*. During the interrogation, for example, the image
of persecution becomes confused with a verbal nonsense comedy
that exploits us while it victimizes Stanley. Although some questions and accusations refer to Stanley's personal life, others transcend his perspective and enter our own.

> What about the Albigensenist heresy?
> Who watered the wicket at Melbourne?
> What about the blessed Oliver Plunkett?
>
> (p. 61)

Indeed, what about him? While understanding that the verbal
sound barrage outweighs the individual question, we cannot help
acknowledging the referential content of the question. Similarly,
Goldberg's clichés constantly divide our focus. In Goldberg's verbal performances, a hackneyed expression is defamiliarized by its
juxtaposition with other clichés, creating a patternless regurgita-
tion that pushes trite sense to the verge of nonsense.

As Pinter's impersonation of the Vice, Goldberg is the funniest
as well as the most frightening character on stage. While Stanley,
Meg, and Lulu refer hesitantly to an absent father, Goldberg draws
from a seemingly inexhaustible supply of anecdotes about a father,
wife, uncle, and dead mother, drowning out and parodying their
emotions. Meg's excitement about the birthday party is mocked by
Goldberg's sinister, hollow-sounding bark:

> What a thing to celebrate—birth! Like getting up in the morning.
> Marvelous!
>
> (p. 55)

Act 3 exposes a seemingly human side to Goldberg—a middle-
aged man worried about losing his teeth and pleasing a boss called
Monty. But the fascination of Goldberg lies in his disjunction from
the world of the boardinghouse, the spiritually uninvolved vantage
point from which he manipulates others. Near the end of the play,

Goldberg drops his social manner; with undisguised malice he terrifies Petey as he flattered Meg by exposing the frailty behind Petey's pose: "Why don't you come with us, Mr. Boles . . . There's plenty of room in the car" (p. 96). Meg offers another proof of Goldberg's insinuating power when she describes her party experience with a Goldbergian cliché: "I was the bell of the ball" (p. 97).

We, too, fall prey to the Vice's power, for at the end Pinter undercuts dramatic irony. We may know more than Meg and Petey about the sequence of events, but we share their ignorance of the motives underlying those events. Laughing at Goldberg while he destroys the Boles household, we have subtly assumed his emotionless stance toward the characters. Yet in the final seconds of *The Birthday Party*, we must test our knowledge against Meg's ignorant "knowing" and see our laughter mirrored in her foolish, self-satisfied smile.

THE CARETAKER

On Pinter's stage, the room is both metaphor and situation. From the insider's perspective the room epitomizes security and privacy; when someone intrudes tensions arise, for the intruder brings new rhythms that must in some way be altered or absorbed or both. The process of absorption implies the subtle frictions, the territorial battles that are the fertile core of Pinter's early drama. Nor does he neglect our room, the theater, for our reactions must be manipulated and absorbed. How do we react to intrusion? The idea can be terrifying, but if the room is a cluttered assemblage of unwanted junk and the intruder a self-serving bum who complains about lack of comfort, there are comic possibilities.

The Caretaker was Pinter's first London success, opening at the Arts Theatre Club on 27 April 1960 and running till May of the following year. Like the other plays discussed in this chapter, *The Caretaker* explores the comic and terrifying effects of intrusion— but with certain differences. *The Room* and *A Slight Ache* involve us in the protagonists' turbulent reactions to intrusion, while in *The Birthday Party* the violent actions of the intruders dominate. In *The Caretaker*, Pinter focuses on the room itself—its ability to shield, to exclude and to impose itself on the characters. For Davies, Aston, and Mick the room has no fixed quality; it is neither the "cosy," "nice" interior in which Rose and Meg are installed, nor Edward's more abstract "here," his comprehensive designation for worldly and emotional authority. Aston's abode is chaotic, not dis-ordered but *unordered*. While the crockery, tea, and newspapers of the other plays suggest traditional "cup-and-saucer" realism, Aston's clutter of buckets, gas stoves, and lawnmower belong to the heavy materiality of our consumer culture. There is nothing proplike about a lawnmower, especially a nonfunctioning lawn-mower. The accumulation of what Mick calls "all this junk here" (p. 70)[73] makes a theatrical statement impossible to ignore: the characters must arrange themselves around the debris.[74] Pinter focuses on the power and chaos of the room as soon as the lights go up. Mick, alone on stage, looks at each object and at the bucket that hangs from the ceiling. Then *"he sits quite still expressionless, looking out front."* Stymied by the room, he gazes blankly in our direction inviting us to examine it as he did and to arrive at the same conclusion.

Located in a concrete, object-filled world, *The Caretaker* is free of symbolic presences; no Riley, no Matchseller, no one with Gold-berg's strange suggestiveness. Instead, the near and total silence of Riley and the Matchseller and the aggressive volubility of Gold-berg are traits in the personalities of Aston and Mick; the ethereal quality of the earlier tramps gives way to the earthy presence of Davies. Unlike the arcane intrusions in *The Room, A Slight Ache,* and *The Birthday Party,* action in *The Caretaker* springs from a banal situation: a man wants a roommate and invites in an old tramp whom he has saved from a scuffle. The tramp's arrival arouses the jealousy of the man's brother who baits and persecutes the intruder. The tramp himself is ungrateful and conniving, and, apparently by mutual consent of the brothers, he is told to leave. Pinter has insisted on the realistic nature of *The Caretaker*: "For me this play is nothing more than a particular situation, that which is created by the relationships between three persons (who are not symbols of anything)".[75]

The particularity of situation and relationship in *The Caretaker* is inseparable from the play's comic action, especially that generated by the character whose bogus title titles the play: Mac Davies, an original creation with a long comic pedigree. Davies's ragged, disheveled appearance immediately recalls the shrewdly bungling tramp-clowns of the circus and early vaudeville;[76] when he chases his trousers and bag or runs from the vacuum cleaner, he unwittingly performs the choreography of the traditional clown butt. But Davies is most comic in his inflated self-aggrandizing speeches, his fantastic posturing that attempts to contradict the statement made by his bum's rags. If Pinter's early protagonists contain elements of the braggart-imposter, Davies fully exhibits the "pretentiousness, swagger, and deceit" of the traditional *alazoneia* who "put up a claim to share in advantages and delights which they have done nothing to deserve."[77] An admitted imposter—he bears one name but answers to another—Davies makes an undeserved claim on Aston's cluttered room and as a result is expelled by Aston and Mick, both of whom play self-deprecating *eiron* to his *alazon*. A more important connection between Pinter's Davies and the briefly sketched Aristophanic *alazoneia* is their unregenerate nature, their consistent comic nastiness even to the point of expulsion.

But Pinter deviates significantly from the pattern of exposure and expulsion. First, the room's tenant and owner, Aston and Mick, invite the intruder into their lives; they, too, are poser-losers, Davies's antagonists and his allies. While Davies's posturing suffices to make him ludicrous, Pinter involves all three characters in gamelike situations in which alliances form, disintegrate, and reform in different combinations. Second, the nature of Davies's intrusion remains ambiguous because the situation into which he intrudes—the brothers' relationship—remains uncertain. The brothers rarely speak or appear together; at one point Mick not Davies seems the intruder in Aston's room. Third, the superiority we typically feel toward a character like Davies is undermined by comic situations in which his bafflement becomes synonymous with our own. While the realism of *The Caretaker* distinguishes it from the other plays of this chapter, Pinter's use of comic action has a similar destabilizing effect. The audience is placed at the nexus of conflicting perspectives, forced to continually revise assumptions on the action.

The play's opening gambit between Davies and Aston illustrates the comic potential of conflicting perspectives:

ASTON: Sit down.
DAVIES: Thanks. (*Looking about.*) Uuh . . .
ASTON: Just a minute.
(ASTON *looks around for a chair, sees one lying on its side by the rolled carpet at the fireplace, and starts to get it out.*)
DAVIES: Sit down? Huh . . . I haven't had a good sit down . . . I haven't had a proper sit down . . . well, I couldn't tell you. . . .
ASTON (*placing the chair*): Here you are.
DAVIES: Ten minutes off for a tea-break in the middle of the night in that place and I couldn't find a seat, not one. All them Greeks

had it, Poles, Greeks, Blacks, the lot of them, all them aliens
had it. And they had me working there . . . they had me
working . . .

ASTON *sits on the bed, takes out a tobacco tin and papers, and begins to
roll himself a cigarette.* DAVIES *watches him.*
Pause.

ASTON: Take a seat.

(pp. 16–17)

Carried away by the rhythm of his tirade (the catchy four-beat
repetition of "Blacks, Greeks, Poles, the lot of them"), Davies
forgets that he wanted "a *good sit down,*" fails to *see* the chair Aston
has made ready for him. The situation created by this exchange—
Davies self-absorption and xenophobic rantings versus Aston's
generosity—becomes, in the course of their first duologue, a kind
of running gag. Aston will offer a chair, a cigarette, shoes, lodging,
money and will volunteer to fetch Davies's bag. Except for the
money, which he immediately accepts, Davies will ignore or reject
Aston's offers, just as he will reject Aston until their last encounter.
Furthering this incongruous interaction, Pinter underscores the
bum's likeness to a traditional *alazon,* the *miles gloriosus* or braggart soldier. Davies foolishly enacts the fighting man's anger ("*exclaims loudly, punches downward with clenched fist*"), and he
spoils for a fight though barely able to control his shaking knees:

I'll get him. One night I'll get him. When I find myself round in that
direction.

(p. 19)

Plautus's Pyrgopolynices (*The Swaggering Soldier*) boasts of fantastic exploits in foreign lands; hardly comparable are Davies's tales
of peripatetic mendicancy. However, the relish with which Davies
recounts his arguments with the Luton monk who refuses to give
him shoes transforms his victimization into a boasting pride. That
Davies prefers to talk about his inability to obtain shoes rather than
to try on the shoes Aston holds for him testifies to his love of verbal
performance and his concomitant blindness to Aston's generosity.
Like the *miles,* too, Davies considers himself irresistible to women.
To Aston's story about the woman in the pub ("how would you like
me to have a look at your body" [p. 34]) Davies responds:

DAVIES: They've said the same thing to me.
ASTON: Have they?

> DAVIES: Women? There's many a time they've come up to me and
> asked me more or less the same question.
>
> (p. 34)

Davies's qualifications—"many a time," "more or less"—belie his
sexual prowess but enhance his resemblance to comic type. Audiences are never to doubt that the *alazon* lies but are to enjoy the
comically exaggerated form of the lie, as when fastidiousness forces
Davies to leave his wife because she piled her unwashed lingerie in
the saucepan.

Davies's most amusing quality is his lying invective. When Aston reproaches him gently for "jabbering" in his sleep, Davies leaps
to the offensive: "I don't jabber, man. Nobody ever told me that
before" (p. 32). Then he adds, as if the possibility were feasible, "I
tell you what, maybe it were them Blacks." Davies's obsession with
"them Blacks," like his obsessions with shoes or Sidcup,
exemplifies the comic rigidity of the *alazon* and of his Renaissance
cousin, the Jonsonian humour.[78] In fact, "the peculiar quality" that
dominates the disposition of the humour character seems an apt
description of Davies's enraged paranoia. Jonson's Asper in
Everyman out of His Humour promises to "scourge the apes," and
Pinter's Davies, in these repetitive rantings, invites the scourging
of contemptuous laughter that Jonson (and later Henri Bergson)
saw as the corrective to antisocial folly.

Mingled with these traditionally comic elements, Davies's curious double identity seems another bit of ludicrous imposture, completely unlike the mysterious and destructive splintering of identity in *The Room* and *A Slight Ache*. Davies's insistence that he is
Jenkins in town, Davies in Sidcup, is funny precisely because he
works so hard to make it seem serious. Unlike Rose and Edward,
who labor to demystify their uncanny intruders, Davies seeks to
mystify the Sidcup connection—the man who has kept his papers
since "oh, must be . . . it was in the war . . . must be . . . about near
on fifteen years ago" (p. 30). He even stirs up mystery about his
origins:

> ASTON: Where were you born?
> DAVIES: I was . . . uh . . . oh, it's a bit hard, like, to set your mind
> back . . .
>
> (p. 34)

Is he ashamed to be Welsh (the name Davies is as Welsh as
McCann is Irish)? Ashamed that if he is anything but English, he

will be classed as a detested "foreigner"? Davies extends to absurdity Pinter's theme of the impossibility of verification (stated in
a program note for the Royal Court production of *The Room* and
The Dumb Waiter just a month before the opening of *The
Caretaker*):

> The desire for verification is understandable but cannot always be
> satisfied. . . . A character on the stage who can present no convincing
> argument or information as to his past experience, his present be-
> haviour or his aspirations, nor give a comprehensive analysis of his
> motives is as legitimate and as worthy of attention as one who, alarm-
> ingly, can do all these things.[79]

What Pinter does not say is that the consistent refusal to "present. . . . a convincing argument . . . as to past experience" can be
extremely funny. Davies balks at committing himself to any past
activity, whether it be his birth or the last time he sat down ("I
haven't had a proper sit down . . . well, I couldn't tell you" [p. 16]).
Evasiveness makes us suspicious in *The Room* and *A Slight Ache;*
Davies, however, is devoid of mystery. Despite and because of the
odd details in his biography we find his nastiness and deceit familiar and typical.

Less typical, apparently, is Aston, whose laconic calm contrib-
utes significantly to our impression of Davies's verbal excess. Yet in
comic duologue the clever *eiron* has precisely this function. He
affects ignorance or stupidity to draw out and expose the *alazon.*
The question for the audience in these early exchanges becomes to
what extent Aston's behavior is ironical. Lighting his cigarette
while Davies *"exclaims and punches"* (p. 17), quietly poking his
plug while Davies whines about the weather, all suggest a subtle
intent. On the other hand, Aston's descriptions of experiences in
the café and pub arise as non sequiturs and betray his own
difficulty with social discourse. Moreover, Aston reveals tendencies that remind us of his guest.

ASTON: I might build a shed out the back.

(p. 26)

DAVIES: I might get down to Wembley later on in the day.

(p. 36)

Both Aston and Davies would find it unbearable not to have plans,
but neither convinces us, even at this early stage, that he is capable
of carrying them out. Like Davies, too, Aston feels misunderstood:

I went into a pub the other day. Ordered a Guinness. They gave it to me in a thick mug. I sat down but I couldn't drink it. I can't drink Guinness from a thick mug. I only like it in a thin glass.

(p. 28)

Such sensitivity recalls Davies's reaction to his wife's lingerie in the saucepan. Excusing Aston from putting up his shed will be an endless series of thick mugs; excusing Davies from the Sidcup journey will be improper shoes or inclement weather. Aston recounts the pub story immediately after giving Davies money, symbolic acknowledgment of his need for Davies's company and his willingness, if necessary, to pay for it. If he is not the clever *eiron*, Aston nevertheless shows an aptitude for maneuvering and manipulation.

For the first Mick-Davies encounter, Pinter repeats the technique he employed in *The Room* when Rose opened the door and discovered to her shock a strange couple on the landing. Here the technique is more theatrical because protracted. While Davies rummages through Aston's belongings, Mick enters, watches for a moment, slips upstage, and attacks. The prowler becomes the prey. Toward this physical maneuver our reactions necessarily depend on our feelings for the participants, and in this scene, Pinter works to divide our sympathies. We do not know Mick, but Davies earns our contempt for his actions toward Aston, and the stalking choreography compels our participation in a game of cat and mouse.

Davies's scream of fear and pain ends comic suspense, but by dropping the curtain after Mick's line ("What's the game?" [p. 38]) and raising it a *"a few seconds later,"* Pinter heightens the gamelike theatricality of Mick's actions and softens their viciousness. In act 2, Mick uses words not muscle to beat down Davies in speeches designed to taunt, madden, insult, and, finally, trap. Like Goldberg, Mick bombards his victim, not with one-line riddles but with comically incoherent anecdotes based on fictional people whom Davies supposedly resembles. With their stunning abundance of detail and rapid short-sentence/phrase delivery, Mick's anecdotes are almost set pieces—verbal performances that seduce us with ludicrous visual comparisons, as that between Uncle Sid who performed "run-ups in the drawing room around Christmas time" (p. 40) and Davies who lies on the floor with his trousers off. And yet, Mick's verbal brilliance is inseparable from the violence of his first attack. Like Freud's tendentious jokes, Mick's anecdotes delight the third party (the audience) not merely for their cleverness but for the antisocial hostility they both displace and release.[80] Hostility finds direct expression in Mick's repetitious interrogations and commentary ("What's your name? . . . Jenkins . . . Jen . . . kins . . . What bed did you sleep in? . . . Choosy. . . . [pp. 41– 42]). Forcing Davies to repeat his answers, Mick widens the significance of his words with the result that Davies implicates himself more deeply with every round of questioning. Davies's offenses are surprisingly diverse, including sleeping in Mick's bed or in Mick's mother's bed, being an old scoundrel, and "stinking the place out" (p. 44) The "unfurnished" apartment that Mick offers to rent not only intimidates Davies, it shuts him out. In this soon-to-be-remodeled flat, Davies will have no place, just as he is unwanted now in the room.

Unwanted but not ejected. At Aston's entrance Mick drops Davies's trousers and his comic aggression as a different game begins. Mick and Davies take new positions, Aston resumes work on his toaster, and a drip in the bucket signals the beginning of play. In the quiet interchange between Aston and Mick, a past relationship is limned; Mick makes overtures that Aston quietly stifles, producing an ambiguous but palpable tension. Mick's sudden diffidence and Aston's equally surprising self-assurance seem to inspire a change in Davies, for he participates in conversation instead of monologuing ("What do you do when that bucket's full?" [p. 46]) However, Davies's interjection reestablishes his contact with Aston and fractures the Mick-Aston duologue, sparking a farce sequence reminiscent of the Marx Brothers' hat trick. Unable to restrain his hostility toward Davies but inhibited by Aston from pursuing verbal tactics, Mick intercepts Davies's bag just as Aston hands it to him. Davies reaches to snatch it back and Aston cuts Mick's taunts with an authoritative "Scrub it" (p. 47). Mick seems to be testing his opponents, trying to irritate Davies without offending Aston. But Aston outwits his brother by placing the bag directly in his hands. Another drop sounds in the bucket, bringing the routine to an end. Aston directs his first words to Davies, completely excluding Mick. As the bully bested, Mick has no recourse but to leave.

Aston's offer of the caretaker's job engenders another sequence, as comic for its attempted coherence as Mick's anecdotes were comic for their dazzling incoherence. Intent on communicating, neither Aston nor Davies can settle on the terms of discussion:

DAVIES: Well, I . . . I never done caretaking before, you know . . . I
mean to say . . . I never . . . what I mean to say is . . . I never
been a caretaker before.
Pause.
ASTON: How do you feel about being one, then?
DAVIES: Well, I reckon . . . Well, I'd have to know . . . you know. . . .
ASTON: What sort of. . . .
DAVIES: Yes, what sort of . . . you know. . . .

(p. 51)

And so on until Aston offers a pair of white overalls that Davies
readily accepts. Costuming for the job is evidently easier than
describing the job. Comically, our sense of reality conflicts with
Aston's. On this junk-filled stage, we have seen the ladder moved
along with the sink, the coal bucket, the shopping trolley, the
lawnmower, and the sideboard drawers. That such an assortment
requires the services of a caretaker is patently ridiculous: the bells
Aston would have Davies polish have not yet been installed.

Yet in hesitating to accept Aston's offer, Davies becomes an un-
witting participant in another game of harassment, playing *alazon*
to Mick's *eiron*. Masking, as Cornford says, "his battery of deceit
behind a show of ordinary good nature," Mick, like the tricky slave
Artorogus in *The Swaggering Soldier*, begins by feeding the vanity
of the braggart:

DAVIES: I don't mind a bit of a joke now and then, but anyone'll tell
you . . . that no one starts anything with me.
MICK: I get what you mean, yes.
DAVIES: I can be pushed so far . . . but . . .
MICK: No further.
DAVIES: That's it.

(p. 55)

A shabby Pyrgopolinices, Davies will later respond to Mick's prodding and boast of an exotic career as a soldier.

MICK: You been in the services. You can tell by your stance.
DAVIES: Oh . . . yes. Spent half my life in them, man.
MICK: In the colonies, weren't you?
DAVIES: I was over there. I was one of the first over there.

(pp. 59–60)

When Davies feels safe enough to join him on the junk pile, Mick
manipulates the bum into admitting his feelings toward Aston.

Masking contempt, Mick plays the callow young man seeking advice from "a man of the world." He even proffers a bit of his meal though noticeably disdains the communal gesture of eating with him. When Davies, in response to Mick's goads, refuses to call Aston "friend" but eagerly rises to hear something "not very nice" about him, he reveals his blindness not only to Aston's generosity but also to Mick's gulling maneuvers.

At this point, when Davies is most comically debased, Pinter loops back to a previous situation: the offer of a caretaker job. Comic as an obvious repetition in the plot, Mick's offer doubles the absurdity of Aston's offer, making the undesirable Davies seem doubly desired, which doubly confuses the audience. Worse, we share our confusion with the least attractive, most transparent character in the play. No more than Davies do we understand Aston and Mick's intentions in offering the caretaker job. Are they competing with or punishing one another? Are they in collusion? What is clear is that the imposture behind at least one of these offers repays Davies for his own ludicrous posturing, just as the two requests for a caretaker mock Davies's own motive with regard to the brothers: to find a way to be taken care *of*. Though inconceivable as a caretaker, Davies seems to fulfill a genuine need in Aston and Mick. Aston's closing speech in act 2, Davies's complaints that open act 3, and, finally, Mick's long interior-decorating speech form a triptych structure symbolizing, like the bag-passing routine, increasingly symbiotic relationships.

Aston's noncomic recollection of the asylum and his shock treatments is the longest realistic speech in the Pinter canon. No rhetorical quirks, no surprising juxtapositions, no insistent verbal repetitions distract us; instead, halting diction seems to express and explain character. During Aston's speech Davies sits silently in the corner and Pinter requests a long slow fade-out, though in play-time we are midmorning. Pinter seems to want Davies thematically present but theatrically absent. That is, he refuses to let Davies represent the audience on stage, preferring that Aston speak to us directly (although Davies refers to "the long chat he gave me" in the following act). For Aston, Davies is there and not there. He needs the old man's friendship or at least his presence, but this need blinds him to deficiencies in Davies himself (the reason perhaps why Davies remains obscured in darkness). Toward the hushed end of his speech Aston comments: "Anyway, I feel much better ncw. But I don't talk to people now" (p. 66).

Yet he does, even "now." And considering Davies's antipathy,

Aston is talking as indiscriminately as before. Interestingly, Pinter has tried to impugn Aston's credibility in this speech: "the one thing that people have missed is that it isn't necessary to conclude that everything Aston says about his experiences in the mental hospital is true."[81] In other words, Aston's discourse should be seen as a verbal performance and not as an example of referential truth. What this suggests is that Aston's noncomic speech can be at least partially aligned with the comic verbal performances earlier in the play. The pathos of Aston's description is undeniable, but the experience itself, Pinter insists, is unverifiable. Aston's words may thus be construed as a Pinterian smoke screen, a type of verbal posturing that differs from Mick's jokes and Davies's boasts in quality but not in kind.

If Aston's speech plunges us into the fictional past, Mick's interior-decorating speech turns us toward the fantastical future: a palatial penthouse that he describes with a clutter of images drawn from home-beautiful magazines.

> Venetian blinds on the window, cork floor, cork tiles. You could have an off-white pile linen rug, a table in . . . afromosia teak veneer, sideboard with matt black drawers, curved chairs with cushioned seats, armchairs in oatmeal tweed. . . .
>
> (p. 69)

In marked contrast to Aston's halting syllables, Mick's discourse blatantly mocks sincerity and referentiality. The piling up of decorator's jargon, the ellipses, and the two instances of the self-congratulatory "yes" testify to Mick's improvisational talents, his creative satisfaction at his own witty labor. Henri Bergson recognized the "laughable results" in the transposition of ideas of everyday life into technical jargon.[82] In this speech, Mick is both parodying the decorator's jargon and displaying its exotic appeal. Jostled together, phrases like "afromosia teak veneer" and "beach frame settee with a woven sea-grass seat" are freed from their signifying function (as descriptions of an actual room) to become part of a comically exaggerated series of orally and aurally pleasing sound images.

Not only does Mick's style differ from his brother's, his monologue reveals different family feeling. Aston's speech shows him cut off from his younger brother by the pains in his head and by his self-imposed isolation. But Mick gives Aston full partnership in his dreams:

DAVIES: Who would live there?
MICK: I would. My brother and me.

(p. 70)

Naturally Davies is excluded from the penthouse, but he does serve as Mick's interlocutor just as he provided the occasion for Aston's monologue. Inverting the traditional pattern of comic imposture, Davies, in spite of himself, has become an enabling presence for Mick and Aston, a kind of emotional caretaker.

Davies' histrionics open act 3, set between the brothers' long speeches; in a practical sense, he has become the link between the brothers. We discover him sitting in a chair ludicrously garbed in the smoking jacket Aston has given him, smoking a pipe filled, probably, with Aston's tobacco. Aston, however, is ruining Davies's life. The latter's harangue, set off by pauses, resembles a reading of official condemnations: "He don't answer me when I talk to him. . . . He don't give me no knife" (p. 67). Soon we learn that Aston will not remove the gas stove; he will not prevent "them Blacks" from using the lavatory; he will not converse; he will not give Davies a clock; and, worst of all, he smiles before leaving the apartment. Like the vicious Informer (another *alazon*) in Aristophanes' *The Birds*, who counts on personal gain by ruining reputations, Davies hopes that his disparagement of Aston will encourage Mick to evict him. And like all *alazoneia*, Davies remains ignorant of the uncertainty of his own position.

Pinter, however, requires *us* to acknowledge Davies's precariousness by admitting darker nuances to the dialogue. Though Davies plays the comic butt when Mick invites him to "listen to some Tchaikovsky," his repetition of the Sidcup story strikes a sadder note. "I've been offered a good job" (p. 74) is his excuse for urgency, but Aston exits unnoticed, leaving the audience to witness his confession. At this point the difference between his present security and the bleakness that was his past seems, for the first time, poignant:

> Don't know as these shoes'll be much good. It's a hard road, I been down there before. Coming the other way, like . . . Last time I left there, it was . . . last time . . . getting on a while back.
>
> (p. 74)

Morbid images ("the rain was coming down, lucky I didn't die there on the road") lend mythic proportions to the road to Sidcup.

This might be Didi and Gogo's endless road or perhaps the treacherous road that challenges Bert in *The Room*. We sense that "getting back all right" required all the pent-up hatred and violence of which Bert was capable. Davies appears to lack the strength for such a road. The red velvet smoking jacket, his symbol of security and even importance in Aston's room, contrasts grimly with his tramp's rags.

Anger, however, resuscitates Davies in a long tirade that swerves giddily between comedy and horror. Recycling Aston's descriptions of the mental hospital with his own now-familiar grievances, Davies fabricates a paranoid scene of persecution with Aston as lunatic torturer, Mick as absent defender, and Davies as innocent victim. Davies constructs his case with hectoring repetitions ("mucking me about," "pincers on your head," "keep your place" [p. 76]), and though this spectacle of unleashed viciousness is terrifying, the audience recognizes the victim role as Davies's most typical imposture and understands that Davies, not Aston, has lost his sense of "place." If these considerations do not mitigate the cruelty of the tirade, Pinter works that purpose with a reprise of *miles gloriosus* behavior; Davies waves his knife at the implacable Aston, who responds with devastating comic understatement: "I . . . think it's about time you found somewhere else. I don't think we're hitting it off" (p. 77). The expulsion of the imposter has begun.

Until this point in the play Pinter has counterpointed two comic structures: the predictable exposure of the poser-imposter and the unpredictable game-playing situations in which alliances form, change, and reform among all three characters. Throughout the play, the simplicity of Davies's character as *alazon* is continually made problematic by his mediating function in the brothers' relationship, a function that baffles Davies as it does us. In Aston's rejection of Davies, Pinter foreshadows the expulsion of the imposter but stages the expulsion in a way that keeps alive the spirit of game playing. The necessary bridge to the final scene is the last Mick-Davies duologue that rehearses the *eiron-alazon* dynamic but suddenly explodes into attack and, on Mick's part, defensive self-revelation.

As the scene opens, Mick pretends to support Davies against Aston's accusations; he then reverses positions, crushing Davies's last hopes of an alliance. Significantly, the reversal occurs not when Davies attacks Aston's sanity but when Mick forces him to confess to an imposture (DAVIES: "I can decorate it out for you" [p. 72]) and

with comic prevarication worthy of Davies himself, Mick accuses
the bum of complicity in the penthouse fantasy. In other words,
Mick uses his own ostentatious verbal performance to expose
Davies's posturing throughout the play. Explicit attack ("You're a
bloody imposter, mate! . . . Most of what you say is lies" [pp. 81–
82]) provokes another verbal performance, executed with an incongruous mixture of overwrought formality ("It's all most regrettable"
[p. 83]) and inventive vulgarity ("you stink from arse-hole to breakfast time" [p. 83]). But Mick strikes an entirely different note
when, after shattering the Buddha against the gas stove, he implies
a contrast between his need for action and Aston's infuriating passivity. The naturalistic diction and rhythm of this speech suggest
that Mick is representing his "real" feelings, and ironically these
reveal a poser-imposter not unlike the reviled Davies.

> MICK: . . . I've got plenty of other interests. I've got my own busi-
> ness to build up, haven't I? I got to think about expanding . . .
> in all directions. I don't stand still. I'm moving about, all the
> time.
>
> (p. 83)

> DAVIES: . . . I get up in the morning, I'm worn out! I got business to
> see to. I got to move myself, I got to sort myself out, I got to
> get fixed up.
>
> (p. 72)

Both Mick and Davies have a vaunted notion of how their time
should be spent, yet both are fastened to Aston's room. In particular, Mick's impassive immobility in the opening seconds of the play
belies his claims to "other interests" and to "moving about."

At Aston's arrival the brothers acknowledge each other by *smiling faintly*—Pinter's only gesture toward conventional comic closure.[83] The smile suggests a tacit understanding that Davies will be
expelled from the room and that family unity will be restored.
Undermining that gesture is the clear ambiguity of the smile. It
may signify communication, it may even replace the Buddha's
mystical smile; but the smile is faint because the bond between the
brothers is tenuous: throughout the play their most important
statements are made in Davies's presence and not to each other.
Pinter has said that *The Caretaker* "is about love."[84] But the relationships mock the fulfillment of love. Aston needs Davies and
attempts to accommodate his peculiarities in order to keep him;
Davies feels contempt for Aston and turns toward Mick for protection. Mick wants no relationship with Davies; he tolerates him only

to be closer to Aston. In other words, Pinter represents these "love" relationships as a conventional love triangle in which each character gropes toward fulfillment with someone who is looking the other way—a comically cruel image of love in which resolution will always be deferred in favor of game playing and maneuvering. That Mick departs just after Aston arrives confirms the instability of their communication. Perhaps the brothers need a new intruder, a new series of gamelike maneuvers, in order to make contact with one another.

The closing duologue between Aston and Davies inverts the emotions expressed in their first scene: to Davies's pleas for recognition Aston responds not with generosity but with four strong "No's." Aston has certainly changed but Davies remains true to his own self-ignorance; and in this scene his habitual rationalizing veers unwittingly between wheedling and invective: pleas become demands. Refusing to acknowledge his groaning, Davies insists that if Aston traded beds, Davies would not feel the draught, would therefore stop groaning. He closes with a bleak reference to Sidcup, which for Davies symbolizes legitimacy and for everyone else the imposture that falsifies all his attempts at legitimacy. However, by bringing down the curtain after Davies's words fade into silence, Pinter weights our response on the side of pity not scorn. *The Caretaker*, Pinter has said, "is funny up to a point. Beyond that point it ceases to be funny, and it was because of that point that I wrote it."[85] "That point" may be the moment when comic rants break into fragmented stutters and then "*a long silence*" while Aston's back remains turned. And yet the inflexibility of Davies's character even to his last pathetic stutterings aligns him with the traditional *alazon* and the Jonsonian humour; he might also be Bergson's typical comic character in *Laughter* whose habit-ridden behavior impresses us as mechanical and antisocial rather than humanly adaptable.[86]

That which is objectlike in Davies's character is reinforced by the stage image:

MICK (*quietly*): All this junk here, it's no good to anyone. It's just a lot of old iron, that's all. Clobber. You couldn't make a home out of this. There's no way you could arrange it. It's junk.

(p. 70)

Aston's junk provides a concrete metaphor for Davies's comic rigidity. His imposture restates in human terms what the room silently suggests, for "there [is] no way you could arrange" the life of Davies/Jenkins. The desire "to make a home" from even useless clobber infects and frustrates both Aston and Mick. Like the cluttered experience of their past, the incoherent assemblage of feelings and memories, Aston's inanimate objects lie around imposing their presence but providing nothing constructive. The brothers must live with the wreckage of their youth as they live with the wreckage of the past. Neither can move the junk or change it or leave it.

Ironically, the irritating Davies provides a kind of relief from the effects of the room. Because of his intrusion the present assumes a fluid quality in which all three characters rebound off one another to create overtly comic routines (gulling Davies, passing the bag). However, Pinter's comic strategy is to induce us to respond to comic elements and, over time, to make us uncomfortable with those responses. Davies qua *alazon* is merely ludicrous, but the game-playing situations in which he participates suggest a function beyond the scope of the stereotypic *alazon*. At the end of the play that suggestion becomes explicit: we have laughed condescendingly when Davies plays the comic butt and when he pretends to be a victim, but in the last *"long silence"* he becomes a victim, a symbol of suffering. Toward the end of the play, as Davies pivots between comedy and crisis, familiar comic images take on a sinister aspect. Davies's colorful self-abuse in the Luton monk story ("What do you think I am, a dog? . . . a wild animal?" [p. 24]) is flung back at him by Mick ("You're nothing else but a wild animal" [p. 82]), and both references are reinforced by Davies's obsession with stinking. Forced to resume the road to Sidcup through what we know will be innumerable detours, we have no reason to think he will arrive. As Pinter's revision of the traditional *alazon*, Davies stinks, above all, of mortality.

The Birthday Party. **Doris Hare as Meg; Brian Pringle as Stanley. Royal Shakespeare Company, 1964. Photo by Zoë Dominic, London.**

The Birthday Party. Robert Symonds as Goldberg; Edward O'Brien as McCann. Actor's Workshop, San Francisco, 1960. Photo by Chic Lloyd. Courtesy of The Billy Rose Theatre Collection, New York Public Library.

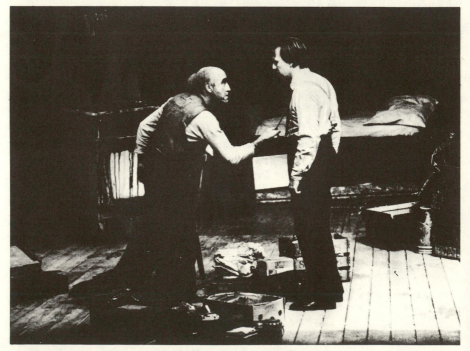

The Caretaker. Warren Mitchell as Davies; Jonathan Pryce as Aston. National Theatre, 1980. Photo by Catherine Ashmore, London.

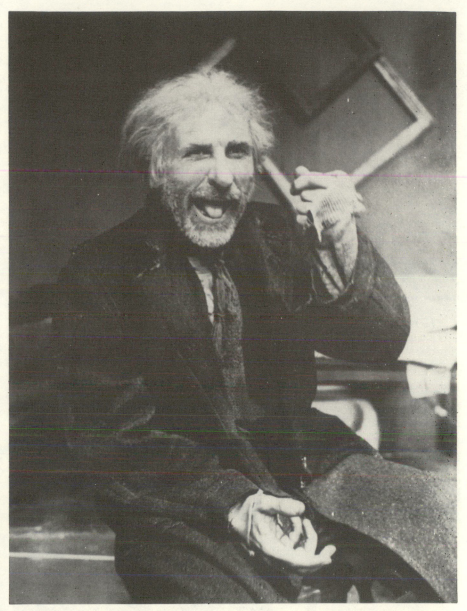

The Caretaker. Barry Morse as Davies. Touring Company Oct.–Nov. 1962. Courtesy of The Billy Rose Theatre Collection, New York Public Library.

The Lover. Vivien Merchant as Sarah; Patrick Allen as Richard. Photo by Zoë Dominic, London.

The Lover. Vivien Merchant as Sarah. Photo by Zoë Dominic, London.

The Homecoming. Vivien Merchant as Ruth; Paul Rogers as Max; Ian Holm as Lenny. Royal Shakespeare Company, 1965. Photo courtesy of The Billy Rose Theatre Collection, New York Public Library.

The Homecoming. Royal Shakespeare Company, 1965. Paul Rogers as Max; Vivien Merchant as Ruth; Terence Rigby as Joey. Photo courtesy of The Billy Rose Theatre Collection, New York Public Library.

The Homecoming. Royal Shakespeare Company, 1965. Michael Bryant as Teddy; Vivien Merchant as Ruth; Terence Rigby as Joey; John Normington as Sam; Paul Rogers as Max. Photo by Zoë Dominic, London.

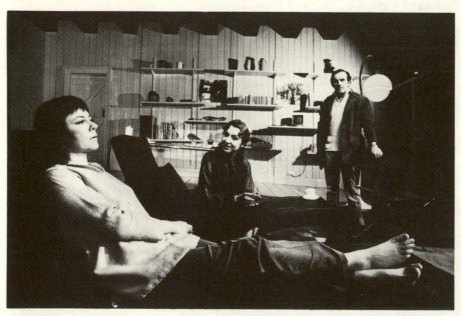

Old Times. Dorothy Tutin as Kate. Vivien Merchant as Anna; Colin Blakely as Deeley. Royal Shakespeare Company, 1971. Photo by Zoë Dominic, London.

Old Times. Dorothy Tutin as Kate; Colin Blakely as Deeley; Vivien Merchant as Anna. Royal Shakespeare Company, 1971. Photo by Zoë Dominic, London.

No Man's Land. Sir Ralph Richardson as Hirst; Sir John Gielgud as Spooner, National Theatre, 1976. Photo by Anthony Crickmay.

2

The Parody Plays

"Parody, says Eric Bentley, "is more important to the modern than to any previous school of comedy."[1] Although critics praise Pinter's comic talents, few before Andrew Kennedy (in *Six Dramatists in Search of a Language*) have seen him as a parodist.[2] Perhaps the emphasis on Pinter's originality seems inconsistent with a form that places a writer in direct communication with his forbears and peers. Perhaps Pinter's own oft-quoted insistence on the spontaneity of his writing process ("I . . . write in a very high state of excitement and frustration. I follow what I see on the paper in front of me—one sentence after another") precludes, or seems to preclude, the idea of his using other literary and theatrical styles as targets.[3] Pinter has said flatly: "I'm not interested in the general context of the theatre."[4]

Yet Pinter the playwright was reared in "the general context of the theatre." At twenty, he became a published poet (two poems accepted in *Poetry London*) and a professional actor (touring for eighteen months in Anew McMaster's Shakespearean company). In 1953, he acted a season in Sir Donald Wolfit's company, and in 1954, under the stage name of David Baron, he toured the provinces as a repertory actor, performing conventional, often stale, West End fare in a grueling schedule of morning rehearsals and evening performances. He wrote *The Room* in four days, between rehearsing for one play and performing another. Later, "I finished *The Birthday Party* while I was touring in some kind of farce, I don't remember the name."[5]

Success brought not less but more immersion in the general context of the theater. Pinter frequently directs, bringing to life not only his own work but plays as diverse as Robert Shaw's *Man in a Glass Booth* and Noel Coward's *Blithe Spirit*. He has written successfully for radio, television, and film, adapting to the limitations

and possibilities of each medium. Moreover, he has continued acting in his own and in the plays of other dramatists.

Have these persistent theatrical activities affected his writing? In
an early interview Pinter mused:

> My experience as an actor has influenced my plays—it must have—
> though it's impossible for me to put my finger on it exactly.[6]

Leslie Smith has put her finger on at least one direct influence,[7]
and Peter Davison has shown links between the music-hall style
and Pinter's dialogue.[8] Pinter himself has drawn comparisons between Wolfit's moment-making gestures (Pinter witnessed them
stage-side) and the kind of theater "I seem to write."[9] Furthermore,
the "fourth-wall" proscenium stage has been stamped on Pinter's
imagination:

> Whenever I write for the stage I merely see the stage I've been used to
> . . . I always think of the normal picture-frame stage.[10]

According to Peter Hall, the much-discussed living-room set in
The Homecoming was inspired by the broad-aproned Aldwych,
where the play began its London run.[11] Thus Pinter's artistic life
thrives in a dialectical tension between what he calls "the large
public activity" of theater and the "completely private activity" that
is writing.[12]

Just such a dialectic informs parody—the tension between the
public domain of literary and theatrical styles and the playwright
inevitably in contact with them. Although recent studies identify
parody as a comically skewed imitation of an author's style or of a
particular work, they also stress the historical moment of the
parodist who ironically plays with and criticizes a tradition even as
he establishes himself within it. Bentley's reference to parody as an
influential school of comedy refers to Shaw's parodies of Scribe,
"[his] way of calling attention to dangerous fallacies."[13] The "Scribe
. . . counter-Scribe" in Shaw is the impulse to debunk a Scribean
device by parodying it: "The very fact that Shaw despised Scribe
helps to explain the particular use he made of him."[14] In Harold
Bloom's theory of poetic influence, "latecomer" poets necessarily
misread their predecessors "so as to clear imaginative space for
themselves."[15] The Russian Formalist concept of "laying bare" or
using a device "without the motivation that traditionally accom-

panies it" is the cornerstone of Bertel Pedersen's study of parody in
modern fiction;[16] the parodist exposes "mockingly and playfully"
the conventions of a genre in order to define and liberate his own
creation.[17] Andrew Kennedy (also in connection with Shaw) defines
parody as the "mimesis of distorting mirrors,"[18] a concept echoed in
Margaret Rose's theoretical work on metafictional parody: "parody
does not attempt to mystify the difference between sign and
signified, or to suggest an identity between itself and its object as
in the mimetic art which parody has so often been used to criti-
cise."[19] In other words, since parody is not a "mirror of nature" but
a deliberately skewed imitation of another representation, it lays
bare the convention of mimesis, exposing it as a device. Stated or
implied in these studies are four ideas relevant to parody in Pinter.
First, the parodist belongs to the "endphase" of a tradition. Second, in response to that endphase he lays bare and playfully recasts
the conventions that inform it. Third, parodists frequently target
the conventions of naïvely mimetic art (well-made realism, television soap opera). Fourth, the parodist's enterprise is inevitably
self-reflexive, for in exposing the limitations of his models he comments on the form of his own creation.

Undeniably Pinter knew intimately the endphase of British theater in the fifties. He memorized the lines and recreated the gestures of the well-made play style that Shaw attacked in the 1890s
but could not kill—a tradition that fostered Somerset Maugham,
J. B. Priestley, Dodie Smith, John Van Druten, and many others—
dramatists whose work still bears revival but who rely on stock
types and conventionally "safe" attitudes. Pinter has called himself
a "traditional" dramatist (liking curtain lines and the suspense they
provoke), but in his polemical address to the 1962 National Student
Drama Festival in Bristol he declared war on tradition. In attacking
moralizing dramatists he implicitly attacks naïvely mimetic art that
uses the stage to mirror conventional social hierarchies. When he
attacks well-made or contrived endings, he prepares us for his own
revised resolutions, the ambiguous tableaux on which his curtains
close. When he decries character labeling and insists that his characters tell him so much and no more, he divorces himself from the
stock characters of well-made drama—those well-educated,
blandly articulate, mildly eccentric types forever lighting ciga-
rettes, pouring drinks, gliding in and out of drawing rooms, talking
not of Michelangelo but of servants, scandals, and motor car excur-
sions. When Pinter evokes the "nausea" of the language trough,

the "stale dead terminology" of our popular culture, he is also
lambasting naturalistic theatrical language that attempts to mirror
social and psychological relationships. Pinter comments:

> But if it is possible to confront this nausea, to follow it to its hilt, to
> move through it and out of it, then it is possible to say that something
> has occurred, that something has been achieved.[20]

What is achieved when a writer follows a dead language "to its hilt"
is parody, as in Pinter's review sketch "Trouble in the Works,"
which owes its comedy to the litany of technical jargon that passes
for dialogue. The impulse to move "through and out of" an out-
moded style is to admit a dialogue with one's predecessors and
peers, and then to demonstrate (subtly, in Pinter's case) one's differences.

In *The Dumb Waiter, The Collection, The Lover,* and *The
Homecoming,* Pinter writes parody. That is, he lays bare the conventions of popular dramatic styles for comic and ironic effect. *The
Dumb Waiter* parodies the gangster movie and the detective plot;
The Collection parodies the conventions of the melodrama and
soap opera; *The Lover* parodies comedies of manners, and *The
Homecoming* parodies domestic family dramas. Written over a period of eight years, these four plays differ in content, form, and
tone; yet they have in common two essential qualities that separate
them from Pinter's other pre-1966 works: one, comic effects can be
traced to the imitation of and parodic departure from other theatrical styles; and two, within the plays themselves, Pinter focuses on
confusing gamelike situations rather than on the emotions aroused
by confusion.

Parody is unabashed gamesmanship. A dramatist creates verbal
and gestural double entendres and leaves it to his audience to
guess his rules. In chapter 3, I discuss the theatrical context of
Pinter's models, but the parodic effects in the plays themselves
would be immediately obvious in the theater. The gangster language and guns in *The Dumb Waiter* are familiar elements of the
crime world; the furtive phone calls and middle-class interiors of
The Collection cue us to expect melodrama or standard television
soap opera; the aphoristic dialogue of *The Lover* echoes the comedy of manners just as the coffee circle ceremony in *The Homecoming* recalls the conventions of family drama in realism. As in all
parody, those elements we identify from past styles are mocked in

the present context, and it is through these mocking elements that Pinter controls our reaction to the work.

Parody, with its gamesmanship, also structures the characters' conflicts, and the word "game" surfaces at crucial moments in the action. Characters fumble because they apply the rules of past behavior to present circumstances, only to discover that the relationship between past and present is a parodic one: the present imitates and distorts the past.[21] Pinter focuses on comic confusion in game playing and steers away from other emotions, an aspect that distinguishes the "parody plays" from the "poser-loser" plays. Parodic elements in *The Birthday Party, A Slight Ache,* or *The Caretaker* (the gangster/comedy duo of Goldberg and McCann; the manners comedy dialogue of Edward and Flora; Mick's interior-decorating fantasy) are interspersed among scenes of stillness in which characters are less confused game players than emotional losers.

The plays in this chapter are unusual in their adherence to the sense of play, the degree to which verbal parodies counterpoint naturalistic speech and maneuvering invades the sphere of action. Pinter in these plays is more obviously the rule maker and controller than in his earlier works. All four have surprise endings that undercut initiative in the characters and mock our sense of superiority with regard to the characters' confusion. Pinter plays games with his audience throughout the plays, making us think we are getting the joke, yet surprising us with the punch line.

THE DUMB WAITER

Hat pulled low over his eyes, breast pocket bulging with his "piece," hunkering buddies at his side, the gangster murdered and met bloody death in the movies while Harold Pinter was growing up. American films on organized crime began in the 1930s, and despite interruptions from World War II and occasional censorship, British audiences became acquainted with all manner of thugs, from Sidney Greenstreet's delicate sadist in *The Maltese Falcon* (1941) to the laconic, overcoated hoods in films like *The Naked City* (1948) and *Night and the City* (1950). In *Odd Man Out* (1947), a film Pinter certainly knew, loose-lipped toughs betray their leader and the "Organization."[22] But crime was comic and gangsters were bumbling clowns in Alexander Mackendrick's *The*

Ladykillers (1955). That Herbert Lom, a popular villain in British
drama, played a serious gangster role in *Night and the City* and a
parodic gangster in *The Ladykillers,* suggests the versatility of the
type.

A fan of American gangster films, Pinter knew a multitude of
stereotypes and could rely on his audience to recognize them. *The
Dumb Waiter,* written just after *The Birthday Party* in 1957, opens
on two men, dressed alike, killing time in a comfortless room. One
reads from the newspaper, the other comments on the crockery
and remarks anxiously: "I hope it won't be a long job, this one"
(p. 131).[23] The hit man's slang is immediately identifiable and
grounds us, as with Goldberg and McCann's "job" talk, in the
gangster idiom. But Goldberg and McCann are surrealistic gangsters; their verbal masquerades soon annihilate the stereotype. In
The Dumb Waiter, Pinter's strategy is parody: he both exploits and
mocks the suspense of hit men waiting to bump off a victim; Gus's
anxiety and Ben's belligerence keep the stereotypes well in view.

Certainly the waiting game is a familiar gangster convention in
film and detective drama. In *Odd Man Out,* for example, two Irish
gunmen, Pat and Nolan, desert their chief and betray the Organization. Just as Gus takes stock of the room in an effort to calm his
nerves, Pat *"moves about the room, prying into silver boxes, exam-
ining various articles and appraising their worth."*[24] Eventually
Pat's movements upset Nolan, and their subsequent exchange is
starkly reminiscent of Gus and Ben's panicked language:

NOLAN'*s hand flies to his jacket and comes out with his revolver.*
NOLAN *(taking fright):* Let's get out of here!
PAT: Shut up! Listen!
NOLAN: I am off!
PAT: Stay where you are, you fool![25]

GUS: I asked you a question.
BEN: Enough!
GUS *(with growing agitation):* I asked you before. Who moved in?
BEN *(hunched):* Shut up.
GUS: I told you, didn't I?
BEN *(standing):* Shut up!

(p. 161)

Staccato, speeded-up attacks record the racing pulse of the killer
who senses a trap, a stereotypical scene in television and film.

Early stage precursors to Ben and Gus are the Cockney toughs in Henry Arthur Jones's *The Silver King* and—a more appropriate example—in William Gillette's *Sherlock Holmes,* a play based on several Conan Doyle stories, which opened in New York in 1899 and sustained long runs in London until 1930. Gillette seems to relish what Doyle had to forgo in giving the narrative point of view to Dr. Watson: a direct presentation of Professor Moriarty's criminal organization. Act 3, scene 1 reveals the boredom and apprehension of Moriarty's hit men, Craigin and Leary, whose target, unknown to them, is Sherlock Holmes. Similar to Gus and Ben's windowless room in *The Dumb Waiter,* Craigin and Leary's den bears a single window "*so grimy and dirty that nothing can be seen through it.*"[26] We find Craigin and Leary engaged in a familiar task—waiting. McTague arrives with a lamp, and Craigin, obscured in semidarkness speaks:

CRAIGIN: Wot's McTague doing here?
MCTAGUE: I was sent 'ere.
LEARY: I thought the Seraph was with us in this job.
MCTAGUE: 'E *ain't.*
LEARY *(after a pause):* 'Oo was the last you put the gas on?
CRAIGIN: I didn't 'ear 'is name. *(Pause)* 'Ed been 'oldin' back money on a deal—that's all I know.
MCTAGUE *(after a long pause):* Wot's this 'ere job he wants done.
CRAIGIN: I ain't been told.[27]

Nor are Gus and Ben told, and like the Cockney assassins, they are also dumb, unable to say who their victim will be. Tension mounts (note Gillette's "Pinteresque" use of the pause) among the killers even as the net closes over the victim.

At pains to incorporate the conventions of standard gangster behavior, Pinter also works to counter them. With Gus he melds gangster and detective roles to create a parodic detective plot. Gus's obsession is not "whodunnit" but "who is doing it" in present time. To the manifest disgust of his partner, but in the best Holmesian tradition, Gus makes observations, gathers clues, and tries to deduce who owns the house they live in, what football matches will be available after hours, and, most important, who is upstairs commanding the dumb waiter. In this game of pre-crime detection, the audience is invited to participate. Since Ben's behavior is constantly suspicious, we, like Gus, wonder why he stopped in the woods when he thought Gus was asleep, why he avoids direct questions. Inquiry, however, is frustrated by the fact that Gus is not a real detective but a ridiculous imitation of one: a parodic detective. His detective impulses undermine his gangster impulses, making him ludicrous in that role as well.

While the nervous gangster and the obsessive detective gave Pinter established conventions for parody, Samuel Beckett's *Waiting for Godot,* which opened in London two years before Pinter wrote *The Dumb Waiter,* provided a comic model of man waiting. Pinter's admiration for Beckett is well known, and many critics note Beckettian echoes in *The Dumb Waiter,* particularly when waiting for Wilson produces the music-hall rhythm and metaphysical resonance of waiting for Godot.[28] Yet the ways in which Pinter "swerves" from his model contribute most fruitfully to his comedy. Beckett subverts naturalism. On his timeless, near-empty stage, artificial scenic devices (the sudden moon, the fast-leafing tree) are deliberately unmimetic signposts in Gogo and Didi's struggle with meaning. Pinter, however, parodies naturalism, exaggerating his stage objects to the level of comic grotesque. The dumb waiter may be construed as symbolic liaison between hirelings and bosses, between this world and the next, but it is also—and mostly—an outdated noisy message machine with a fantastic assortment of demands. Differentiating his pair of waiters from Beckett's, Pinter permits no self-awareness or understanding. When revelation comes at the end of their wait, Gus and Ben are frozen in a silent tableau. Though Gogo and Didi are also frozen (they *"do not move"* at the end), Beckett endows them with awesome understanding:

> ESTRAGON: I can't go on like this.
> VLADIMIR: That's what you think.[29]

However, Pinter freely borrows and exploits the Beckettian comic mime and music-hall style—or, rather, he takes advantage of the fact that Beckett made nonliterary popular styles acceptable.[30] Derby-hatted, feisty, yet vulnerable, Beckett's tramps have been compared to Chaplin's tramp, and all have been likened to Everyman in the representation of the human comedy. Pinter's Gus and Ben are closer to another derby-hatted comedy team, Laurel and Hardy, whose mime often resembles Chaplin's—not surprising since Laurel and Chaplin, both English, received early training together in Fred Karno's pantomine company.[31] The comedy of Laurel and Hardy lies less in their universal resonance than in their relationship. Both are incompetent, but Hardy bullies and blames Laurel for their catastrophes while Laurel, chastened, pauses, then resumes his delicately choreographed mischief. Laurel's wail and Hardy's long-suffering "take" to the camera may seem unrelated to the stage behavior of Gus and Ben, yet the basics of their relationship are parallel. Ultimately Ben knows little more about the world they inhabit than does Gus, but his contemptuous stares and bullying convince himself and Gus that he is superior.

Interspersed, then, with parodic treatment of gangsters and detectives is this mirthful strain derived from the English music halls. Pinter's comic strategy is based on the incongruous blend of parodic elements: that a gangster can behave like an amateur detective; that two gangsters' behavior reminds us of a music-hall act; and that, conversely, two clownlike characters carry guns and work as assassins.

Furthermore, parody provides counterpoint to the growing fear of the characters. A game analogy may clarify this contrapuntal tension. The givens of Pinter's play situation resemble Johan Huizinga's description of any play action: "It proceeds within its own proper boundaries of time and space according to fixed rules and in an orderly manner."[32] Gus and Ben go to an anonymous room, wait for a certain period of time, then shoot the first person who walks through the door. Within this larger game, the killers play routine games to pass the time. However, *this* time, before the victim's arrival, unexpected intrusions alter the rules of the old game, heralding a new one whose object is not clear to either audience or characters until the last seconds of the play. It is the conflict between the old and new game plans that triggers terror for the characters, suspense for us. Moreover, the game-altering intrusions, the envelope and the dumb waiter, divide the play into three sections. In the first two sections, Ben's gangster and Gus's detective behavior mix fluidly with clownlike actions; in the complex third section, roles congeal, but parody remains Pinter's technique for molding and mocking audience expectation.

Pantomime opens *The Dumb Waiter* and establishes its comic context. Pinter's stage directions for the mime merit full quotation as they reveal his shrewd understanding of the comic routine:

> BEN *is lying on a bed, left, reading a paper.* GUS *is sitting on a bed, right, tying his shoe-laces, with difficulty. Both are dressed in shirts, trousers and braces.*
> *Silence.*
> GUS *ties his laces, rises, yawns and begins to walk slowly to the door, left. He stops, looks down, and shakes his foot.*

> BEN *lowers his paper and watches him.* GUS *kneels and unties his shoe-lace and slowly takes off the shoe. He looks inside it and brings out a flattened matchbox. He shakes it and examines it. Their eyes meet.* BEN *rattles his paper and reads.* GUS *puts the matchbox in his pocket and bends down to put on his shoe. He ties his lace, with difficulty.* BEN *lowers his paper and watches him.* GUS *walks to the door, left, stops, and shakes the other foot. He kneels, unties his shoe-lace, and slowly takes off the shoe. He looks inside it and brings out a flattened cigarette packet. He shakes it and examines it. Their eyes meet.* BEN *rattles his paper and reads.* GUS *puts the packet in his pocket, bends down, puts on his shoe and ties the lace.*
>
> *He wanders off, left.*
>
> BEN *slams the paper down on the bed and glares after him. He picks up the paper and lies on his back, reading.*
> *Silence.*
> *A lavatory chain is pulled twice off, left, but the lavatory does not flush.*
> *Silence.*
> GUS *re-enters, left, and halts at the door, scratching his head.*
>
> (p. 129)

This silent action, which could describe a typical Laurel and Hardy gag, telegraphs the nature of the Gus-Ben partnership and plants seeds of suspense. The comedian's gag arouses laughter through absurd action and repetition. We laugh not only because Gus finds an object in one of his shoes but because he *then* finds an object in the other shoe. Similarly, the first time Ben rattles his newspaper he shows annoyance; the second time his annoyance is mocked because Gus continues unearthing objects. Like Laurel, Gus simply acts, oblivious to criticism. Like Hardy, Ben shares his irritation with the audience, glaring and rattling his newspaper. Like Hardy, too, Ben's disdain makes him seem dominant; he looks, then hides, so that Gus, under his scrutiny, assumes the aspect of a victim. A cat-and-mouse game has begun for which we have no explanation.[33]

Gus's clownish behavior deserves consideration. He has *"difficulty"* tying his shoes, a child's problem typical of the clown's interaction with all props. Not even the lavatory chain works for Gus though he pulls it twice—a repetition confirming his ineptitude. That he finds a cigarette packet and a matchbox in his shoes is the clown's parody of the logic of logistics. That he *"shakes"* each item is more irrational reasoning: he hopes to retrieve a smokeable cigarette from a packet he has been standing on. Distracted by

Ben's furtive behavior, we do not think to ask how these items arrived in Gus's shoes. Yet our acceptance of Gus's eccentricities means we already view him as a clown, and, by implication, we become a clown's audience—that is, an audience prepared to laugh. Pinter may hope for this reaction; the stage directions at the end of the mime indicate: *"Gus re-enters . . . scratching his head"*—the clown's gesture of befuddlement.

After the comic mime, until the first intrusion, Pinter introduces all the parodic motifs, intertwining them, as he did in the mime, in a careful pattern of repetition. Ben reads lurid lines from the newspaper about a man run over by a lorry while Gus responds like a music-hall feed: "He what?"; "Go on!"; "It's unbelievable" (p. 130). Then Gus exits and returns with: "I want to ask you something" (p. 130). Ben interrupts, telling Gus to make the tea. Instead Gus describes the crockery and refers back to the question he has not asked, at which point Ben interrupts him with another recital from the newspaper. Through repetition we understand the rules of the newspaper game: Ben reads aloud and Gus makes interested comments. The game begins when Ben slams down the paper with "Kaw!" and ends when commentary exhausts itself. Moreover Ben establishes the limits of the game when he reminds Gus: "Time's getting on" (p. 131). A deadline looms over them. The newspaper game passes the time, and the audience acknowledges time passing.

Gus's detective aptitude is revealed and parodied immediately. Even in the newspaper routine he probes for causes behind effects. About the man who crawled under the lorry: "Who advised him to do a thing like that?" (p. 130). Persistent, he sets out three times to ask Ben "something." Ruminating over the funereal color of the plates, Gus meticulously hunts for significance:

There's a white stripe . . .
You know, sort of round the cup. Round the rim. All the rest of it's black, you see. Then the saucer's black, except for right in the middle, where the cup goes, where it's white. [ellipses mine]

(p. 131)

When Ben reads about the cat killing, Gus makes an intuitive leap worthy of Sherlock Holmes: "I'll bet [the brother] did it" (p. 132).

Soon, though, detection dovetails into clownlike confusion. After the first recital from the newspaper, Gus attempts an interrogation:

GUS:	I want to ask you something.
BEN:	What are you doing out there?
GUS:	Well, I was just—
BEN:	What about the tea?
GUS:	I'm just going to make it.
BEN:	Well, go on, make it.
GUS:	Yes, I will. *(He sits in a chair.)*

(p. 130)

In a sketch Laurel wrote for a tour of the English music halls, he constantly interrupts Hardy who is trying to introduce himself. Suddenly Hardy turns on Laurel and the latter, flustered, loses his train of thought and wails. Then interrupts again.[34] Similarly, Gus is cowed by Ben's aggressiveness and forgets, or agrees to forget, his question. But his sitting down signals his obstinacy and soon he gets his question asked: "Have you noticed the time that tank takes to fill?" (p. 133). Of course the question deflates the suspense created by his persistence, and the joke is compounded by Ben's absurdly technical response to the problem ("It's got a deficient ballcock, that's all" [p. 133]), yet the response reassures Gus, recalling Stanley's absolute faith in Ollie's wisdom.

Having mocked Gus's pattern of questioning, Pinter launches a real suspense plot through one of Gus's probes.

GUS:	Eh, I've been meaning to ask you.
BEN:	What the hell is it now?
GUS:	Why did you stop the car this morning, in the middle of the road?
BEN *(lowering the paper):*	I thought you were asleep.

(p. 135)

Ben's conventionally dramatic gesture of lowering the paper, of responding guardedly, piques our curiosity and echoes his behavior in the opening mime. Suspicious behavior and unanswered questions are, of course, the grist of the detective plot that Pinter parodies through Gus's stumbling manner. But to parody means to incorporate the conventions of the model and this Pinter does, releasing bits of information in the guise of colloquial banter, challenging us to figure out not only what is peculiar about Ben and Gus's relationship but what, simply, they are doing there. In addition to the clues we pick up when we recognize the gangster parody, Gus gives us direct information:

I mean, you come into a place when it's still dark, you come into a room you've never seen before, you sleep all day, you do your job, and then you go away in the night again.

(p. 134)

We learn that they must "be on tap . . . in case a call comes" (p. 134), that they are waiting now for "him" to get in touch, and that things have "tightened up" (p. 137). This timed release of information is, as John Russell Brown points out, authorial game playing,[35] an idea that Pinter himself acknowledges at the close of this first section of the play.

The subject now is sports. Earlier Pinter had Gus discover a picture—the only picture on the wall—of cricketers. At this juncture, Gus interrupts Ben's third recital from the newspaper by recalling a close football match between the Villa and the Spurs. Twice he uses theatrical metaphors:

Their opponents won by a penalty. *Talk about drama.*

(p. 137)

He went down just inside the area. Then they said he was *just acting.* [emphasis mine]

(p. 137)

Gus's expressions flow perfectly into description, and sports is a logical topic for two bored men to discuss. Nevertheless, though an audience may miss Pinter's reference to games and theater, the reader should not. Actors are players in the game of drama, and just as games defy the rigidity of their rules, ending abruptly in "disputed penalties," the play on stage, whose rules are in the process of being defined, may also defy expectation. Immediately following this sports argument, a new kind of game playing begins.

"An envelope slides under the door, right." Since the door stage right is the outside door, a new player must be arriving, introducing Ben and Gus to a new game. With nothing in their rule book to prepare them, they panic:

BEN:	What's that?
GUS:	I don't know.
BEN:	Where did it come from?
GUS:	Under the door.
BEN:	Well, what is it?
GUS:	I don't know.
	They stare at it.

(p. 139)

The anonymous message is a device dear to mystery writers, for those on the receiving end feel toyed with, watched. Yet Pinter parodies the device: the "message"—twelve matches—is so cryptic as to be incomprehensible. Though the incident moves Ben and Gus to brandish revolvers, Gus is too frightened to venture forth, and Ben's comment, "They must have been pretty quick" (p. 140), ludicrously rationalizes his stalling. Completing the parody of the symbolic intruder, Pinter has Gus pick his ear with one of the matches.

In this second section of the play, the counterpoint between parody and suspense grows more incisive. Gus and Ben's semantic argument ("light the kettle" / "light the gas") reads like a traditional music-hall routine, its absurdity enhanced by the fact that both phrases flank the argument, each uttered by the one who denies saying it. Fear soon explodes into violence, yet the action is reminiscent of a primitive gag. Two clowns at opposite ends of a room back away from strange noises and collide, bouncing off each other's backsides. Both scream with fright. Then, furious at losing his aplomb, Ollie hits Stanley; Ben throttles Gus. That Ben grabs Gus's throat *"at arm's length"* reveals the harmless theatricality of the gesture. And Gus's clownlike insouciance during this routine is one of the best comic touches in the play. Conceding that the correct phrase is "light the kettle," Gus now tries to light the matches, first on his crushed matchbox, then on his shoe. Ben's mounting frustration, expressed in *"stares,"* fails to deter him. In an early film, Chaplin played a pawnbroker's assistant who dismantles a client's watch with an augur, a can opener, a plumber's hammer, and a dental forceps in a mock effort to determine its worth. The client's shocked stares and gestures fail to deter him.[36] If Gus played the feed in the newspaper game, Ben now plays the straight man, the one who chokes on his anger. *"Wearily"* he utters the phrase he claims never to say, then *slams his paper down"*—not to launch the newspaper game but to vent his ridiculously inflated irritation.

Yet the atmosphere is thickening. Gus asks, albeit *"tentatively"*: "have you got any idea who it's going to be tonight?" (p. 144). This is to defy the rules, which say that the victim will be unknown. However, Gus, apparently for the first time, tries to understand the ramifications of the game they play for the Organization. His associative meditations take him from the room, to Wilson, to "just thinking about that girl" (p. 146), a former female victim. Pinter has never written a more ghoulish speech.

She wasn't much to look at, I know, but still. It was a mess though, wasn't it? What a mess. Honest, I can't remember a mess like that one. They don't seem to hold together like men, women. A looser texture, like. Didn't she spread, eh? She didn't half spread. Kaw! But I've been meaning to ask you.

BEN *sits up and clenches his eyes.*

Who clears up after we've gone? I'm curious about that. Who does the clearing up?

(pp. 146–47)

Gus's repetitious colloquialisms ("mess," "half spread") and his obvious fascination with the image render it grotesquely comic. Ben, *"clenching his eyes,"* joins other Pinter characters (Rose, Stanley, Edward, Disson) who develop eye problems when confronting their deepest fears. Ben reasserts his authority by denigrating Gus ("Have a bit of common"; "you birk"), but the audience has caught the odor of corpses. These clowns kill people, are waiting to kill someone. At the end of this middle section, Pinter displays his full parodic spectrum. Gangsters, clowns, and a dubious detective mingle with increasing complexity, and suspense mounts.

In the tense conflict between the two hit men, Gus leans toward dialogue, Ben toward avoiding it. Refusing to answer questions about their present situation, Ben also withholds verification of their mutual past (the football game). The newspaper both camouflages Ben and symbolizes his compulsion to play by the rules: if he performs his habitual action, events should unravel in the habitual way. His references to time ("Time's getting on"; "We'll be on the job in a minute") define his attitude: a perfect functionary, Ben follows the clock, does not anticipate, does not delay. By comparison, Gus is a hounded existentialist obsessed with present circumstances as potential indicators of the highly complex Organization. His observations seem random, but at this point in the play, nearing the end of the second section, he aims for clear self-expression.

It's his place all right. Look at all the other places. You go to this address, there's a key there, there's a teapot, there's never a soul in sight—*(He pauses.)* Eh, nobody ever hears a thing, have you ever thought of that? We never get complaints, do we, too much noise or anything like that?

(p. 145)

No longer complaining about the lack of windows, the lack of tea, Gus stumbles inductively toward revelation. He wants Ben to "think about" the whole game, not just their small part of it; and especially to think about "that girl." However, Pinter blocks ratiocination in a pointed juxtaposition of word and action:

> GUS: No, it was that girl made me start to think—
> *There is a loud clatter and racket . . . of something descending.*
>
> (p. 147)

Enter the dumb waiter, and the complex third section of the play.

Through the inspired use of this farcical rising and falling object, Pinter combines parody with gamesmanship at its zaniest level. Forgetting past tensions, Ben and Gus are fully engaged in present time in yet another game: satisfy the dumb waiter. Like Chaplin on the assembly line in *Modern Times,* Ben and Gus exemplify the Bergsonian description of the comic character—one whose behavior "reminds us of a mere machine."[37] In Eric Bentley's theory of farce:

> Human life . . . is horribly attenuated . . . It is a question of the speeding up of human behavior so that it becomes less than human.[38]

Trying to match the automated pace of the assembly line, Chaplin's gestures are "less than human," for he must become machinelike to work with a machine. Once they decide to play the dumb waiter's game (an irrational decision but one that relieves their tension), Ben and Gus also become creatures of farce. They scramble to put their food on a plate and itemize their offering in frenzied assembly-line fashion:

> GUS *(calling up the hatch):* Three McVitie and Price! One Lyons Red
>   Label! One Smith's Crisps! One Eccles cake! One Fruit and Nut!
> BEN: Cadbury's.
> GUS *(up the hatch):* Cadbury's!
> BEN *(handing the milk):* One bottle of milk.
> GUS *(up the hatch):* One bottle of milk! Half a pint!
>   *(He looks at the label.)* Express Dairy! *(He puts the bottle in the box.)*
>   *The box goes up.*
>
> (p. 152)

Supplying the dumb waiter brings out the Laurel and Hardy dynamic in Pinter's gangsters. Ben concocts an explanation for the dumb waiter's appearance and, as Ollie would, bullies Gus into accepting it. However, Ben's involvement with the dumb waiter tends to demystify him, a detail often overlooked. His first verbal contact with the presence upstairs begins with an abbreviated comic mime typifying the clown's awkwardness with props:

> *He brings the tube slowly to his ear.*
> What?
> *To mouth.*
> What?

(p. 155)

Believing the dumb waiter to be a sort of Orwellian eye that would see Gus withholding his Eccles cake, Ben is childishly delighted when the voice corroborates his usage of "light the kettle." He crumbles when Gus reminds him: "There's no gas."

> BEN *(clapping hand to head):* Now what do we do? . . .
>   What do we do now? [ellipses mine]

(p. 157)

The clown's gesture of confusion—"*clapping hand to head*"—reveals Ben's growing vulnerability, but his question, "What do we do now?" refers back to his role as game player, *doing* certain actions in a structured context. Gus's question, "What about us?" (p. 157), undermines game playing by focusing on their personal needs, not only to eat but to live.

The instruction catechism that follows directly responds to both questions. For Ben the recital-response means playing at the old game, reaffirming the continuum that has suffered such devastating shocks. By participating in the established rule-bound duologue, Gus verifies Ben's reality and recreates the feeling of "us" in their relationship. The passage sounds like a standard routine performed by music-hall duos, and Pinter, seating them together on the bed, reinforces the image of partnership. The instructions routine crystalizes the interplay between parodic material and suspense plot: gangsters performing a music-hall routine—with Gus detecting and correcting Ben's error—prepare themselves, and us, for a killing.

In the section that follows, marked off distinctly by "*silence*," parody evaporates, and the parodic models, gangster and detective, step boldly into view and into combat. The clownlike behavior that always serves to undercut these roles is temporarily sus-

pended, only to be reinvoked as a playwright's geste in the final
image of the play. Emerging from the lavatory, Gus *"stands thinking,"* then embarks on a fierce interrogation, a detective's hunt for
the truth. Because the audience is familiar with the issues (the
intrusion of the envelope, the lack of gas, the dumb waiter), because we, too, have no explanation for them, and because Pinter
chooses not to undercut him, Gus's detective work becomes valid,
even compelling. Just as Holmes infers the existence of Moriarty
from various seemingly unrelated crimes, Gus senses links between various incidents. Asking *"nervously":* "What's one thing to
do with another?" (p. 161), Ben unconsciously pays tribute to Gus's
method; connecting one thing to another is precisely how detectives solve mysteries.[39] Gus even develops the detective's manner.
Like Bogart's Sam Spade he spits questions, and, unresponsive to
Ben's blows, he advances threateningly toward him. For the first
time the word "game" surfaces in the dialogue when Gus attempts
to label the mystery:

> What's he doing it for? . . . We've proved ourselves before now, haven't
> we? We've always done our job. What's he doing all this for? What's the
> idea? What's he playing these games for?
> *The box in the shaft comes down behind them.* [ellipses mine]
>
> (p. 162)

When Wilson, impersonated by the dumb waiter, descends with
his coy reprimand ("scampi" puns on scamp), Gus's worst fears are
confirmed. Wilson has been playing games and has not yet finished.

For Ben, however, Wilson's games confirm Wilson's existence
and, by extension, his own. The more Gus grows into his detective
role, the more Ben behaves like a model thug. In contrast to his
arm's-length imitation of choking, Ben hits Gus *"viciously"* on the
shoulder, then silences him with a conventional but resonating
threat: "I'm warning you!" Detectives by necessity, we sense the
subtext of both Gus's interrogation and his silence; what he dares
not discover is the possibility of Ben's betrayal. In the next section,
present action parodies past action and records the damage done
by Wilson's war of nerves. Ben and Gus resume the positions of
their opening tableau, Ben lying on the bed with his newspaper,
Gus sitting on his. They replay the newspaper game but stripped of
content, mouthing the catchwords only. Brutalized, Gus barely

manages his text while Ben performs the charade (indeed, insists on it) without flinching. For the first time, Pinter plainly invites sympathy for Gus. We recognize this adulterated newspaper game as parody, not of a past theatrical style, but of the past in our experience of the play. Laughter at this point stems directly from our sense of recognition—not of the particulars but of Gus's emotional devastation. We are aware, too, of the change in Ben. Clownish awkwardness forgotten, he responds to the speaking tube whistle with superb finesse, coordinating mouth and ear to speaking and listening. Finally—

> *He takes out a comb and combs his hair, adjusts his jacket to diminish the bulge of the revolver.*
>
> (p. 164)

Here is the model gangster Pinter has parodied, breast pocket bulging with his piece, a polished tool ready for service.

Yet at this moment Pinter reintroduces the clown motif. Hurtled into the room like a circus *stupidus* is Gus, and the effect for us is a pie in the face, the rug pulled from under our feet. Only now can we appreciate Pinter's comic manipulations, his blend of parodic materials with the techniques of suspense. When he had Ben respond to the speaking tube whistle, Pinter confirmed Gus's suspicions of Wilson's presence upstairs. When Ben called Gus to assist him, we learned that he did not plan treachery. But when Gus comes through the door, we learn that all we have learned up to this point has been inadequate to prepare us for the shock. Revelations crowd in too quickly to be absorbed. When the door stage right swings open, who really expects to see Gus?

Davison points out that authors who make use of popular traditions such as the music hall create a multifaceted theatrical experience. In Pinter's case, I think Davison is wrong when he suggests that we will be aware of actors acting.[40] We will, however, be aware of the playwright writing, especially on rereading the play. We will appreciate the brilliant parody of the detective play, in which the fatal clue is not a gaslight dimming but a toilet flushing. We will note that the fast accumulation of contradictory details at the end parodies plays like Agatha Christie's *Love from a Stranger* in which Pinter acted in repertory in August 1956, a year after Beckett's *Waiting for Godot* reached London.[41] And we will certainly recognize Pinter's dexterity in exploiting the conventions those two plays represent: the surprise ending that turns tables on our expectations and the image of clowns waiting, victims and unwilling perpetrators of an irrational design.

Reviewing the play's language affirms the parodist's careful and ironic overlay of material, making double entendres from colloquialisms just as he makes gags from simple movements. "It's down here in black and white" (p. 130); that banality sits snugly in Gus and Ben's humorous newspaper routine, a mild comment on our typical catch phrases. Hearing the same words uttered in a routine stripped of content—nothing is down there in black and white—we make an immediate connection to the human relationship, also emptied of content, and to Gus's shout:

> WE'VE GOT NOTHING LEFT! NOTHING! DO YOU UNDER-
> STAND?
>
> (p. 162)

And the other meaning of "black and white" resonates; in a present severed from the past, black-and-white clarity ceases to obtain. The newspaper articles, parodies of our own lurid headlines, sound the first morbid notes which are echoed by colloquialisms that pun on death: "You kill me"; "You were sitting up dead straight." Pinter also reaps comedy from the overuse of exotic words, and from the contrast between Wilson's list of international dishes and Gus and Ben's Eccles cake and crisps. Exotic labeling also intimidates, and it is no coincidence that Ben, an Organization man, bullies Gus by pretending familiarity with le mot juste, be it "ballcock" or "Ormitha." The many evocations of verbal and physical gags from music-hall and clown traditions sting ironically, for such gags rely on perfect cooperation and coordination, and the final stage image shows partners severed, set on each other like dogs. And of course Gus's unanswered questions ring hollowly when we realize he has been hunting down the details of his own demise.

In the theater, however, Pinter's playful theatrical tricks prevent our dwelling on metaphysical ironies. Through a *"long silence,"* we stare at the tableau of Ben aiming his gun at Gus. Once again they are dumb waiters. So are we: on the edge of our seats wondering if the gun will go off. The fact that it does not go off mocks our tension and reminds us that Pinter's parody lays bare the conventions of realism. Pinter's guns are props and his characters richly parodic pawns, tough and desperate but mostly funny. Placing them in tableau, Pinter imitates and, of course, parodies the well-made play: we are given the solution to certain problems in *The Dumb Waiter*, only to be faced with a final question mark. We can almost sense the playwright in the wings, bringing down the curtain.

THE COLLECTION

Like *The Dumb Waiter*, *The Collection* involves a search for the truth. In the former, however, Pinter mocks the search; in the latter he mocks the truth. James and Stella, Harry and Bill, are sophisticated West End fashion designers whose lives intertwine when James seeks the truth about Stella's confessed adultery with Bill at a dress collection showing in Leeds. During the play we receive no less than five different versions of the adultery, including the possibility that it never occurred. Because everyone lies at some point during the play, "the truth" about the incident becomes splintered into a series of subjective truths based on personal and unknowable motives. According to the playwright:

> When an event occurs—some kind of sexual event in *The Collection*, for example—it is made up of many little events. Each person will take away and remember what is most significant to him. The more other people try to verify, the less they know.[42]

But the less they know, the more they speculate, creating an atmosphere of anxious uncertainty.

Written for television in 1961, *The Collection* parodies two related popular dramatic styles: the late nineteenth-century domestic melodrama and the television soap opera. That is, Pinter parodies the melodramatic plot convention in which past sins create emotional chaos in the present, as well as the soap-opera convention of the unending problem, which unravels in an atmosphere of unanswered questions, stammering, accusations, and tears. In fact, *The Collection* is a fine test case for parody. The play's comic incongruities are purchased at the cost of the conventions, the character types, and the gloom-and-tears mood of both these popular genres.

At first glance, it seems incongruous to link the domestic melodrama in which fallen women soliloquized to tearful audiences with the bloodless soap opera encased in its sterile electronic box. Yet radio and television soap operas, consistently popular in the United States and Britain since before World War II, are the mod-

ern incarnation of domestic melodrama. Both are based on a for-
mula of flat characters and broad coincidence; both focus on problems of love, marriage, and family; both reinforce conventional
morality; and both are afflicted with a disease Robert Heilman calls
"monopathy," in which emotions, like the characters themselves,
are unifaceted and unqualified to the point of being obsessional:[43]
the kind of stock representations Pinter objected to in his "Writing
for the Theatre." In *Lost in London* and *East Lynne*, two popular
melodramas of the 1860s, the protracted sufferings of the heroines
(both fallen women) monopolize the action. In *East Lynne*, Isabel
Archer leaves husband and children to run off with the scheming
Sir Francis Levison, who deserts her after she bears their illegiti-
mate child. She returns to East Lynne as a governess (her sin-worn
face her only disguise), witnesses the death of one child and finally
expires, recognized and forgiven, in her husband's arms.

With the move toward social realism, the fallen woman was less
a blight than a "problem," and monopathetic suffering was replaced
by a more complex anxiety. Jones's *Mrs. Dane's Defense* and
Pinero's *The Second Mrs. Tanqueray* both treat the subject of the
woman with a past who tries to rehabilitate herself through marriage. The past catches up with Mrs. Dane in the person of Sir
Daniel Cateret, a trial judge and guardian of Mrs. Dane's young
fiancé. In a brilliantly theatrical scene, Sir Daniel cross-examines
Mrs. Dane, peeling off layer upon layer of lies until he exposes her
true identity. In Pinero's drama, Paula Ray's past is known to her
husband when they marry but she stands condemned by his
daughter, by his own ineptitude, and, most of all, by her obsessively guilty conscience: "I'm tainted through and through; any-
body can see it."[44] A brooding anxiety hangs over both women, but
Paula Tanqueray, the more pathological of the two, analyzes her
situation in strikingly modern terms: "I believe the future is only
the past again, entered through another gate" (p. 62).

Contributing to psychological complexity is an element that links
these plays to the soap opera: the nonending. At the final curtain of
Mrs. Dane's Defense, the heartbroken fiancé, asleep on the couch,
receives a chaste kiss from a more suitable girl, and Lady Eastley
(Mrs. Dane's good friend) and Sir Daniel walk off arm in arm. They
will marry. One imagines their doily-covered path stretching into
the future, crossed periodically by interesting domestic problems.
Despite oneself, one would like a sequel. *The Second Mrs. Tanqueray* ends with Paula's suicide, and the final lines are spoken by
her ungrateful stepdaughter:

Killed—herself? Yes—yes. So everybody will say. But I know—I helped to kill her. If I'd only been merciful!

(p. 64)

Before *"she faints upon the ottoman,"* she thus reiterates the central concern of this problem play: can individuals sanction behavior that society condemns? Implying that there is no easy answer, Pinero choreographs with care the movements of the family friend in the final seconds of the play. After the stepdaughter faints, he pauses *"irresolutely—then goes to the door, opens it, and stands looking out."* Neither in nor out of the room, he creates an impression of uncertainty and inconclusiveness.

Perhaps the most soap-opera-like ending to plays of this period occurs in Jones's *The Lie*, a melodrama about a good sister defamed by a bad sister. Eventually the long-suffering Elinor is vindicated, but she has lost to her sister the man she wanted to marry. In the end, she receives a proposal from a man she does not love:

NOLL: . . . Dear, let me scrape together a little bit of happiness for
          you out of it all—you will, won't you?
ELINOR: Not yet—oh, I don't know—perhaps—
          CURTAIN[45]

If this cliffhanger finish was acceptable to the reading public, who were accustomed to receiving their fiction in installments, Elinor's indecisiveness also points toward the anxiety-ridden soap opera world in which "people agonize over decisions, and worry about the results of their actions. Should Barbara marry Tony when she is not sure she loves him? Should Tara [identify] the father of her unborn child?"[46] The monopathy of anxiety—this endless agonizing over decisions—is made possible and nurtured by the nonending.

Fundamental to the conception of soap opera is that every cloud's silver lining has a tear: contained in the resolution of one problem lie the seeds of another. Eventually everyone's problems intertwine and spin off in endless permutations, as in Britain's working-class soap opera, *Coronation Street*, launched in 1960 and still playing to high ratings. Quoted in a journalist's article, the former producer of the program comments:

The problems of writing *Coronation Street* are never that one is faced with a lack of material but rather that there is almost too much for comfort. The material proliferates like yeast. . . . Every happening on

> Coronation Street . . . sets off an elaborate chain reaction, from the incident to the characters, from the characters to one another.[47]

This octopuslike profusion of incident and complication permits little variety. The television camera brings into close range the signifiers of interminable agonizing—darting eyes, quivering lips, twitching and furrowed brows—gestures that are similar to but no more complex than the heroine wringing her hands or fainting upon the ottoman. They telegraph the obsessional gloom and anxiety that soap opera has inherited from domestic melodrama.

What about *The Collection?* No one would accuse Harold Pinter of emotional transparency. The instant gratifications of melodrama and soap opera are characteristically absent from Pinter's emotional spectrum. Feelings are filtered through a highly contrived arrangement of pause and silence and verbal maneuvering. For Pinter, "the more acute the experience the less articulate its expression."[48] In *The Collection,* however, feelings and experience are attached to a banal incident suggestive of conventional tears and gloom. Into the lives of James and Stella, Harry and Bill comes the discovery of Stella's apparent adultery with Bill. In a typical Victorian melodrama, Stella would suffer hideous remorse, James would suffer spasms of rage mingled with heartbreak, a suffering Harry would intercede with the couple, and the insufferable Bill would melt from his posture of cold uncaring. One of the four would die of grief. The soap-opera version would naturally be less exciting as the writer would endeavor to extend the aftermath for at least a month, return to it constantly for three months, then intermittently for the next six to eight months.

Essential to the humor of *The Collection* is Pinter's parody of the sin-suffering dynamic in melodrama and soap opera—a parody we best appreciate by noting Pinter's use and abuse of the conventions. *The Collection* contains an unusual number of typical melodramatic signifiers. For example, James's recriminations provoke real tears from Stella, recalling melodrama's tormented fallen women.

> I don't know what you're . . . I just don't know what you're . . . I just . . . hoped you'd understand . . .
> *She covers her face, crying.*[49]

> (p. 143)

As the villain was identified by black clothing and wig, Stella is identified with her white kitten, suggesting a feline seductress who guards claws under a guise of softness and fragility.[50] Music, another traditional labeling device, provides commentary on both Stella and Bill.[51] When she puts on a Charlie Parker record in her darkened apartment, then lies back on the sofa stroking the kitten, she creates an impression of both loneliness and sexual readiness. Vivaldi as background music shows Bill's desire to appear refined, but the transistor radio suggests his transitory position in Harry's house. Finally, name labels, a device as old as the morality play and rampant in Victorian melodrama, gloss ironically the personalities of three of the characters. Harry's surname "Kane," puns on the Biblical Cain ("Am I my brother's keeper?"[52]); Harry "keeps" Bill economically and probably sexually and also "canes" him verbally at the end of the play. James Horne is "horned" or cuckolded by his wife's adultery and reacts by horning in on the private lives of Harry and Bill. Stella, not quite a fixed star, illuminates nothing and appears unreachable at the play's conclusion.

As he placed us in an atmosphere of clown gags during the opening mime of *The Dumb Waiter,* Pinter establishes the world of melodrama and soap opera at the outset of *The Collection.* Conceived initially for television, the scenic directions reveal the kind of sketched-in realism and class labeling we associate with television soap opera. Harry's Belgravia house sports *"Elegant decor. Period furnishing";* James's Chelsea flat has *"Tasteful contemporary furnishing."* The prominent position of the telephone booth (upstage, *"on promontory"*) sketches in the street and our modern world of electronic communication. Moreover, the opening action of the play plunges us into a mood of mystery and soap-opera anxiety. A *"figure . . . dimly observed"* (p. 121) enters the telephone booth and calls Harry, but maliciously refuses to identify himself. Even in the printed text, Pinter conceals his identity, "Voice" concluding the conversation with an ominous "Tell him I'll be in touch" (p. 121). Pinter supplements verbal mystery with a visual tableau: Harry replaces the receiver and *"stands still,"* radiating perplexity, suspicion, perhaps fear. On television the camera naturally closes in, combing the actor's face, inviting us to wonder less about the characters of the two men than about what the call means. In the best tradition of soap opera, we are instantly launched into the action, anticipating more information.

Immediately following is the first scene with James and Stella, a tour de force imitation of monopathetic soap opera tension. Stella is about to leave for the shop; James sits on the sofa smoking. To her simple yet resonating question, "What are you going to do?"

James *"looks at her with a brief smile, then away"* (p. 122). His silence causes her to stammer:

STELLA: Jimmy . . .
        Pause.
        Are you going out?
        Pause.
        Will you . . . be in tonight?

(p. 122)

JAMES *reaches for a glass ashtray, flicks ash, regards the ashtray.* STELLA *turns, leaves the room. The front door slams.* JAMES *continues regarding the ashtray.*

The characters know more than we do, but the situation is fraught with so many familiar soap-opera signals—the ash flicked, the door slammed, the tableau of the lone figure fixing his gaze on anything but the cause of his tension—that we feel at least superficially informed. This is marital tension in the soap-opera world. We know there will be a sequel.

In fact the double-set image and the steady to-and-fro movement of the lights are sufficient to plant the expectation of a sequel; even before we understand that James has appointed himself truth finder with regard to his wife's infidelity, we anticipate a causal relationship between the two worlds. Consistent with conventions of melodrama and soap opera, Pinter uses fade-ups and fade-outs to frame tableaux, build tension, and comment on character relationships. Within the play there are three blackouts that, like act divisions, define major segments of the action. The first blackout signals James's phone call to Bill (Harry answers) and launches the intruder's assault on Harry's world. We then meet Stella and Bill and hear Harry's initial reaction to the call. Finally James makes contact in person and finds Harry again. Second blackout. After a brief appearance from Stella in the flat, the focus is on Harry's house. Bill and James meet and the audience learns the nature of the problem. A third blackout culminates this interview. Now we see the repercussions of James's visit. For the first time all four characters are visible on stage. The symmetry is perfect: Harry picks a quarrel with Bill, James with Stella. Then a phone call at Harry's house—a titillating wrong number—triggers attacks at both residences.

HARRY: . . . but the fact of the matter is, old chap, that I don't like strangers coming in my house without an invitation.

(p. 140)

JAMES: . . . No, really, I think I should thank you, rather than anything else. After two years of marriage it looks as though by
accident, you've opened up a whole new world for me.

(p. 144)

Now, a mirror reflection of the opening action, Harry is the "*figure
dimly seen*" in the phone booth. Soon Harry and Stella are illuminated on one side of the stage, Bill and James on the other.
Symmetrical choreography reinforces contrapuntal motives: James
tries to probe further, and Harry tries to end all further probing.
Ultimately, while Harry eavesdrops, James orchestrates his own
scene à faire, a "mock duel" with Bill. But nothing is settled. As a
final humiliation to both James and Harry, Bill produces yet
another version of the story. In the last tableau, Bill and Harry,
James and Stella stare at each other in silence; the interiors fade to
half-light then blackout.

The image of stalemate at the close of *The Collection* subverts
the conventions of its precursor styles. Fundamental to the plots of
domestic melodrama and soap opera is the verifiability of the past;
the sins of Isabel Archer, Mrs. Dane, and Paula Tanqueray must be
real in order to justify their long and instructive suffering. What
leads James to Bill and back to Stella is the belief that the truth lies
buried in the past and that if it were known the incident itself could
be purged. James discovers of course that the past is not only
uncertain but unknowable, and the accretion of details produces
only one clear conclusion: everyone is lying. Parodying the moral
logic of fallen-women melodramas in which sinners stand confronted by their sins, *The Collection* explores the existential logic
of uncertainty. The past twists and turns in on itself. As the play
progresses in time, James moves back in knowledge, sure of less at
the end than at the beginning.

The sequential logic in soap operas and melodramas hinges on
the rhetoric of the question. Correctly posed questions yield answers that establish facts and become truths. Pinter parodies the
interrogation process in *The Room* and *The Birthday Party*, using
questions not to elicit answers but to intimidate and victimize
characters. In *The Collection*, interrogations are subtler, as fact
finding becomes a game of comic evasion. Having drawn the cuckold's card, James taunts Stella either by refusing to answer her
questions (in their first exchange) or by asking her questions to
which there can be no right answer. "What is your aim?"; "You
know what you've got?" (p. 139). With Bill the game is more enter-

taining, for unlike Stella, Bill is an apt and intriguing opponent. His first move is to refuse to be interrogated, leaving the house before James arrives. Once caught, Bill coolly patronizes James as though he were a beggar or an imbecile:

> JAMES: Well, there's something I'd like to talk to you about.
> BILL: I'm terribly sorry, I'm busy.
> JAMES: It won't take long.
> BILL: I'm awfully sorry. Perhaps you'd like to put it down on paper and send it to me.
>
> (p. 128)

James, reduced to using physical aggression, puts his foot in the door. Throughout this confrontation scene, Bill scores repeatedly on the verbal level, leaving the more obtuse physical moves to James. For example, Bill easily adopts James's method of parrying questions with questions:

> JAMES: Got any olives?
> BILL: How did you know my name?
>
> (p. 129)

He trades insults adroitly:

> JAMES: You're not a bad looking bloke . . .
> BILL: Oh thanks.
> JAMES: You're not a film star, but you're quite tolerable looking, I suppose.
> BILL: That's more than I can say for you.
> JAMES: I'm not interested in what you can say for me.
> BILL: To put it quite bluntly, old chap, I'm even less interested than you are.
>
> (p. 129)

He jokes when interrogated and is funniest when James, like Sir Daniel in *Mrs. Dane's Defense*, launches a careful cross-examination:

> JAMES: You booked into 142. But you didn't stay there.
> BILL: Well, that's a bit silly, isn't it? Booking a room and not staying in it?
> JAMES: 165 is just along the passage to 142; you're not far away.
> BILL: Oh well, that's a relief.
>
> (pp. 130–31)

In this verbal play of hide and deceit, Bill's witty riposte strikes an appropriately callous note. It also testifies to his stubborn unwillingness to be intimidated by a physically stronger male. Eventually, Bill parodies James's interrogation with one of his own:

BILL: Is she supposed to have resisted me at all?
JAMES: A little. . . .
BILL: Did she bite at all?
JAMES: No.
BILL: Scratch?
JAMES: A little.
BILL: . . . She scratched a little, did she? Where? *(Holds up hand.)* On the hand? No scar . . . Absolutely unscarred. We can go before a commissioner of oaths, if you like. I'll strip and show you my unscarred body. Yes, what we need is an independent witness. You got any chambermaids on your side or anything? [ellipses mine]

(pp. 132–33)

Since James is obsessed with the logistics of the bedrooms and the color of Bill's pajamas, Bill adds the detail of tattling chambermaids, transforming the Leeds hotel into a backdrop for a French farce. He even appropriates a traditional comic device: the telltale scar. James applauds Bill's clever performance, cuing audience laughter.

Now they play a game of "how far will you go?" James, taking over the bar, calls Bill a "wag," then a "wow"; then they spin off together in a completely irrelevant discussion about Harry's allergies. They are jockeying for position, James calling the plays, Bill participating—but only up to a point:

BILL: Ah, well, it's been very nice meeting you, old chap. You must come back again when the weather's better.
         JAMES *makes a sudden move forward.* BILL *starts back, and falls over a pouffe on to the floor, flat.* JAMES *chuckles.*

(p. 135)

Pinter returns us to the dynamic of the beginning: Bill dismissing James, James asserting his authority with an aggressive physical maneuver. As in the beginning, Bill's verbal games mock James's trite physical ones. When James disbelieves Bill's first "confession" and presses for the truth, Bill responds with a derisive pun; he was not sitting on the bed but "lying," and may be lying still.

At their next meeting, verbal and physical games lose their subtlety. Bill taunts the cuckold, making a homosexual allusion with a
cheese knife: "Try it. Hold the blade. It won't cut you. Not if you
handle it properly. Not if you grasp it firmly up to the hilt" (p. 150).
Martin Esslin finds homosexual tendencies in James, even
speculating that Stella's dissatisfaction may stem from James's being "a latent homosexual."[53] What seems equally likely is that
James's emotional limitations prevent him from responding deeply
to any feelings beyond his own sense of crisis. During this interview, James treats Bill much as he treats Stella—he bickers in
conversation and refuses the olives Bill offers. His response to
Bill's sexual challenge is to defend in—as Bill says—an "unsubtle
way" his manly honor: "JAMES *stands, goes to the fruit bowl, picks
up fruit knife. He runs his finger along blade.*" Taunting the
homosexual, James rehearses the symbolism Bill employed, then
concretizes the symbol, using the knife as a weapon that he throws
at Bill's face. Defending himself, Bill receives a scar and the details
of the first version of the Leeds incident have been verified. Once
again, James has created a game he can win.

The absurdity of this game is obvious, and it caps a pattern
reminiscent of a comic gag. With scattered materials, James attempts to erect a bridge to the past, but each time he places a brick
on the structure someone sneaks up behind and undoes his labor.
Sabotaging James's efforts, Harry lies to James about Stella and to
Stella about James in order—perhaps—to salvage his shaky relationship with Bill. Stella seems to be the victim of everyone else's
games—or is she? At the end she enters the ring with a low blow of
her own. She mimics James's silence at their opening dialogue and,
in response to his question, *"looks at him, neither confirming nor
denying."* Pinter suggests that her face appear *"friendly, sym-
pathetic,"* but of course neither of these sentiments can be verified.

This unverifiability of motive and feeling is the result of the
gamelike distortions that riddle Pinter's parodic text. Adapted from
television, Pinter's double set creates a double focus for the audience that undermines the mimetic validity of either world. Shifting
between sets becomes less a matter of realistic visitation than a
metaphor for the fast-changing versions of the adultery story. Furthermore, the set provokes internal parody, scenes mirror scenes
with increasing distortion. The verbal gamesmanship in James's
first scene with Bill is parodied by aggressive physical games in his
second scene, as truth hunting is mocked by the parodic truth
James asserts by scarring Bill's hand. Ultimately the fade-ups and

fade-outs that open and close each mini-installment parody the resolutions of melodrama and the cliffhanger conclusions of soap opera. Pinter's tableaux offer fleeting, unstable images, and the closing image, two couples at stalemate, neither resolves the action nor points toward a future resolution.

The internal distortions produced by the double set and the shifting versions of the event in Leeds are enhanced by verbal play. Characters fix labels to define or clarify relationships as when James labels Bill a "wag" (jokester or entertainer) and assumes for himself the patronizing audience role. Similarly, labeling comforts Stella and Harry, at least temporarily, for during their visit she lies and he lies and both agree to accept their lies as truth:

STELLA: . . . my husband has suddenly dreamed up [this] fantastic story, for no reason at all.
HARRY: That's what I said it was. I said it was a fantastic story.
STELLA: It is.
HARRY: That's what I said and that's what Bill says. We both think it's a fantastic story.

(p. 148)

They exchange the phrase "fantastic story" like acolytes fingering a talisman, although Harry will revise this story by claiming that Stella alone had concocted it—another fantastic story. But with this agreed-upon label for the disruption in their lives, Stella and Harry can part gracefully. In his long tirade near the end of the play, Harry's needling repetition of "slum" metonymically denigrates Bills' character, and as his rage builds he free associates from "putrid" to discover a shockingly comic metaphoric label: "slum slug." However, Bill wriggles out from under all labels; changing the story of the adultery yet another time, he demonstrates the futility of trying to fix meaning through verbal description. Simon Trussler has complained the "the characters [in *The Collection*] talk not like members of the upper-middle class pretending to be classless, but like upper-middle class characters imitating people in plays."[54] This is an astute observation, and it supports the argument for parody in the text. Pinter imitates and fractures the banal, mimetic language of soap-opera confrontation. *The Collection* is packed with double entendres from puns on fruit knives to Bill's ironical "I'm going to be Minister for Home Affairs" (p. 131). The "collection" refers to the dresses shown at Leeds and to Harry's Chinese vases. Both are fragile, expensive luxury items and serve to objectify the relationships of the characters—made for exhibit but incapable of taking stress. The characters also resemble a collection of pawns and are the purveyors of a collection of lies. As is typical with Pinter, repetition in phatic interchanges produces an ironic pattern. Although the characters perpetrate deceit they parrot clarity:

> JAMES: . . . I can see it both ways, three ways, all ways . . . every way. It's perfectly clear. . . .
>
> (pp. 143–44)

> HARRY: It's all quite clear now.
> STELLA: I'm glad.
>
> (p. 150)

> JAMES: Well, thanks very much, Mr. Kane, for clearing my mind.
>
> (p. 155)

Such clarities are ironic refractions, images of each person's memory of the incident at Leeds.

Verbal refractions are themselves imaged in the "deceptive" mirror to which we are introduced in Bill's second scene with James (p. 146). Mirroring reality, mimetic art presents us with characters, action, and dialogue corresponding to the behavior and speech of recognizable people—the kind we meet on television soap opera. But the characters in *The Collection* are deliberately truncated, impossible to identify with. The double set and the constant play of lights break emotional continuity by heightening our awareness of theatrical devices at work. These fashion designers move like mannequins, set up and controlled by their maker. Similarly, while dialogue reflects familiar emotional anxieties, the play's language contains the comic potential to mock those anxieties. And the adultery itself, an event that would usually launch a series of predictable soap-opera reactions, is subtly transformed into a metaphor for metaphysical uncertainty.

Through James, Pinter lays bare the mimetic assumptions underlying domestic melodrama and soap opera. Like a conventional moralist, James believes that the turth is knowable and will out with enough probing. He fails to see that the mirror might be deceptive just as he fails to see that artificial representations of reality (the fictions of Bill and Stella) are no more or no less valid than his own representations. James is both a monopathetic sufferer and a throwback to naïve realism. In Pinter's parodic reworking of melodrama and soap opera, he is also a comic butt.

The Collection works at another level of comedy: the audience's recognition of Pinter's self-parody, his self-reflexive gestures in the text. Bill's lines to James, "You're not my guest, you're an intruder. What can I do for you?" (p. 129), evoke the dangerous intruders of Pinter's early plays and mockingly neutralize the reference in repartee. James's line to Stella, "He [Bill] entirely confirmed your story" (p. 143), reuses Pinter's "impossibility of verification" theme in a context of ironic prevarication. And Bill, the worst liar in the play, is allowed to mouth Pinter's worst untruth:

> Surely the wound heals when you know the truth, doesn't it? I mean when the truth is verified? I would have thought it did.
>
> (p. 151)

With James's reference to the mirror, self-reflexiveness dovetails into parody; that is, Pinter's own philosophy of unverifiability becomes the impetus for laying bare the conventions of melodrama and soap opera. At the end of the play, Pinter applies one final wrench to his models. James, his wound far from healed, asks Stella to verify Bill's last story: "That's the truth, isn't it?" In response, Stella's noncommital smile "neither confirms nor denies"—giving us not a cliffhanger ending but a parody of one; there will never be a true answer to James's question.

THE LOVER

FAINALL: . . . marriage is honourable as you say; and if so, wherefore should cuckoldom be a discredit, being derived from so honourable a root?
>
> William Congreve, *The Way of the World*

ALGERNON: You don't seem to realize that in married life, three is company, two is none.
>
> Oscar Wilde, *The Importance of Being Earnest*

CONSTANCE: Perhaps it's natural that a man and wife should differ in the estimate of her prospective lover.
>
> Somerset Maugham, *The Constant Wife*

RICHARD *(amiably)*: Is your lover coming today?
>
> Harold Pinter, *The Lover*

For centuries English comedy has been chuckling over the same lopsided proposition: if marriage is the happy reward of the love chase, adultery is the less happy recognition that the chase should

never have ended. Frustrated but usually appealing lovers become
bored disillusioned mates who yearn to reenter the love game
without, however, losing the benefits of marriage. The marital
dance à deux, à trois, even à quatre has oiled the machinery of
comic plots since the Restoration comedy of manners. Two years
after *The Collection,* Pinter examines the more amusing aspects of
adultery; in his one-act play *The Lover,* first presented on television, he parodies the conventions of Restoration and twentieth-
century manners comedy.

In the long tradition of English manners comedy, certain themes
recur. Wit, that verbial florescence of good taste and intelligence,
is a virtue; jealousy in marriage a vice; and an intelligent marriage
always considers money and property. Dryden, Wycherley, Congreve, and Vanbrugh, as well as their modern counterparts, Wilde,
Maugham, and Coward, approve of love but not of love's conse-
quences; they would agree with Vanbrugh's Rasor: "Marriage is a
slippery thing."[55] Restoration manners comedy hurtles us into the
"bustle" of life; witty ladies and gallants (married and unmarried)
dart in and out of plots and counterplots chasing ephemeral images
of happiness while the lesser crowd of "wit-woulds," cuckolded
husbands, and foolish wives try and always fail to thwart them. As
soap-opera rhetoric hinges on the unanswered question, so manners comedy depends on the rhetorical complications of the double
entendre, enabling witty lovers to express desire even as they obey
the limitations of polite discourse.[56]

Verbal ornamentation, satirical handling of town manners, cyni-
cism toward the material side of marriage—these aspects link Restoration comedy to *The Importance of Being Earnest,* Wilde's
parody of the well-made play. Like Vanbrugh's Heartfree and Constant and Farquhar's Aimwell and Archer, Wilde's Algy and Jack
contrive to further their love ambitions; in a blaze of last-act maneuvering, all the gallants triumph. Congreve's Lady Wishfort resembles Wilde's Lady Bracknell in that both are loving mothers—
that is, strict money managers—but the differences between the
dowagers are more interesting for they point to differences in the
playwrights' social and theatrical world views. Lady Wishfort, as
her name suggests, exists in a state of unfulfilled desire; while
affecting a "sort of dyingness," she is terrified at the death of her
youth and labors at her rejuvenation with varnish and powder.
Lady Bracknell pontificates from her iron fortress of respectability;
stuffiness and greed are her humors and she never deviates. Lady
Wishfort is comic in her weakness, Lady Bracknell comic in her

strength. It is this strength, this shatterproof surface, that distinguishes Wilde's characters and dialogue; in *Earnest,* repartee becomes an end in itself, deliberately undercutting feeling and sense. Wilde's people wear the high, bright colors of their Restoration forbears, but they lack their passionate blood.

In the drawing rooms of Coward's *Blithe Spirit* and Maugham's *The Constant Wife,* the absence of passion is not only felt, it generates conversation. These plays look past the wedding day to marriage itself, and beyond to the triangular "arrangement." Yet the treatment of actual adultery is cautious, and in this sense we come full circle. Despite the titillation of extramarital affairs, the ranks of witty gallants eager to divert the Mrs. Sullens and Lady Brutes from dreary mates, most English manners comedies treat adultery with caution.[57] Both Dryden's *Marriage à la Mode* and Maugham's *The Constant Wife* pose the question: how do sensitive, intelligent couples confront marital boredom? Dryden's Rhodophil and Dorilice play at adultery, comic business arises in the name of adultery, but, finally, neither husband nor wife is unfaithful. When the curtain rises on *The Constant Wife,* John is already carrying on an affair, but the onstage meeting between husband and mistress (who is, of course, a trivial woman) reveals John's embarrassment. In drawing-room as in manners comedy, pleasure lies in the anticipation of adultery not in its fulfillment.

The Lover is Harold Pinter's contribution to the manners comedy tradition, and in certain ways Pinter echoes his predecessors faithfully. The triangular arrangement of drawing-room comedy is recalled in Sarah's "arrangement" with Richard. The Restoration visor masks, long cloaks, and fans, all disguises to facilitate and heighten the excitement of adultery, are recalled in the modified costumes and role playing of *The Lover*. Richard plays Max as well as a would-be rapist, then a "park-keeper," while Sarah plays Dolores and Mary. The misogyny rampant in both Restoration and drawing-room comedy also shapes the sexual interaction in Pinter's play. We recall that Wycherley's Horner compares women unfavorably to dogs and Maugham's Mrs. Culver finds women guiltier than men. "These are excuses for him. There are none for a woman."[58] Pinter's Max echoes both sentiments:

MAX: Perhaps I should meet him and have a word with him.
SARAH: Are you drunk?
MAX: Perhaps I should do that. After all, he's a man, like me. We're both men. You're just a bloody woman.[59]

(pp. 182–83)

The battle of the sexes becomes a complicated image of sexual attraction in both public and private spheres.[60] When Richard reveals how much he loves his wife, he refers not to her personality but to her public image:

> Yes, I find you very beautiful. I have great pride in being seen with you. . . .
>
> Great pride to walk with you as my wife on my arm. To see you smile, laugh, walk, talk, bend, be still. To hear your command of contemporary phraseology, your delicate use of the very latest idiomatic expression, so subtly employed. Yes. To feel the envy of others, their attempts to gain favour with you. [ellipses mine]
>
> (p. 187)

This objectification of Sarah as a series of various well-executed physical and verbal gestures describes another form of misogyny. Yet such gestures are what society means by "manners." Insofar as Sarah displays her wit and beauty (her good manners) society approves of her, and this gives Richard "great pride." Sparkish, in *The Country Wife*, for whom manners are everything, speaks to the issue directly:

> I love to be envied and would not marry a wife that I alone could love.[61]

In 1962, however, Pinter did not write comedy of manners; he wrote a parody of that style. The triangular arrangement in *The Lover* is the conscious invention of husband and wife, each coolly in possession of double roles, each playing those roles to and for each other. They act out the illusion of an adulterous arrangement during the afternoons and play out their marital roles in the mornings and evenings. Careful actors, Richard and Sarah use standard adulteress/cuckold behavior—tense questions, unsubtle evasions—to make the illusion work. Noel Coward's *Blithe Spirit*, a play Pinter has directed, may be labeled a quasi-parodic manners comedy. Coward also mocks marital infidelity, as one side of his adulterous triangle is played by a ghost. Yet "grey" Elvira is still a presence on stage; in a whimsical but theatrically viable sense, the triangle remains intact. In Pinter's *The Lover*, the role-playing game itself becomes the focus, and what Pinter suggests about desire and fantasy stirs our interest even as comic situations develop.

The Lover is divided into seven short scenes, each a compact collation of clues and comic effects. Pinter like Wilde chooses to emphasize the artificiality of his creation not only verbally but structurally. Each scene begins with a light cue and physical mime, silent seconds that are vital to Pinter's comic strategy. Since our eyes absorb faster than our ears, Pinter makes us comfortable with a trite stage image, then with a verbal image he shocks us.

At the opening of *The Lover*, we see a bedroom, balcony, and living room area whose *"tasteful, comfortable"* furnishings establish an atmosphere of typical middle-class life. Sarah, not a maid, empties and dusts the ashtrays—a sign of bourgeois practicality. Richard passes from bathroom to bedroom to living room, opening up all areas of the house (and leaving no secretively closed doors). Holding his conventional breadwinner's briefcase, Richard kisses Sarah's cheek, signifying domesticated sexuality, completing the picture of a safe, suburban marriage. Then Pinter smashes the icon. Richard inquires *"(amiably):* Is your lover coming today?" (p. 161). Richard and Sarah's "amiable" treatment of infidelity corresponds with their dialogue of harmonious sounds. "Mmmnnn" seems to mean "yes," "I don't know," and even "thank you, I will" (p. 161). (Presumably *they* know what they mean.) In this prologue of seventeen lines, Pinter introduces his comic method, his players, and one important rule of their game: while the lover is visiting, Richard may not come home.

The second scene (Richard's return from work) upsets the pattern of amiable stability. After kisses Sarah hands Richard a drink—token of homey comforts—and he hands her the newspaper—token of the hectic, outside world to which he belongs. Their question-and-answer exchange proceeds, but with modification:

RICHARD: What about this afternoon? Pleasant afternoon?
SARAH: Oh yes. Quite marvellous.
RICHARD: Your lover came, did he?
SARAH: Mmnn. Oh yes.
RICHARD: Did you show him the hollyhocks?
        Slight pause.
SARAH: The hollyhocks?

(p. 163)

A *"slight pause"* in a Pinter play may or may not indicate a "look," but it certainly translates as a "moment," a quick mental inhalation. Our interest is piqued because Sarah seems surprised; in their habitual game of verbal catch, Richard has thrown a curve. However, with the aplomb of a Restoration wit, Sarah regains balance.

Her remark, "Not all that interested, actually" (p. 163), intimates that her lover does more with his afternoons than look at holly-hocks. To Richard's precise questions about the weather, the wireless, she answers equivocally; she puns good-humoredly on Venetian blinds and blinding sunlight and though Richard turns her joke into another probe, she parries successfully until he changes the subject.

In all manners comedies, a wife's infidelity is discussed in terms of money and property. Thus Sarah prefaces her statement of affection ("But it's you I love") by acknowledging her inferior status as a wife: "But I'm in your house" (p. 166). However, the notion that their house is not communal property makes Sarah's adultery more wicked and Richard's position more ludicrous, as Wycherley's Pinchwife observes:

> The gallant treats, and gives a ball
> But tis the absent cuckold pays for all.

> (p. 76)

Pecuniary matters become the shrill theme of Maugham's *The Constant Wife* when Constance berates Marie-Louise, her husband's lover—not for marital infidelity but for sexual stinginess:

> I should respect you more if you were an honest prostitute. She at least does what she does to earn her bread and butter. You take everything from your husband and give him nothing he pays for.

> (p. 491)

Such polemic is not Pinter's style, but the distinction (or lack of) between wife and prostitute clearly interests him. Richard's whore is a "functionary who either pleases or displeases," while "dignity," "respect," and "sensibility" are qualities in his marriage.

The game metaphor becomes fully applicable when Sarah refers to Richard's "mistress." As Richard probed Sarah's extramarital affair she now "discusses" his. Such dialogue evokes an image of flamboyant Restoration gamblers: he has placed a bet, now she calls. At stake, perhaps, is their marriage, but at this point comic behavior distances us from feelings of sympathy; Richard after all is a participant, not a victim, in the adultery game. Sarah plays her next card in the bedroom scene where the "tit-for-tat" structure becomes an amusing version of Wildean symmetry. In *The Importance of Being Earnest*, Jack comes to town for relief from the

country, Algernon goes to the country to escape obligations in
town. Jack has an imaginary wicked brother, Algy an imaginary sick
friend. In the middle of act 2 they use the same name; at the
beginning of act 3 they speak at the same time. In *The Lover*,
Richard asks if Sarah imagines him at his desk while she is with her
lover; now Sarah asks: "Do you think about me at all . . . when
you're with her?" (p. 170). Thinking of Richard is "piquant"; conjur-
ing Sarah means "titillation." Both claim not to be jealous; then,
standing by the window, they pronounce nearly echoing lines:

RICHARD: What would happen if I came home early one day, I won-
            der?
            Pause.
SARAH: What would happen if I followed you one day, I wonder?
                                                              (p. 171)

Side-by-side, they each switch off a bedside lamp, and Sarah comments on their mutual loves while Pinter comments on his own
technique: "I think things are beautifully balanced, Richard"
(p. 173). The dialogue in this scene, like the presence of *"moonlight
on [the] balcony,"* is absurdly mannered. The audience may even
experience a heady feeling of doubleness, for the obstrusive presence of the bed and the sexual emphasis in the dialogue are the
props of farce, but the sexless ease with which this couple functions
reminds us of antiseptic television "sit-com" sex; after bedroom
lamps are extinguished, we imagine nothing more interesting than
station identification.

In the next two scenes, Pinter tells two jokes, one old, one new.
Richard learns, before leaving, that his wife's lover "is coming
again today" (p. 174), and when the lights fade up, we see Sarah
prepared to receive him. The doorbell rings. It is not the lover but
the milkman, that proverbial functionary whom the children of
bored housewives are supposed to resemble. In Pinter's rendition
of the joke, the milkman stubbornly tries to sell "cream," an unsubtle allusion to semen. Apparently Mrs. Owen has had three jars.
Sarah refuses, but the obscene suggestion has been made; the next
visitor peddling cream may not be refused.

However, when Sarah greets her lover Max at the door,
"RICHARD *comes in*" (p. 175), and the butt of this second joke is the
audience: the ménage à trois we have been led to believe in proves
a blind for a sexual game between mates. At this confusing and
unsettling point in the action, game playing begins in earnest with

the couple's nonverbal seduction ritual, a conga drum for catalyst, after which they ridicule marriage. Richard, a would-be rapist, mouths lewd euphemisms ("Where's your lighter?"; "I'm dying for a puff" [pp. 176–77]), while Sarah waves her futile distress signal: "I'm waiting for my husband!" (p. 177). Then, without a pause, the assailant transforms into a rescuing park-keeper and leads the woman into his shelter (atmospheric conditions having conveniently worsened). Now *she* seduces while *he* protests: "My wife's waiting for me" (p. 178). Soon Max seduces Dolores, who naturally protests: "I'm a married woman!" (p. 179), then traps her and tells Mary that it is "teatime." The final act is Sarah's solo. Lurking under the table, Max grabs Sarah's legs and pulls her down, while she *"looks about, grimaces, grits her teeth, and gradually sinks* (p. 179), a frantic mugging routine that sums up and parodies the violent physicality and the assailant-victim dynamic of the previous scenes.

We sense that these rituals developed out of improvisations after Sarah and Richard's illicit afternoons became as routine as their marriage—an affair symbolized by the teapot and milk jug. In order to make sex more illicit they added a near rape, a heroic rescue, and sex in a park-keeper's hut. We sense, too, that variety titillates. Sarah makes love to Richard via her lover and a priggish park-keeper. Sex improves for Richard not only when he is Max but also when he is Max playing at violating a married woman. Significantly, the setting for the couple's fantasies is, as in Restoration comedy, the park, that symbol of uncivilized nature in the midst of civilized and repressive city life. Enhancing the enjoyment of game playing and play acting, Pinter and the Restoration dramatists give their characters a coded double language. While Lord Fidget, behind a partition, chats with his wife, Mr. Horner shows her his "china." "Teatime," that innocent and most conventional institution, is, in *The Lover,* a euphemism for sex under the table. Just before she is pulled down, Sarah becomes Mary—an exciting combination of virgin and whore.

Sarah and Richard's afternoon scenario is also cleverly executed parody. She seduces him with B-movie gestures—arching her back, crossing and uncrossing her legs. Together they scratch the drum, a parody of sexual foreplay but also Pinter's self-reflexive parody of the silent action that introduces each scene of *The Lover.* Instead of polite kisses on the cheek, she scratches his hands, he grabs hers. The seduction episodes in the park are edited parodies of real sexual fantasies that are, in turn, related to real situations.

Richard and Sarah, enacting these fantasies at a double remove
from real life, resemble the married ladies and gentlemen of the
Restoration court who delighted in seeing their manners mirrored
in plays set in conventional drawing rooms and in the byways of
familiar London parks.

Like all games, Richard and Sarah's play acting depends on the
willingness of each player to stick to the rules. One rule becomes
obvious to the audience: the autonomy of each world must be
respected. The conga drum and Sarah's high-heeled shoes are the
props for the afternoon just as Richard's briefcase, Sarah's low-
heeled shoes, the newspaper and drinks are the props for the
evening. Understandably, Richard feels annoyed when Sarah
forgets to change shoes—a sign, perhaps, that she like Gus in *The
Dumb Waiter* is getting "slack." Understandably, too, Sarah is in-
credulous when Richard broaches the subject of Max (SARAH: "You
never asked me that before" [p. 165]) and when Max inquires after
Richard (SARAH: "Why are you suddenly talking about him"
[p. 180]). Richard and Max seem to be consolidating, a move that
would topple Sarah's beautifully balanced game.

However, Richard intends merely to change the rules to trip and
confuse Sarah until she agrees to play in a new way. He works these
changes by blurring Sarah's habitual roles. Before Max's arrival,
Richard claimed that he had no mistress, only a whore. Now Max
has a wife. Is she also Richard's mistress? Sarah's hesitations make
it obvious that this is new territory, yet when she tries to retaliate
she makes the mistake of relying on a *past* statement, namely, that
(according to Max) his whore/mistress is too bony.

SARAH:	How's your whore?
RICHARD:	Splendid.
SARAH:	Fatter or thinner?
RICHARD:	I beg your pardon?
SARAH:	Is she fatter or thinner?
RICHARD:	She gets thinner every day.
SARAH:	That must displease you.
RICHARD:	Not at all. I'm fond of thin ladies.
SARAH:	I thought the contrary.
RICHARD:	Really? Why would you have thought that?

(p. 188)

The pause spotlights Sarah's error. Now she, not Richard, breaks
the rules by importing data from their "play" world into the dialogue of their "serious" world. The strength of Richard's maneuver-

ing is that he will not be consistent. Soon he *"opens the cupboard and takes out the bongo drum"* (p. 192), thus exposing the afternoon prop in the evening and invalidating their adultery game. Sarah's protest ranges from anger ("You shouldn't touch that"; "Put it back" [p. 192]) to begging ("Please. Don't don't" [p. 193]); her vulnerability recalls momentarily Stella's tears in *The Collection*. However, consistent with the game-playing spirit of *The Lover*, Sarah meets deceit with deceit and tosses in a counterplot:

> You stupid. . . ! *(She looks at him coolly.)* Do you think he's the only one who comes! Do you! Do you think he's the only one I entertain! Mmmnn? Don't be silly. I have other visitors, other visitors all the time. When neither of you know, neither of you. I give them strawberries in season. With cream. Strangers, total strangers. But not to me, not while they're here. They come to see the hollyhocks. And then they stay for tea. Always. Always.
>
> (p. 193)

Unable to compete with Richard in his present maneuverings, Sarah invents a past that he cannot refute. Cleverly employing their sexual code words, she insists that their games are merely a blind for assignations with "other visitors" on "other afternoons."

Richard wins. Not because he destroys the game but because he plays for "real." He *does* take Sarah unawares, *does* force himself on her. Mixing all roles, he becomes Max (playing the drum), the rapist ("Got a light?"), and Dolores's boyfriend ("You're trapped") while Sarah *"jerks away, to behind the table"* (p. 194). Forcing Sarah to improvise, Richard revives the feeling of the love chase, and when she capitulates, rapidly knitting together elements from the old and new games ("Why are you wearing this strange suit. . . ? [p. 195]), he feels justified in asserting his needs: with the resonating meaning of "change," Richard combines "lovely wife" and lust-engendering whore to transform Sarah into his "lovely whore."

The delicate adjustments of play that *The Lover* dramatizes have been analyzed by play theorists Huizinga and Caillois whose differentiation between the play world and workaday reality provides a model for Richard and Sarah's "old" game.[62] With briefcase and newspaper, Richard establishes the surface reality of the serious business world, while afternoon tea, with its connotations of leisure, locates the play field. Yet Richard apparently feels unfulfilled in a crucial play element identified by Caillois: "uncertainty." Thus Richard "discovers" Max's drums so that he can once again *and* for

the first time trap and seduce Sarah. "Change," repeated three
times at the end of play, puns on Sarah's clothes change and the
need for a changed game. Jacques Ehrmann, revising Caillois and
Huizinga, points to another interpretation of Richard's behavior.
Ehrmann asserts that the "dialectic" of reality-play, seriousness-
gratuitousness is fundamentally false; Huizinga and Caillois "fail to
see that the interior occupied by play can only be defined by and
with the exterior of the world,"[63] a view Pinter's Richard would
share. Sarah would like to keep "tea" separate from the banality of
morning and evening conjugality; Richard wants to integrate, to
rediscover play within their "serious" routine. Thus in *The Lover*,
Pinter points to both the necessity of play and the difficulty of
defining its status in our lives. Ridiculing marriage, he suggests
that marital conduct is merely highly programmed play whose
rules must occasionally be broken. If adultery mocks marriage in
The Collection, mock-adultery sustains marriage in *The Lover*.

Moving his characters from one game to another, Pinter effects
subtle alterations in his verbal score, producing comic reversals
and revelations. Elaborate verbal symmetry establishes the couple's "beautifully balanced" relationship in the second scene:

SARAH:	Tired?
RICHARD:	Just a little.
SARAH:	Bad traffic?
RICHARD:	No. Quite good traffic, actually.
SARAH:	Oh, good.
RICHARD:	Very smooth.
	Pause.
SARAH:	It seemed to me you were just a little late.
RICHARD:	Am I?
SARAH:	Just a little.
RICHARD:	There was a bit of a jam on the bridge.

(p. 162)

Long lines balance short lines; good traffic balances bad traffic;
both utter "just a little," and the euphemistic possibilities of "a bit
of a jam on the bridge" are nicely constrained by the deliberateness
of polite badinage. When Richard chooses to change the game his
diction becomes formal and eccentric: "I was looking . . . for someone who could express and engender lust with all lust's cunning.
Nothing more" (p 169). And when he announces that Max can no
longer visit—which really means that he is becoming Max—formal
syntax combines with vulgar diction to release what Richard pre-

tends is pent-up aggression: "Take him out into the fields. Find a ditch. Or slag heap. Find a rubbish dump. Mmmm?" (p 191). However, after he succeeds in redirecting the game, Richard integrates less ferociously with Max: "You can't get out, darling. You're trapped" (p. 195). The use of "darling," Richard's addition to Max's dialogue, indicates that lover and husband have at last united.

Aggressiveness, which Freud places at the heart of tendentious jokes, is simultaneously released and contained in comedy of manners repartee.[64] Sharp rejoinders point to unresolved tensions in sexual relationships, but formal diction tacitly consents to the discourse of civilized restraint. The sexual pressure within witty repartee, this double exposure of desire and discord, naturally yields pleasure for the audience who can guiltlessly and without inhibition observe its effects. In *Blithe Spirit*, Coward modified the Restoration thrust-and-parry convention by adding an extra riposte that considerably raised the level of verbal aggressiveness, and Pinter in *The Lover* followed suit:

CHARLES: It's discouraging to think how many people are shocked by honesty and how few by deceit.
RUTH: Write that down, you might forget it.
CHARLES: You underrate me.[65]

RICHARD: . . . I mean if I, for instance, were called upon to fulfill the function of a lover and felt disposed, shall we say, to accept the job, well, I'd as soon give it up as be found incapable of executing its proper and consistent obligation.
SARAH: You do use long words.
RICHARD: Would you prefer me to use short ones?

(pp. 186–87)

Both Charles and Richard have the last word in these exchanges and in the action of their respective plays (although Richard's victory is dubious at the end of *The Lover* while Charles's status has truly changed). In Wildean repartee, pompous language mocks romantic sentiment; Algernon Moncrieff declares his love as much to appreciators of parodic wit as to Cecily Cardew:

ALGERNON: I hope, Cecily, I shall not offend you if I state quite frankly and openly that you seem to me to be in every way the visible personification of absolute perfection.[66]

Andrew Kennedy aptly labels such language "costume speech": "a theatrical language that functions somewhat like costume jewelry

. . . more ostentatious than the 'real' thing, but just right for display and illusionism."[67] "Costume speech" works strategically in Richard's adjustment of his marital game; the illusion he tries to achieve is distance from Sarah without, however, causing a confrontation. Considering the importance of fantasy in their lives, such maneuvering demands the utmost subtlety. Sarah herself is not without wiles.

SARAH: You've had a hard day . . . at the office. All those overseas people. It's so tiring. But it's silly, it's so silly, to talk like this. I'm here. For you. And you've always appreciated . . . how much these afternoons . . . mean. You've always understood.
She presses her cheek to his.
Understanding is so rare, so dear.

RICHARD: Do you think it's pleasant to know that your wife is unfaithful to you two or three times a week, with great regularity?
(p. 190)

The audience laughs at this orchestrated conflict between drawing-room formality and bedroom informality, but Richard's "costume speech" works to deflect their tension to a stylistic rather than a personal confrontation, thereby cushioning their relationship from the shock of change.

Pinter's own modification of manners comedy repartee is his use of repetition for the purpose of needling. A Pinter character will repeat a line or force his interlocutor to repeat a line that deliberately slows down the rhythm of exchange and hints at hidden meanings. When Sarah lists qualities Richard would look for in a mistress, Richard adds "wit," and Sarah repeats, "And wit, yes." Then Richard attacks: "Wit, yes. Terribly important, wit, for a man." Repetition trounces referentiality, opening up a range of indeterminate euphemistic meanings. However, Sarah chooses to ignore Richard's attack. Her line, "Is she witty?" is itself a witty parry and earns a laugh from Richard. But Sarah cannot deflect Richard's more subtle use of repetition when the couple discuss their own relationship:

SARAH: How could I forget you?
RICHARD: Quite easily, I should think.
SARAH: But I'm in your house.
RICHARD: With another.
SARAH: But it's you I love.

RICHARD:	I beg your pardon?
SARAH:	But it's you I love.
	Pause. He looks at her, proffers his glass.
RICHARD:	Let's have another drink.

(p. 166)

Forced to repeat her words in the void of his silence Sarah sounds trivial, and his request that she serve him exacerbates her humiliation. The exchange passes with the speed of typical repartee, but clearly Sarah fails in Richard's view to distinguish adequately between *her* lover and *their* love.

Apart from repartee and needling repetition, double entendre enriches *The Lover's* language, particularly the words "trap" and "game." Erotically trapped inside the park-keeper's hut and inside her conception of their fantasy world, Sarah traps herself by applying old rules to confusing present circumstances. However, Richard is also trapped, for despite his artful variations on the marriage theme, a sinister sameness underlies the "change" he has won from (and for) Sarah. Pinter has no appreciation for the drawing-room morality of Maugham's *The Constant Wife* in which John learns to accept Constance's infidelity as her economic and emotional privilege. Nor does he choose the optimism of Congreve or Dryden in whose plays lovers and marital partners square their shoulders, determined to cherish each other more. Pinter's attitude is closer to Wycherley's in *The Country Wife.* After Horner debauches Margery and tricks her husband into silence, Wycherley calls for a "dance of the cuckolds." The leering gaiety of these "vain fops" assures us that selfishness is its own reward and deception pays. At the end of Pinter's *The Lover,* the renewed marital embrace remains a triangular fantasy. Or rather a quadrangular fantasy: the "lovely whore" joins Richard, Sarah, and the lover for "tea." Kneeling together, Richard and Sarah grotesquely parody a bride and groom at a high church wedding, but of course marriage is hardly new to them. Undermining Richard's last words, Pinter shows us modification but very little change.

"Game," a word used repeatedly in this chapter, resonates during Sarah and Richard's crisis:

SARAH:	Stop it! What's the matter with you? What's happened to you? *(Quietly.)* Please, please, stop it. What are you doing, playing a game?
MAX:	A game? I don't play games.

SARAH: Don't you? You do. Oh, you do. You do. Usually I like
              them.
MAX: I've played my last game.

(p. 183)

The multiplicity of the games played in *The Lover* is reflected in
the multiplicity of meanings. In the first sense, "game" is synonymous with "trick," a deliberate sleight-of-hand, recalling Gus's
meaning in *The Dumb Waiter:* "What's he playing all these games
for?" Countered by Max's denial, Sarah refers to their private
games, activities they enjoy at a certain time and place. When
Richard insists, "I've played my last game," he finally answers her
in kind and extends the meaning with existential literalness. Max's
presence *is* the game. When he walks out the door, he has indeed
ended the game.

Game playing involves the playwright as well and comments on
his relationship to his characters and the audience. As in *The
Dumb Waiter* and *The Collection*, Pinter's verbal and physical sty-
lization distances us from the characters. Richard and Sarah are
parodic mixtures of Restoration wits, urbane drawing-room types,
and two-dimensional stick figures who fill out the scenario of sexual
fantasy. They are also parodies of the conventionally "nice" middle-
class couple, the businessman husband, his cleverly modern wife.
Nor is Pinter without self-parody. The "germ" of his plays, he says,
derives from the physical image, the sitting, lying, and standing
postures of people in a room.[68] Richard and Sarah, playwrights in
their living room, are also inspired by physical images, but their
movements mock Pinter's carefully choreographed gestures. With
their drum-scratching, leg-crossing, and Sarah's medley of
grimaces, Pinter's characters turn posture into posturing, parodying their creator's obsession with stage pictures.

If Pinter mocks his method he also mocks his audience. As in all
parody plays, Pinter invites us to trust our assumptions, exploiting
our desire for the pleasure of "getting the joke."[69] However, when
Richard enters as, and later seems to dispose of, Max, we are
caught off balance: our comic pleasure is inseparable from surprise
and discomfort. The funniest moments in *The Lover* occur when
past conflicts with present, when the new game jolts the old, when
action is most fluid, words most volatile. Is the game a trap or the
trap a game? Is change the game or does the game change? Pinter's
comedy is a caution against assuming, like Sarah, that the game we
know is the game we play.

THE HOMECOMING

Western drama thrives on the family. Paradoxically united, divided, creative, destructive, immortal, and time-bound, the family means above all human beings in dynamic relationship. Traditional comedy focuses on the family *forming*. Old alliances corrupted by selfishness give way to new, healthier unions cemented by love, sanctioned by marriage. From the Forest of Arden through St. James's Park to the Chelsea drawing room, comedy urges that which is creative and affirmative in family relationships. The tragic vision casts the family at the center of chaos. Unnatural upheavals in Lear's kingdom and cosmos are personified by the disintegration of family ties. The myth of the House of Atreus makes a tragic example of a simple truth: no child chooses to be born, nor does a parent choose the nature of his offspring. Both are locked, will-less, in a lifelong struggle. Furthermore, the past, represented by the parent, imposes patterns on the present and directs the future. Blood ties can prove heroic, as in the love of Antigone for her blind father, of Edgar *(King Lear)* for his. More often than not, tragedy underscores the burden of filial obligation. Hamlet's hysteria after the ghost pronounces his horrible edict is partly his recognition that the autonomy of his own life is over.

In twentieth-century English drama before 1956, the family was, with remarkably few exceptions, conventional and well-behaved. John Russell Taylor speaks of the "typical Dodie Smith-Esther McCracken family—fussy scatter-brained mother, stolid inarticulate father, bossy tomboy daughter, arty varsity-bound son" as the donnée of light comedy.[70] However, two very different dramatists, whose work was particularly influential for Harold Pinter, proposed different versions of the family model. In *Hay Fever* (1925), Noel Coward parodies the family with the eccentric Blisses, reaping comedy by systematically undercutting the expectations of "normal" people, the Blisses' weekend guests. Coward also mocks the idea of healthy new alliances growing out of youthful love: Sorel and Simon act out courtship rituals with more attention to performance than to emotion, and their love objects flee before the final curtain. The Blisses are intolerant and intolerable in their reactions to others. They seduce outsiders but refuse to admit them, preferring their own inbred alliances.

In *The Family Reunion* (1939), T. S. Eliot explores the pathology of family ties, interweaving Aeschuylus's *Oresteia* with the Christian themes of sin and expiation. Harry, the neurasthenic inheritor of Wishwood, returns for his mother's birthday after eight years of wandering. He is pursued by the Eumenides because he murdered his wife (or thinks he did). In the last act, however, Harry learns that his hatred for his wife recapitulates his parents' loveless marriage and, armed with this "consciousness," Harry breaks the "chain" of inheritance binding him to the "shrieking forms in a circular desert" and becomes a Christian missionary.

The Family Reunion deliberately shatters the mimetic surface of stage realism, and it may be argued that Eliot parodied the family model to a greater degree than Coward did. Employing the conventional signifiers of well-made light comedy, the play is set in a dowager's drawing room. A collection of bland aristocrats gather, uttering commonplaces, waiting for the family reunion. However, outside the drawing room the Eumenides hover; the characters speak in verse and periodically chant in chorus. The conflict between generations is resolved comedically, but with an ironic twist: Harry triumphs and marries, not a woman but a faith, and the family reunion ends in an eerie wake. Of course, Eliot's parodic changes were intended to enlighten not amuse. By placing elements from Greek tragedy and Christian doctrine in a familiar theatrical context, Eliot hoped to make spiritual truths accessible.

To the dramatists of Pinter's generation the drastically different styles of Coward and Eliot seemed to offer little. Coward was too light and commercial, Eliot too esoteric. But Eliot raised issues about family life that later dramatists echoed, and it was perhaps significant that *The Family Reunion* was revived in London during the run of Osborne's *Look Back in Anger* at the Royal Court. A few years later, two plays in Arnold Wesker's trilogy, *Chicken Soup with Barley* (1958) and *I'm Talking about Jerusalem* (1960) presented an East End Jewish version of the family model John Russell Taylor describes. A strong mother, Sarah Kahn, dominates her husband, Harry; the daughter Ada, while not a tomboy, is a political activist (usually a man's role), and the artistic son Ronnie is a poet and dreamer. Though Wesker's earthy characters and setting are far removed from Eliot's drama, Wesker is as preoccupied as Eliot with cyclical family history. The idealistic Ronnie loses his bearings and becomes weak and lost like his father, while Sarah Kahn, tenaciously keeping the family together, resembles Amy, Dowager Lady Monchensey of *The Family Reunion:*

AMY: I keep Wishwood alive
       To keep the family alive, to keep them together,
       To keep me alive, and I live to keep them.[71]

Amy's rapacity ("and I live to keep them") may be fiercer than
Sarah's, but in both the Wesker plays and *The Family Reunion*,
mothers try to mold sons in their own image and lash out bitterly
when the sons rebel.

In Peter Shaffer's *Five Finger Exercise* (1958), stylistically and
structurally the type of Coward's London successes, Clive, another
neurasthenic son, explains his family to an outsider:

> . . . let me give you a warning. This isn't a family. It's a tribe of wild
> cannibals . . . Between us we eat everyone we can . . . Actually, we're
> very choosy in our victims. We only eat other members of the family.[72]
> [ellipses mine]

Shaffer probes the pathology in mother-son relationships, and
again a passage from *The Family Reunion* proves relevant:

HARRY: . . . What about my mother?
          Everything has always been referred back to mother.
          When we were children, before we went to school,
          The rule of conduct was simply pleasing mother;
          Misconduct was simply being unkind to mother;
          What was wrong was whatever made her suffer,
          And whatever made her happy was what was virtuous—
          Though never very happy, I remember. That was why
          We all felt like failures, before we had begun.[73]

This passage goes to the heart of Clive's resentment and eventual
betrayal of his mother. That everything always refers back to father
is one of the themes in *No Trams to Lime Street* (1959) by Pinter's
friend Alun Owen. Taff and Cass, two sailors on the first night of
shore leave in Liverpool, confront difficult fathers. While Tass
takes comic revenge by mimicking his father's bullying, Cass,
whose needs are more repressed, is unable to break inveterate
patterns of animosity.

To consider *The Homecoming* (1965), Harold Pinter's version of a
family reunion, in relation to the previously mentioned plays
seems unfair to all concerned. It is separated by its nonnaturalistic
compactness, its surreal presentation of family pathology, its unre-
lenting viciousness. Yet Pinter shares the concerns of his contem-

poraries: the recurring family cycles (Max's three sons paralleled by Teddy's three sons; the wife/mother/whore role, remembered in Jessie, incarnated in Ruth); the guilt-aggression patterns in relations between parents and children (the verbal abusiveness that passes for communication between Max and his sons); and most of all, the experimental attempts to render these issues honestly. In their individual ways, Coward, Eliot, Wesker, Shaffer, Owen, and Pinter are hacking away at the same family model. However, Pinter carries his rebellion into parody. More vehemently than Coward and Eliot, Pinter lays bare the conventions of family life in polite society—social introductions, the family coffee circle—undercutting them for ironic effect.

Pinter goes even further, parodying both contemporary themes and Oedipal conflicts. Everyone "refers back" to mother, but in completely contradictory ways: Jessie is both "slut-bitch" and "charming woman." Wesker's theme of the returning son is replayed in *The Homecoming* but with a comic reversal: it is Ruth not Teddy who comes home. Like Wesker's Kahns, Pinter's North London family is Jewish, but with none of the Kahns' social concerns. Pinter's working-class men occupy peripheral or illegal jobs; their focus is inward, consciously tribal. Max combines Amy Monchensey's rage and Sarah Kahn's constant nagging, replacing the latter's naturalistic language of confrontation with invective so extreme as to rouse nervous laughter. More mother than father (and even more than most mothers), Max suffered the pain of childbirth and "gave birth to three grown men . . . all on my own bat" (p. 56).[74] Eliot's use of the Atreus myth in *The Family Reunion* seems relevant to *The Homecoming;* certainly the curse of betrayal is present in succeeding generations. But instead of the hovering Eumenides in Eliot's play, an adulterous couple, MacGregor and Jessie, haunt the characters in Pinter's play. Sam's last-scene revelation about MacGregor and Jessie's copulation in the back of his cab, what some critics view as the key to the family's behavior, is treated by the characters as ludicrously inconsequential. Reversing the Greek and Eliotic theme of acceptance through suffering, Teddy's long night's journey into a bleak afternoon ends in denial and vacancy.

The Homecoming incorporates and extends elements of the other plays in this chapter. Like *The Dumb Waiter,* language in *The Homecoming* contains music-hall rhythms (less in duologue than in monologue), but the routines that characterize Gus and Ben's teamwork on a job are instinctual family behavior for the North

London tribe. Slapstick arises not from the intrusion of an object but from the presence of a woman who enters the family rough-and-tumble. The sexual event that haunts *The Collection,* that is mock-ritualized in *The Lover,* climaxes a growing tension between Ruth and the family of men and is enacted with deliberate, non-ritualistic candor on stage.

As in all the parody plays, game playing is central to the behavior of the characters; that is, each character must make adjustments as the old game is refashioned surprisingly, and with ambiguous results, into a new game. Pinter maintains that "the game is the least of it . . . a chosen device. It's the way the characters face each other under the game that interests me."[75] The emotional confrontations "under the game" are especially affecting in *The Homecoming.* By their nature, family reunions are dramatic events involving emotions that are, to a certain extent, recognizable to everyone.

But the comedy of *The Homecoming* lies in what we do not recognize. A conventional ritual—the family circle in act 2—is brought into view and then is undercut mercilessly: "as soon as a situation looks as if it were attaining a recognizable meaning, [Pinter] introduces some nonsense, wild improbability or verbal play, and we fall once more through the trap-door."[76] *The Homecoming* reflects life in a cracked mirror; in one fragment we recognize the familiar actions of family drama, in another fragment the same image is grotesquely distorted, parodied. Charting a naturalistic or psychological trajectory through the play both reduces its complexity and fails to represent our response as we experience the play in the theater.

The Homecoming is shocking; Pinter intends it to be. No Gus or James or Sarah appears—no character whose evident confusion and persistent questioning give credence to our own gaps in understanding. Events are, in the order in which they occur, undeniably strange and estranging. After six years teaching philosophy in an American university, Teddy comes home to introduce his wife Ruth to his father Max, his uncle Sam, and his brothers Lenny and Joey. Within twelve hours, the brothers make love to the wife; the husband leaves and the wife stays with his family, becoming some combination of wife, mother, and whore. Intensifying the strangeness of events is the characters' behavior. They seem to dart in and out of realistic frames of reference, alternately playing out and parodying conventional roles. When Ruth remarks that the family is "lovely" for asking her to stay, she uses conventional terms of gratitude, although the behavior leading up to that invitation has been anything but conventional. Pinter has said that the play came to him as "a dark dream,"[77] and, like a dream, the real and surreal blend with horrific ease and humor.

As in all the parody plays, the tension between past and present behavior creates comic incongruities in *The Homecoming*. In this play, however, characters use the past not to respond to confusion but to manipulate and impress other members of the family. Behind their anger seems to lie different versions of the family history according to which the mother Jessie is both loathed and cherished. The conflict arises when another family member offers a different representation of the past (especially Jesse's past) or when he focuses directly on the present. Undercutting, then, is the family game that Max dominates but that they all play. Game playing, Pinter's "chosen device," structures the first four scenes of act 1 and supplies information about the family. After Ruth's arrival the game is altered and in act 2 extended until it is finally played out.

In act 1, before the first blackout, we meet each member of the family, beginning with Max and Lenny. Max enters looking for the scissors; Lenny ignores him until he approaches.

> MAX: . . . Do you hear what I'm saying? I'm talking to you! Where's the scissors?
> LENNY (*looking up, quietly*): Why don't you shut up, you daft prat?
> MAX *lifts his stick and points it at him.*
> MAX: Don't you talk to me like that. I'm warning you.
> *He sits in large armchair.*
>
> (pp. 23–24)

Shocking our expectations of filial relationships, Lenny's verbal insult immediately draws laughter: we may recognize the parent's nagging but not the calculated viciousness of the son. Undermining Max's authority, Lenny responds not to what Max asks but to the noise he makes, his irritating presence in the room. In return, Max, like the traditional enraged *sennex*, lifts his stick—the token of his authority—then settles into an armchair, too old for physical combat. More important, he appears to be accustomed to the abuse. The audience learns in the opening seconds of the play that threats and insults are acceptable fare in this family. Like two animals testing each other, one pokes and prods until the other swipes; neither draws blood.

Since noise irritates Lenny, Max chooses to monologue, mixing biography and reverie in terms that are both colloquial and violent:

he was a "tearaway," he "knocked about" with MacGregor. Like
Goldberg and McCann, Max and Mac were a team, "two of the
worst hated men in the West End of London" (p. 24). MacGregor
was "fond" of Jessie, but it made Max sick "just to look at her rotten
stinking face" (p. 25). Lenny stems the flow of reverie: "Plug it, you
stupid sod" (p. 25). Max shouts abuse and Lenny calmly replies:
"You know what, you're getting demented" (p. 25). Dementia and
senility, diseases of the aged, remind Max of his future (if not his
present) condition. Lenny extends the insult by asking advice on a
horse race, then ignoring the advice; thus he attacks Max's most
cherished bit of autobiography.

> MAX: He talks to me about horses.
> *Pause.*
> I used to live on the course. One of the loves of my life. Epsom?
> I knew it like the back of my hand. I was one of the best-known
> faces down at the paddock. What a marvellous open-air life.
>
> (p. 25)

Comical self-aggrandizement, the use of clichéd hyperbole, and
the Jewish inflection all connect Max to Pinter's Goldberg. However, his question-and-answer style and hectoring tone are also
characteristic of music-hall monologues. Even parts of the content
resemble a Dan Leno routine, "The Huntsman," which describes
the comically incongruous attempts of a working-class man to fit
into posh horsey society. Max, too, had important connections:

> I should have been a trainer. Many times I was offered the job—you
> know, a proper post, by the Duke of . . . I forget his name . . . one of
> the Dukes.
>
> (p. 26)

Foolishly pluming himself, Max tries to undercut Lenny who
knows "nothing" about horses.

Lenny's ironic politeness ("Dad, do you mind if I change the
subject?" [p. 26]) returns the insult, and then Lenny throws his
lowest punch. He forces Max to acknowledge his present role as
family cook, implying that horse expertise has dwindled to dog
cooking. When Max raises his stick for the second time, Lenny
mocks the gesture with a recital of little-boy terror: "Oh Daddy,
you're not going to use your stick on me" (p. 27). The memory of
the frightened child revives the era when Max and his stick had

power, a painful contrast to the winded geriatric in the present. Lenny has triumphed in this round: "*Max sits hunched*" and silent.

Sam enters next. Quieter than Max, he, too, likes to tell stories about himself.

> Yes, he thought I was the best driver he'd ever had. They all say that, you know. They won't have anyone else, they only ask for me. They say I'm the best chauffeur in the firm.
>
> (p. 29)

While Lenny undercuts Max with references to his age and possible senility ("you daft prat" [p. 23]), Max needles Sam about his sexual inadequacies ("You paralysed prat" [p. 31]) and embellishes his mockery with crude images:

> MAX: What have you been doing, banging away at your lady customers . . . having a few crafty reefs in a layby?
>
> (p. 30)

But Sam silences Max with a reverie that revises the character of Jessie in the family romance. Referring back to Jessie, it appears, is like pushing an emotional buzzer; Max uses her to provoke Lenny, Sam to quell Max.

Joey, entering next, offers the most abbreviated version of his autobiography: "I've been training down at the gym" (p. 32). The youngest son, Joey is the least abused. And yet, at the slightest mention of self-flattery ("I wasn't in bad trim" [p. 33]), Max cuts him with a hilarious Groucho Marx-style put-down:

> I'll tell you what you've got to do. What you've got to do is you've got to learn how to defend yourself, and you've got to learn how to attack. That's your only trouble as a boxer. You don't know how to defend yourself and you don't know how to attack.
>
> (p. 33)

One wonders what Joey *does* do in the boxing ring.

Our response to this pattern of undercutting is carefully orchestrated by the playwright. Pinter's considerable acting experience in repertory made him aware of both the conventions of family decorum and the comic undercutting techniques of West End dramatists and their imitators. In the drawing rooms of Rattigan and Coward, upper-class stuffiness is so well established by accent and manner that undercutting becomes a healthy revolt. In Wesker's Jewish family, deflation is colloquial and direct. But no family in the history of English drama has been as violently abusive as Pinter's North London brood, nor has that abuse mined such creative gems as Max's line: "I'll chop your spine off" (p. 25)—even from a butcher this is a remarkable image. What tilts our response toward laughter is that no one, at least in these introductory scenes, suffers noticeably from the invective. Made contemptible by Max's put-down, even the laconic Joey seems simply the brunt of a joke rather than a victim.

Essential to Pinter's comic strategy, then, is that we apprehend the patterns of family malice while enjoying the game dynamic behind that malice. Through Lenny's jibes at "Dad" and Max's sinister reminiscence of "our father," Pinter sounds the theme of generational inheritance: Max, a fearful child, raises sons who hate and fear him. It is, however, the common past of this particular family that relates to the undercutting game. Because they *share* a history, no one's personal version of family life is safe from criticism or debunking. At the first blackout, then, we have met the family and experienced its precariously comic balance of power.

BLACKOUT.
LIGHTS UP.
Night.
TEDDY and RUTH *stand at the threshold of the room.*

(p. 35)

Pinter's archetypal dramatic situation now unfolds: two people walk into a room: they will change the aspect of that room. If the four opening scenes reveal the noisy, crudely funny side of the undercutting game, the four nocturnal scenes (Ruth-Teddy, Teddy-Lenny, Lenny-Ruth, Max-Lenny) reveal the game's subtlety, its potential for brilliant comic reversal. Teddy and Ruth arrive in the middle of the night; he unlocks the door with his own key, introducing his wife to the family home in which "Nothing's changed. Still the same" (p. 38). Acting the host, Teddy asks Ruth to sit down, to have a drink, to go to bed. His security in the house seems linked in controlling Ruth's movements in it. Revealing her opposition to Teddy, Ruth resists positioning; she refuses to sit down, tells *him* to go to bed, takes possession of the key, and goes out for a walk as if he, not she, were the new arrival.

Ruth's maneuvers are reminiscent of many Pinter scenes in

which gesture makes visible a character's emotional needs. In *The Dumb Waiter,* Gus's comically erratic movements infuriate Ben but also reveal Gus's unwillingness to follow the old rules of their game; in *The Collection,* James tries to score points by forcing Bill to move; in *The Room,* sitting or perching is a key maneuver in the Sandses' game of dominance; and getting the tramp to sit down is vital to Edward's security in *A Slight Ache.* For Teddy and Ruth's arrival scene, Pinter borrows the nonsense language of logistics from *The Birthday Party,* when Petey and Meg prattle about whether or not Stanley is up and coming down:

> TEDDY: Shall I go *up?*
> *He goes into the hall, looks up the stairs, comes back.*
> Why don't you sit *down?*
> *Pause.*
> I'll just go *up* . . . have a look.
> *He goes up the stairs stealthily.*
> RUTH *stands, then walks slowly across the room.* [emphasis mine]
>
> (pp. 36–37)

Ruth's moves, her standing, sitting, and walking, provoke a tension missing from the earlier plays. Unlike Gus, for example, she manipulates movement to subvert authority; luring Teddy into making a command, she shows him (and us) how little his commands mean. At the end of the scene, when he tries to take control sexually ("*He puts his arms on her shoulders and kisses her*" [p. 40]), Ruth retreats completely out into the night.

In the theater the scene between Teddy and Ruth excites more fascination than laughter, but significantly it foregrounds the relationship between past and present that will dominate the rest of the action. Ruth, more than any other Pinter character, lives fully in the present, in the second-by-second fluctuations at the heart of any human interaction. This gives her tremendous power, especially when interacting with a family whose basis for aggression is the manipulation of the past. Having not shared the humiliations of this family with this family, Ruth is not subject to the family taboos. According to Pinter, she exists in a kind of free-floating state:

> The woman is not a nymphomaniac as some critics claimed. In fact she's not very sexy. She's in a kind of despair which gives her a kind of freedom. Certain facts like marriage and the family for this woman have clearly ceased to have any meaning.[78]

A year before *The Homecoming*, Pinter wrote the screenplay to
The Pumpkin Eater, in which a woman's entire sense of self-worth
is bound up in producing children. As the woman drifts away from
her husband's active life, her behavior takes on a certain self-
directed logic that shields her from criticism or change. Ruth oper-
ates similarly; her condition of "despair" frees her from acting logi-
cally and removes the necessity (or even the advisability) of
hunting down motives for her behavior. And yet, Ruth's despair
translates into the dramatic terms already established in the play;
by responding fully to the present needs and fears of the male
household, she demonstrates her expertise in the undercutting
game.

From the outset, Ruth's sense of the present moment separates
her from Teddy.

> TEDDY: Well, the key worked.
> *Pause.*
> They haven't changed the lock.
> *Pause.*
> RUTH: No one's here.
>
> (pp. 35–36)

Teddy's information links the house to his past life in it, while
Ruth's comment speaks to the present reality: a room is shaped by
the people inhabiting it; the most compelling thing about this room
is its emptiness. Moreover, Ruth's attention to objects (Max's chair
in this scene, the glass of water with Lenny) focuses our attention
on the configurations of space—just as Mick's silent moment at the
opening of *The Caretaker* causes us to absorb the junk. But again
Ruth's behavior disturbs us; Teddy moves *"stealthily"* but she
moves deliberately, as if taking stock.

Tension mounts in the short scene between Teddy and Lenny. In
this interchange Pinter prepares us for the parody that will be
Teddy's homecoming and foreshadows Teddy's abdication as Ruth's
husband. After six years the reunion between brothers bristles
with hostile evasion. Lenny feigns indifference while Teddy reveals
the comic potential in Pinter's statement about speech and silence:
"The speech we hear is an indication of that which we don't hear."[79]
As a stratagem to cover his naked embarrassment, Teddy answers
the polite questions Lenny refuses to ask: "I've been keeping well"
(How are you?); "I've just come back for a few days" (How long will
you be staying?). Teddy himself makes a comedy of evasion by

never mentioning Ruth: "*I've* just come back . . . *I've* been keeping well" [emphasis mine] (p. 42), and his physical language carries the omission further. He abandons the living room area without waiting for Ruth to return, leaving her to a private homecoming with Lenny.

Ruth's scene with Lenny is one of the highlights of *The Homecoming*. They have not met, but we have met them; we know Lenny is malicious and we have just seen that he hates Teddy. Now, holding a "small clock" as if to tick off the minutes, he waits for Ruth. Outdoors, Ruth must pass through the living room to go upstairs; the audience is primed for a confrontation.

Lenny, like Teddy, immediately tries to position Ruth—not logistically but emotionally and sexually. First he lets her know that he can play the host: he offers drinks, comments about the weather, and delivers a line that sounds like Sorel Bliss greeting one of Simon's friends:

> You must be connected with my brother in some way.
> The one who's been abroad.
>
> (p. 44)

Next he splatters her, Goldberg-style, with observations and information that turn on the contrast between day and night, the normality of the daytime, the unpredictability of nighttime, the fact that she is dressed and he wears pajamas. He challenges her to recognize the sexual possibilities in their situation; like his clock, Lenny might be capable of "letting out a bit of a tick" (p. 49). Using another Goldberg technique, Lenny seeks to dominate Ruth by discrediting her biography. When she twice mentions her married connection to Teddy, Lenny changes the subject; when she mentions their vacation in Venice, Lenny supplants her story with one of his own. And like Goldberg in his interrogation scenes, Lenny attempts to confuse by rapidly switching contexts:

> . . . otherwise I've got a pretty shrewd idea I'd probably have gone through Venice. Yes, I'd almost certainly gone through it with my batallion. Do you mind if I hold your hand?
>
> (p. 46)

When Ruth asks "Why?" Lenny answers with two long speeches that exploit the family talent for self-flattery and non sequitur. In the first he describes how he beat up a pox-ridden "lady" who was

"making a certain proposal" down by the docks; in the second he
describes how he jabs an "old lady" who asked him to move a heavy
iron mangle. Like Mick and Goldberg, Lenny embroiders his violent themes with drawing-room euphemisms ("I wasn't financially
embarrassed") and clichés ("no one about, all quiet on the Western
Front"). He enjoys the grandiose expostulation:

> What I anticipated with a good deal of pleasure was the brisk cold bite
> in the air in the early morning.
>
> (p. 48)

And he enjoys undercutting it:

> And I was right. I had to get my snowboots on and I had to stand on a
> corner, at about five-thirty in the morning. . . . Bloody freezing.
> [ellipses mine]
>
> (p. 48)

Clearly Lenny is improvising, borrowing technical jargon in order
to sound informative. Jargon can backfire; "jibbing the boom" is an
archaism, "playing about with the yardarm" an absurdity. But then,
narrative accuracy hardly matters; hoping to intimidate Ruth,
Lenny struts out his intellect, demonstrating by the inventiveness
and spontaneity of his speech that he can dominate her and control
their dialogue. These speeches, like Max's in the first scene of the
play, are excellent parodies of the front cloth music-hall monologue, the "there-I-was-and-who-do-you-think-should-come-up-to-
me" variety. Max locates his action "down at the paddocks," Lenny
"down at the docks." The parody lies not only in the content but in
the explicitness. While the comedian trusts to innuendo for effec-
tiveness (along with the sly wink, the coy smile), Lenny's narratives combine the rambling eloquence of the stand-up comedian
with the malice of Anthony Burgess's *Clockwork Orange* yobs.

However, Ruth is not impressed, or if she is, she obeys the
dictates of the undercutting game: "The rules . . . are that nobody
ever shows a blow actually register."[80] Ruth coolly undercuts the
first story by deliberately missing the point, focusing on a detail in
the narrative and ignoring the violence. After the second narrative,
Lenny again tries to position her, this time with respect to the
ashtray. She protests: "It's not in my way" (p. 49), but he moves it
anyway. Next he wants to remove the glass of water, but now she
takes control. Indirectly addressing Lenny's hatred of women, she
taunts him by *enacting*, in present time, the female roles he most

despises: the prostitute and the mother. Like the aggressive whore, Ruth proposes to "take" Lenny; like the sadistic mother (who bestowed the hated name "Leonard" and whose memory weighs on Lenny like the heavy iron mangle), Ruth proposes to nurse him, offering her lap and a sip from her glass.

John Russell Brown, discussing the life Pinter gives to objects, suggests that Ruth's sipping from, proffering, and finally draining the glass enacts in miniature a powerful drama of seduction and rejection.[81] By giving "life" to the glass and ashtray, Pinter is parodying their conventional function as signifiers of a realistic setting. Activating this parody is Ruth, whose "freedom" from the "facts" of marriage and family (the "facts" of conventional realism) translates dramatically into a talent for improvising in present time. In this scene, Ruth exploits Lenny's thinly disguised fear and hatred of female sexuality by challenging him with her own quasi-incestuous sexuality: "Why don't I just take you? (p. 50)"

Lenny's response registers the depth of his defeat. His fantasies invaded and flung back at him, Lenny ironically assumes the conventionally moral stance that he has so ostentatiously attacked in his narratives:

> You're in love, anyway, with another man. You've had a secret liaison with another man.
>
> (p. 50)

To this incongruous recital of Oedipal pain, Ruth responds with a mocking offer of nurture. Lenny's gesture, shouting up the stairs after Ruth departs, resembles Max waving his stick, and is equally ineffective. He, not Ruth, has been positioned, and the audience has the satisfaction of witnessing a genuine comic reversal—the attacker victimized, the biter bit.

Max's entrance recaptures the feeling of suspense, for conceivably Lenny could inform him of the new arrivals. Pinter works up the possibility when Max insists on an explanation for Lenny's shouting. Pinter's human jungle has been compared to Jonson's sick world; certainly Max rages with the monomaniacal fixation of a Jonsonian humour:

> He was talking to someone. Who could he have been talking to? They're all asleep. He was having a conversation with someone. He won't tell me who it was. He pretends he was thinking aloud. What are you doing, hiding someone here?
>
> (pp. 51–52)

Lenny answers with an elaborate reprise of the undercutting game, derailing Max's questions by probing a different event in the past: the source of Max's fatherhood, the image of his parents "at it." For the first time, Lenny parodies his philosopher brother; "in a spirit of inquiry" he needles his father "about the true facts of that particular night" (p. 52), and Max, pushed to the brink of horror, responds abusively. When Jessie is mentioned he spits. His comment, "You'll drown in your own blood," implies that Lenny's hatred will end in murder, but it also refers back to Lenny's interlude with Ruth. Lenny *is* drowning in his own blood, so immersed in the family pathology that he obsessively replays the mother-hating scenes of his family romance.

Four evening scenes and four night scenes terminate in a family reunion in the morning. Pinter prepares the reunion by extending the one-on-one combats of the first scenes to rebounding confrontations. Artfully prefiguring the violence of the scene, Pinter has Joey shadowboxing in the mirror. Max, nursing a grudge from the previous night, intimidates Joey with a silent stare. He complains about Sam's kitchen noises, then invites Joey to a football game, but Joey refuses. Retaliating, Max calls Sam out from the kitchen and, in Joey's presence, attacks Sam's impotence. Then Teddy appears and stunningly undercuts Max by making him a "laughing-stock" (p. 57). Punishing Teddy by insulting Ruth, Max orders Joey to "chuck them out" (p. 58), but instead Joey apologizes to the newcomers: "He's an old man" (p. 58). Lenny's arrival is Max's final humiliation. Catching Joey unawares, Max slugs him in the stomach, then crowns Sam. His strength finally vindicated, Max ends physical violence with a physical truce, calling loudly for a "cuddle and a kiss" (p. 59).

The farcical slapstick elements in this scene are unmistakable. Violence erupts after a potboiler exchange in which Max acts the role of fast-talking comic and Teddy acts the straight man:

MAX: Who's this?
TEDDY: I was just going to introduce you.
MAX: Who asked you to bring tarts in here?
TEDDY: Tarts?
MAX: Who asked you to bring dirty tarts into this house?
TEDDY: Listen, don't be silly—

(p. 57)

The momentum of misunderstanding builds until Teddy explodes with: "She's my wife! We're married!" The pace and misdirection of this duologue resemble a typical Groucho Marx "conversation"—here with a groom in Cocoanut Manor:

GROUCHO: You must call on me sometime.
GROOM: I was just about to say . . .
GROUCHO: Yes, come up and see my flowerbeds.
GROOM: Well I intended to . . . say . . . was . . .
GROUCHO: I want you to see my pansies . . .
GROOM: Well, uh . . .
GROUCHO: I have short pansies and long pansies.[82]

Both Max and Groucho pursue their own maniacal course against a straight man trying politely to have his say. Physicalizing the disjunction of verbal styles, Pinter parodies realistic movement with clown choreography:

In the clown boxing match, dirty tactics are the preferred method of winning the fight, and it is likely that the referee, who usually favors the dishonest fighter, will get pummelled at least once . . . It is . . . particularly humorous if a dwarf boxer knocks out a tall opponent.[83]

Using John Towson's description, we recognize Max as dwarf boxer and dirty fighter, Joey as the tall (or at least strong) opponent, and Sam as the unlucky referee, who tries to help Max and gets pummelled. Pinter need never have seen a clown boxing match to produce this parody of a fair fight in the ring. Yet the similarity between Towson's description and Pinter's action demonstrates the range of Pinter's comic physical vocabulary that he began to develop in *The Dumb Waiter* and used to comic effect in *The Caretaker* and *The Lover*.

Thus, after the calculated undercutting dynamic of the first four scenes and the reversals in the duologues of the nocturnal scenes, homecomers and family collide, and the force of impact is registered by a slapstick tussle and a wild mélange of verbal styles. The surface fracture in this scene prepares us for the contrapuntal comic and horrific explosions in act 2. Conventional images of domestic life and realistic dialogue are juxtaposed with their parodic counterparts so that the audience perceives events as though in double exposure. We have the sense that real and surreal blur, as in Pinter's "dark dream," with no reason or discernible motive. Yet the game playing of act 1 continues; this family can relate in no other way. What we have seen of Ruth's method with Lenny and Teddy remains consistent but grows more sexual; the game she plays with her body is finally echoed in the prostitution "game" the family proposes at the end of the play. As Ruth enters the family group, events take on the strangely free-floating quality of her personality. Unlike act 1, act 2 unravels not as a series of scenes but as a series of shocks, separated by only one blackout.

Our feeling of double exposure is established at the beginning of act 2, when the family gathers in decorous arrangement for after-dinner coffee. Having traded compliments with his daughter-in-law, Max launches into after-dinner speech making. First he presents an idyllic portrait of the butcher as a young man, eulogizing the morals, heart, and mind of his dead wife. Then he paints a scene that resembles a Victorian frontispiece: loving parents surrounded by freshly scrubbed, pretty children. In seconds he alters to diatribe: Jessie is a "slut-bitch," the boys bastards, and families on both sides are crippled or crazy. What turns the mood sour is Ruth's question: "What happened to the group of butchers?" (p. 63); as with Lenny she responds deliberately to a detail in the narrative, thus undercutting the bellicose embroidery. If the audience is unaware of the strategy of her question, they cannot fail to appreciate its impact—what Andrew Kennedy calls the shock of "ceremony and its violation."[84]

Elements of ceremony permeate Max's first speech. He ritually bathes the children one by one, covers Jessie with offerings ("I'm going to treat you to a couple of items" [p. 62]), pours her libations ("a drop of cherry brandy" [p. 62]), and compares his ceremony with another ("I tell you, it was like Christmas" [p. 62]). Heightening the pictorial arrangement in his speech is the family ritual being enacted in present time. Ruth, filling the mother's role, pours coffee and receives compliments on her cooking. When Max shatters his heavily gilded portrait we not only feel the shock but see one of its effects; Sam is ostracized from the family circle.

The next double exposure concerns Teddy's life. He responds, shakily, to Max's cue ("You've got a wonderful family, a marvelous career" [p. 65]) with his own idyllic vision: "It's a great life, at the University . . . we've got everything we want" (p. 66). Against Teddy's mundane description, Lenny flings a parody of the philosopher's jargon, which Teddy impotently sidesteps: "That doesn't fall within my province." Is Teddy a respectable academician or an idiot? For Pinter he is clearly both, or rather both are the same. Parodying a phenomenological description of an object, Lenny mocks his philosopher brother:

LENNY: . . . Take a table, take it. All right I say, *take* it, *take* a table, but
once you've taken it, what you going to do with it? Once
you've got hold of it, where you going to take it?
MAX: You'd probably sell it.
LENNY: You wouldn't get much for it.
JOEY: Chop it up for firewood.
LENNY *looks at him and laughs.*

(p. 68)

Even the laggard Joey takes part in this Marx Brothers-like chorus
of one liners, and Lenny's laughter cues our own. This scene is an
excellent illustration of the comedy of unmasking in Freud.[85] Teddy's position of dignity and respect is grounded in his status as a
philosopher; by mocking philosophical ideas, the family makes his
authority seem fraudulent. Unable or unwilling to strike back,
Teddy confirms his isolation from the group.

Ruth, however, joins the group. She undercuts Lenny's jibes
just as she undercuts his stories, by relating his abstractions to a
sexual performance enacted in present time. Lenny interrogates
Teddy first about the "known and unknown," then about "this business of being and not-being" (p. 68). In the course of her short
speech, Ruth responds to both oppositions: the "known and unknown" are, respectively her moving leg and her underwear; "being and not being" are her fragmented words and the mechanical
movement of her lips. As a former photographer's model, Ruth
understands how to manipulate images: she superimposes on a
conventional cross-legged posture a close-up of her moving leg; she
transforms a realistic image of her face during conversation with a
fast close-up on her moving mouth. These crude silent images are
the stuff of pornography that dehumanize even as they arouse.
Reductive and impersonal, Ruth's "self-images" also recall
Richard's impressions of a doll-like Sarah in *The Lover:* "I have
great pride in being seen with you. To see you smile, laugh, walk,
talk, bend, be still" (p. 187). But while Sarah's body language
confirms her social position, Ruth's sensuality parodies and mocks
convention. Sarah separates marital decorum from afternoon
games while Ruth makes shocking innuendoes during after-dinner
coffee.

Yet just as Max swings from sentimentality to abuse, Ruth swings
from the impersonal to the deeply personal. Her life, it seems,
began "quite near here" (p. 69) and ended when Teddy took her to

America, a sterile wasteland and, we assume, a metaphor for marriage to a sterile intellectual. Ruth's use of the present tense in her description of America, with an incantatory repetition of the last two lines ("And there's lots of insects there . . . And there's lots of insects there" [p. 69]), suggests the everlasting present of a soul in purgatory. Her fragmented language contrasts poignantly with Max and Lenny's music-hall verbosity and with Teddy's arrogant abstractions. Emphasizing its uniqueness, Pinter opens and closes the passage with *"silence."*

However, Ruth's audience shares neither her tastes nor her style. Her ambiguous images are comically undercut by the prosaic and time-bound:

> MAX *stands.*
>
> MAX: Well, it's time to go to the gym. Time for your workout, Joey.
> LENNY *(standing):* I'll come with you.
> JOEY *sits looking at* RUTH.
> MAX: Joe.
> JOEY *stands. The three go out.*
>
> (p. 69)

That Lenny willingly follows Max is a wonderful comic irony, and Joey's stupefied stare becomes a brief comic gag. Yet in the physical language of the play Ruth has scored a victory: her complex verbal messages have emptied the room. Earlier she took possession of the key; now she controls the central room of the house. Perhaps in appreciation of the comic reversals that she herself has instigated, Ruth allows Teddy to take her hand and *"smiles at him."*

These contrapuntal swings from sentimentality to abuse, from pornography to poetry, loosen the connection between the real and surreal. After the sheepish exit of Max, Lenny and Joey, Teddy tries to reestablish a "real" connection to children and home in America. He specifically locates the children in time ("about eleven o'clock") and space ("at the pool"), then reminds Ruth of his work timetable and her relation to it. Prodded by Ruth, he displaces his hatred of his family onto a hatred of filth, comparing the clean pools of America to the "filthy urinal" of the London neighborhood. Finally he locates the two of them on vacation in Venice, but in this comic and telling exchange, even the recent past diverges from the present:

> TEDDY: You liked Venice, didn't you? It was lovely, wasn't it. You had a good week. I mean . . . I took you there. I can speak Italian.

RUTH: But if I'd been a nurse in the Italian campaign I would have been there before.

(p. 71)

Using Lenny's tactics as well as his story, Ruth creates a past unfamiliar to Teddy, thus discrediting their mutual biography. This is precisely Sarah's method in *The Lover,* when she suggests that she entertained visitors other than Max and Richard. Even if the audience fails to connect Ruth's odd response to Lenny's story of the Italian campaign, Pinter underscores the significance of the exchange. After a *"pause,"* Teddy says, "You just rest. I'll go and pack" (p. 71). In his haste to remove Ruth, Teddy errs again; he deserts the space and Lenny arrives, as he did earlier, to usurp his place.

Ruth's exchange with Lenny reveals a startling contrast from their previous scene. Now she monologues and he listens selectively, breaking in to banter about a Victorian hat (an oblique reference to the idealized Jessie in a silk dress "heavily encrusted in pearls" [p. 62]). Then Lenny asks Ruth to dance, and this time *he* enacts the sexual subtext of Ruth's disjointed description of house and lake: "LENNY *kisses* RUTH. *They stand, kissing"* (p. 74). In a rapid series of grotesque stage images, Joey takes Ruth to the couch, lies on her, kissing, while Max capers from the couch to the silent standing Teddy on whom he rains a speeded-up parody of parental admonitions which alternately deny and confirm, but always mock Ruth and Teddy's marriage. The violation of ceremony is complete.

Critics provide explanations for the overt sexuality of this scene: we read that Ruth's marriage is finished anyway, she longs for the familiar filth of the Old World, she needs to be needed.[86] However, explanations did not mitigate the shock in performance. Pinter's own ironic interpretation of events should caution us against easy rationalizations:

There are thousands of women in this very country who at this very moment are rolling off couches with their brothers, or cousins, or their next-door neighbors. The most respectable women do this. It's a splendid activity. It's a little curious, certainly, when your husband is looking on, but it doesn't mean you're a harlot.[87]

Indeed, we are prevented from forming one opinion or another since Max, acting as chorus, provides fantastic commentary on the action. He calls Ruth "a lovely girl," "a beautiful woman," "a woman of feeling" (pp. 75–76), at which point Joey and Ruth roll off the sofa. Clearly, Pinter aims to maximize what Bert O. States calls "the shock of non-recognition,"[88] our realization that the characters are more informed than we are. More than any work in the Pinter canon, act 2 of *The Homecoming* dramatizes Pinter's theme of "the impossibility of verification" and proves "that there can be no hard distinctions between what is real and what is unreal, nor between what is true and what is false."[89] Well versed in these tenets of modernism, we will still find that Teddy's defensive stand on "intellectual equilibrium" (his belated analysis of the action) directly reflects our own attitude. Witnessing the quasi-incestuous couplings on stage, we, like Teddy, feel that we are not "lost in it." Or are we?

Avoiding dramatic irony up to this point, Pinter now makes us accomplices in "it." After Joey's entrance we learn the whereabouts of Ruth and observe the family's protracted discussion about keeping her—could they put her "on the game?" Could Teddy send them sufficient clientele? Their grotesquely objective approach is reminiscent of Joe Orton's *Entertaining Mr. Sloane*, when Kath and Ed bargain for the favors of Mr. Sloane. But there the brother-sister contract scene ends the play (Sloane is never confronted with the arrangement), whereas Pinter prepares for a confrontation with ceremonious care:

> RUTH *comes down the stairs, dressed.*
> *She comes into the room.*
> *She smiles at the gathering, and sits.*
> *Silence.*
>
> (p. 90)

Having witnessed the family's negotiations, we are in a privileged position of knowing more than Ruth, just as in *Hay Fever* we know more than the guests who arrive without knowledge of each other for a weekend with the Blisses. Milking the irony, Pinter employs the polite language of drawing-room comedy:

> TEDDY: Ruth . . . the family have invited you to stay, for a little while longer. As a . . . as a kind of guest. If you like the idea I don't mind. We can manage very easily at home . . . until you come back.
>
> (p. 91)

After the blunt discussion before Ruth's entrance, Teddy's careful euphemisms are, of course, both terrible and funny. Her response, however, undercuts our position of authority. She is quite willing to bandy euphemisms, because she will remold their proposal to suit herself. The family offers to set her up on Greek Street as a prostitute, an illegal game proposed in the same spirit as the family games with Teddy: they hope to undercut her by pushing her to extremes. Unlike Teddy, however, Ruth does not retreat. An ironic revision of the biblical Ruth, Pinter's Ruth accepts her husband's family, thereby undermining all their games. In a tableau representing her triumph, Ruth sits stage center, the object of desire around whom the others cluster.

However, to say Ruth has won is to ignore the ambiguities that resonate in the last moments of the play. Though the others are silenced (Teddy gone, Sam prostrate), Max paces, worrying—with good reason—that she'll "do the dirty on us" (p. 97). Suddenly he falls to his knees and begins to sob: Pinter replaces tit-for-tat undercutting with a painful spectacle of human rejection, fear of aging, and loss. Then the tears stop; Max crawls over to Ruth and looks up at her. Our perspective now changes from the tragic to the cruelly comic, for having received his comeuppance, Max rejoins the family circle in whatever way he can. Moreover, he remains characteristically unrepentant—physically obeisant but verbally aggressive. His last three lines contain an assertion ("I'm not an old man" [p. 97]), a nagging question ("Do you hear me?" [p. 97]), and a command ("Kiss me" [p. 98]). As Austin Quigley points out, the London family will affect Ruth as much as she them.[90] In this unstable stage tableau, no one can be called victorious.

The tableau at the end may be viewed as Pinter's ultimate parodic geste: instead of finalizing the action, it provides another shock of nonrecognition. No psychologically coherent explanation can account for Ruth's emblematically serene presence on stage. We feel like witnesses of a spectacle whose action has unraveled with the force of inevitability, yet throughout the play the concatenation of verbal styles as well as the parodies of realistic speech and behavior have made us incapable of comprehending an overarching design.

Typical of the parody plays, however, Pinter's language supplies pointers. Before the arrival of Teddy and Ruth, Pinter inflates the diction to an absurd degree, thus preparing us for frequent deflation. Sam informs us:

> I don't press myself on people, you see. The big businessmen, men of affairs, they don't want the driver jawing all the time, they like to sit in

the back, have a bit of peace and quiet. After all they're sitting in a Humber Super Snipe, they can afford to relax. At the same time, though, this is what makes me really special . . . I do know how to pass the time of day when required.
Pause.

(p. 29)

Sam's coy parenthesis ("this is what makes me really special") and his pontificating tone shatter the surface of naturalistic exchange.

As in *The Lover,* the tone, diction, and mere quantity of words indicate the status of relationships. Ruth and Teddy, in marked contrast to the rest of Teddy's family, speak to each other without rhetorical flourish, at least in the beginning; the ambiguity of their feelings is charted in what they say and do not say, not in *how* they speak. As Ruth allies herself increasingly with Lenny, her speech becomes more fragmented and personal while Teddy's language grows more abstract. Marking the point where a husband proposes prostitution to his wife, Pinter suddenly gives Ruth and Teddy the smooth speech of the drawing room. In her last line: "Eddie . . . don't become a stranger," Pinter traces the course from intimacy to estrangement, for we know "Eddie" has already become a stranger.[91]

The "contract" scene of act 2 recalls the final scene in act 1. As speeded-up parodies record the shock waves of collision, the stilted jargon of legal documents records the nightmarish turn of the action. Mundane rhetoric could not encompass the situation; like Swift, Pinter deepens the horror with a dehumanizing discourse. And yet disjunction in language and action characterizes the verbal strategy throughout the play. Parodying the family drama, *The Homecoming* scourges traditional playgoing instincts: all possible motives are unverifiable, all displays of emotion erratic and contradictory. The undercutting game, which we understand and laugh at, also suffers mutation, becoming a past norm that present revelations break down or recast. In *The Homecoming,* as in the other parody plays, Pinter shocks us into laughter, then defies us to rationalize what we are laughing at.

3

Playing on the Past

After writing *The Homecoming*, Harold Pinter claimed to be finished with "room" plays: "I couldn't any longer stay in the room with this bunch of people who opened doors and came in and went out."[1] In the early "poser-loser" plays, room-bound terrified characters defend their territories against alarming intruders. In the "parody plays," characters still in rooms battle for authority in relationships. In the full-length plays of the 1970s, highly articulate, self-conscious professionals fight a subtler battle. At stake is less the security of territory or the status of a relationship; at stake is the integrity of the self—or, rather, the ability to constitute a convincing version of the self in language. Characters in *Old Times*, *No Man's Land*, and even *Betrayal* are comically obsessed with the creative and destructive possibilities of verbal play in that treacherous Pinterian play field: the unverifiable past.

As a prelude to the plays of the 1970s, Pinter's shorter works after *The Homecoming* offer useful insights. *The Basement* (1967), a television play, marks Pinter's defiant answer to his artistic imprisonment in the room.[2] Law and Stott work through elaborate scenarios for sexual mastery, first one, and then the other dominating the room and sleeping with Jane. As relationships alter, the room itself alters—from Law's shabby hominess to Stott's Swedish decor, to an overdone Italian baroque interior that comments on the stifling, phony decadence of the ménage à trois. With its themes of athletic competition, the unresolved love between the men, the sexual rapacity of the woman, *The Basement* foreshadows *Betrayal*, the changing decor of the television play echoed in the revolving set of the stage play. As television allowed Pinter freedom from the confined stage room, it also freed him from narrative time. Action in the theater unfolds sequentially in the continuous present, but the televised fragments in *The Basement* undermine

our perception of sequence: rather than "follow" a narrative we
absorb a pattern of images. Writing for film allowed Pinter even
greater freedom; fast cuts to the past in *Accident* (1967) and *The
Go-Between* (1969) create a weave of past/present images,
metaphors for the confusion of memory and pain.

In *Landscape* (1968), originally a radio play, Pinter experi-
mented with subjectivity and memory. Beth's incantatory evocations of sun, sea, and the warmth of a lover's touch counterpoint
her husband Duff's crude descriptions of a beer handler's duties
("Hammer the spile through the centre of the bung").[3] Like Mouth
in *Not I*, Beth encircles one scene, the memory of the beach, and
recalls both liberating and terrifying elements that she cannot resolve. The sensuousness of her lover combines in memory with
anxiety about witnessing eyes; guilt over a possible adultery mixes
with ardor for her husband. When Pinter transferred *Landscape* to
the stage, he eschewed—typically—Beckett's abstract scene design, yet his physical concept for the play differs significantly from
The Homecoming, three years earlier. The stage directions for
Landscape place Beth in an armchair, Duff in a chair near a long
table. Their room is a kitchen, as befits their position of manser-
vant and maid to the deceased Mr. Sykes, but *"the background, of
a sink, stove, etc., and a window, is dim."* In this room, props and
furniture, the *physical* elements of their world, fade. Beth's
armchair holds her body; it does not signify, as does Max's, her
mastery of and identification with the room. Unlike any former
Pinter character, Beth speaks from her interior landscape, never
referring to Duff, apparently unaware of his presence. Like the
monologuists in Virginia Woolf's *The Waves*,[4] she is mind speaking,
moving effortlessly in time, meshing past and present.

> Women turn, look at me . . . Two women looked at me, turned and
> stared. No. I was walking, they were still. I turned. [ellipses mine]
> (p. 177–78)

With Beth, Pinter undermines the audience's anticipation of narrative. We may have been tempted to discover explanations for
Goldberg's pursuit of Stanley, for Ruth's shocking adultery; in
Landscape, the "dim" room and Beth's monologue style obviate
such inquiry. How do we verify spoken thoughts?

In *Silence* (1969), the short companion play to *Landscape*, the
walls of Pinter's room are completely down. Characters occupy
stage areas as ephemeral as the relationships they discuss. Though

Ellen crosses to Rumsey and Bates (verifying her affairs with and betrayal of the two), dialogue is minimal; monologue dominates the play. Continuing his experiments in breaking up stage time, Pinter plays with circularity; the closing lines in *Silence* consist of a short-hand repetition of earlier speeches, creating a stichomythia devoid of coherence. *Silence* abjures the illusion of action unraveling in time and charts the way for the scenic non sequiturs of *Old Times,* and the complete break from conventional sequential movement in *Betrayal.*

Like *Silence, Landscape* is barely comic, but Pinter creates juxtapositions with comic overtones. Duff addresses his unhearing wife:

> DUFF: Do you like me to tell you about all the things I've been doing?
> *Pause.*
> About all the things I've been thinking?
> *Pause.*
> Mmmmnn?
> *Pause.*
> I think you do.

but at this point Beth completes the image of her lover's embrace:

> BETH: And cuddled me.

> (p. 189)

Beth's reconstructions of an imaginary past conflict with Duff's desire for affirmation in the present. Such verbal juxtapositions become overtly comic in *Old Times* when Deeley attempts to block Kate and Anna's retreat into the past.

Verbal artifice, a consistent comic device in the Pinter canon, reaches its apex in *The Homecoming* with its dizzying parodies of drawing-room and domestic realism. More obliquely comic than earlier works, *Old Times, No Man's Land,* and even *Betrayal* add self-consciousness and perceptual distortion to verbal play; characters themselves control tonal shifts, and in the case of Deeley and Spooner—Pinter's educated *alazoneia*—they become ironical word critics. Always highly volatile in Pinter's work, words in these plays become the sole means of delimiting and defending one's perception of reality—and hence, oneself. Replacing the visible boundaries of the room are the characters' unbounded word-worlds, exuberant and desperate performances generated by memory, fantasy, and desire.

Pinter's own verbal worlds, and our memory of them, enter his work of the 1970s. As in the "parody plays," the battle for ascendancy is accompanied by elaborate gamesmanship; like the "poser-loser" plays, these works close (or in the case of *Betrayal*, begin) with pompous illusions shattered. Recognition of Pinter's past themes in the plays we view in present time creates a new comic dimension. Yet *Old Times, No Man's Land,* and *Betrayal* breed familiar Pinter tensions and comic situations. The past is still inscrutable, the present still ambiguous, comedy still listing precariously between the two.

OLD TIMES

In *Old Times* (1971), his first full-length play since *The Homecoming,* Pinter charts new territory and reworks the old: he creates drama about the presentness of the past while dramatizing his past themes in comic present-time situations. A married couple, Kate and Deeley, living in elegant seclusion, are visited by Anna, Kate's friend of twenty years ago. Reminiscences about postwar London become grist for sexual combat as Deeley, Kate, and Anna avoid, confront, and finally reinact a problematic scene from their past. However, Pinter's comic manipulations—imposture and exposure, game playing, nonnaturalistic verbal performance—obviate "primal scene" motive hunting; unverifiability, always linked to Pinter comedy, now becomes its playful theme. In *Old Times,* more than in any previous work, Pinter gives prominence to the power of language not only to describe but to create experience:

> The fact that [Deeley and Anna] discuss something that [Deeley] says took place—even if it did not take place—actually seems to me to recreate the time and the moments vividly in the present, so that it is actually taking place before your very eyes—by the words he is using.[5]

These unverifiable acts of memory in the form of song, anecdote, and repartee allow Anna and Deely to claim intimacy with (and possession of) Kate. In fact, each plays *eiron* to the other's *alazon,* continually raising the stakes on intimacy in order to expose the other's claim as lying imposture. Comically, their competition becomes self-revelatory; in "remembering" Kate, Anna and Deeley eroticize her and thus expose their own frustrated desire. But their frustration inspires dazzling word performances, pleasurable not only because they release sexual hostility[6] but because they become an occasion for, in Roland Barthes' terms, "verbal display."[7] Unlike the partners in *The Lover* and *The Homecoming,* the trio in *Old Times* touch only through words but, as Pinter implies, the words *play.* Like the characters, we are seduced into voyeuristic acts of imagination, taking pleasure in the cruel finesse of these sexual combatants even as we "see" into their "past."

As he was writing *Old Times,* Pinter worked the ideas of erotic perception, power, and memory into a short "Poem."

Poem

they kissed I turned they stared
with bright eyes turning to me blind
I saw that here where we were joined
the light that fell upon us burned
so bright the darkness that we shared
while they with blind eyes turning to me turned
and I their blind kiss formed.[8]

In every event a perceiver and a perceived are locked into relationship by their connection to the event. Because passion is self-absorbed or "blind," only the perceiver "sees" objectively; only he can "form" the kiss. When "they" who kiss become aware of the "I" who sees, all are "joined" in a moment of burning consciousness. But what if the perceiver distorts what he sees, malforms the kiss? Suppose the "I" is contained in the "they," the mind viewing the self acting. Will the self remembered be a truthful representation? Is the truth about any event—especially a sexually charged event—ever accessible?

Perception, memory, and erotic interaction are themes in both Pinter's *Old Times* and Sartre's *No Exit* (*Huis Clos,* 1944), in which Pinter acted the role of Garcin for B.B.C. television (1965). In Sartre's claustrophobic drawing-room Hell, three characters meet, each becoming victim and victimizer of the other. Their mutual torture is explicitly connected to Sartre's concept of "the look" that "fixes" the subject as object in the perception of the "Other." Sartre's farcical example of the keyhole watcher illustrates the transformation of subject into object: at the moment of the Other's look, the self ceases to be merely jealous within his own experience; he becomes a spy in the experience of the other. For Sartre the power of the look confirms our contingency in social relationships; unable to escape the Other we also depend on him for whatever image of self we hope to maintain.[9] Thus in *No Exit,* Inez needs Estelle, who needs Garcin, who needs Inez to verify his self-image. However, in Dorothy McCall's words, "The look becomes hell when the other refuses the image of myself I want him to see . . . Garcin is fixed as a coward in the eyes of Inez, Estelle as an infanticide in the eyes of Garcin, Inez as a nothing in the eyes of Estelle."[10]

Pinter the writer may have absorbed elements of Sartre's philosophy; Pinter the actor certainly absorbed the sexual interplay between the tormented Garcin, the lesbian Inez, and the nymphomaniac Estelle. Like Garcin, Deely in *Old Times* tries to assert his masculinity with one woman, then the other; in both plays, lesbian sexuality seems to block heterosexual contact; in both plays, sexual tension heightens the problem of perception. In *Old Times*, however, the power of the perceiver to affect the self-image of the perceived generates comic material: Deeley and Anna do battle with perceptions. Sartre says that "in looking at [others] I measure my power";[11] in denigrating each other Deeley and Anna rise in power. In their texts, their versions of the past, each describes the other in compromising positions and him/herself in close proximity to Kate. Such image making, however, has its dangerous side: Kate is given the power to verify or deny these verbal images, a power she exercises brutally at the end of the play.

Past and present interweave in *No Exit* to dramatize the problem of existential choice, but in *Old Times* past and present are a matter of linguistic choice mirroring the characters' perceptions and desires. However, Pinter borrows the Sartrian technique of wresting action from dialogue. Estelle, Garcin, and Inez narrate their crimes; in a brilliant theatrical climax, they then enact them. In Deeley's story and in present time, Anna, wearing black, sits across from him on a low sofa. In the story (and possibly in present time), she is aware of him gazing up her skirt. Pinter comments reflexively on this technique in one of Anna's speeches—

ANNA: . . . There are things I remember which may never have happened but as I recall them so they take place.[12]

(p. 28)

—thus giving warning that in *Old Times* a character's story might become an acting text. Indeed, Anna's memory of the sobbing man will "take place" at the end of the play.

Allowing his characters to generate their own scenes, Pinter draws attention to the process of creation, the play as artifact that imitates not life, but the artist's particular and clever arrangement of life. Always a punctilious craftsman, Pinter in *Old Times* lays bare the materials of his craft. That is, he weaves other art forms (Carol Reed's film *Odd Man Out* and the Gershwin-Kern lyrics of the thirties and forties) into *Old Times*, creating a comic pattern of recollection for his audience as well as for his characters.

Odd Man Out, 1948, enters *Old Times* at four levels. First, it provides a possible meeting place for Deeley, Anna, and Kate; did they see the film together or apart? Second, the title glosses the gamelike behavior of the characters in which two play, leaving the other "out." Third, Pinter uses the flashback technique of the film for the Anna-Kate scenes (although in *Odd Man Out*, delirium inspires the flashback while in *Old Times* present time cuts to past without psychological transition). Fourth, the scenario of the movie evokes the theme of perceptual distortion. In a crucial closing scene, a doctor and an artist fight each other to save the life of Johnny McQueen, a dying IRA chief: the doctor wants to save his body, the artist his soul. Robert Newton, Deeley's hero in the movie, plays the artist Lukey (Luke is mentioned in act 2 of *Old Times* as Deeley's competition for Anna), who would capture Johnny's likeness for his portrait gallery. The artist cares only for the image of death-in-life and ignores the reality of the man's pain. It is revealing that Anna admires F. J. McCormick who plays Shell, the scavenger trying to sell Johnny to the highest bidder. Shell and Lukey are roommates in a dilapidated Victorian, and though they detest one another, they are, with respect to Johnny, partners in crime.[13] Similarly, Deeley and Anna collude in dehumanizing Kate despite the affection they express for her. The filmmaker frames Kate in a language of cinematic shots:

> She likes taking long walks. All that. You know. Raincoat on. Off down the lane, hands deep in pockets.
> (p. 20)

Anna, too, renders Kate in photo images that draw attention to (and perhaps defend against) her "look":

> Sometimes, walking, in the park, I'd say to her, you're dreaming, you're dreaming, wake up, what are you dreaming? and she'd look round at me, *flicking her hair, and look at me as if I were part of her dream.* [emphasis mine]
> (pp. 20–21)

Deeley and Anna's descriptions are, of course, interpretations of Kate, romantic and simplistic fictions that reduce her to an object of reminiscence, a means of validating their own versions of experience.

This multitextured surface may not yield all its riches to an audience, but through its comedy, *Old Times* is among Pinter's most accessible plays. Motives and memories are unverifiable but sexual combat is not. Tension builds palpably with every revision, new look at, old times. Since characters create stories out of details we have just heard, we participate in the sparring comedy, now joining Anna in one-upping Deeley, now joining Deeley in undercutting Anna. But this text of combat is itself continually and comically revised by the perspective of a third party who produces a new text, a new version of experience. The opening scene of the play artfully establishes triangular wordplay—when the lights dim, *"three figures are discerned"*; as Kate and Deeley discuss Anna, she remains in *"dim light at the window."* About the ambiguity of this opening Pinter said: "it's true that in *Old Times* the woman is there, but not there, which pleased me when I managed to do that, when that came through to me."[14] Particularly interesting is the way in which Anna comes through during the opening exchange:

KATE *(Reflectively.)*: Dark.
Pause.
DEELEY: Fat or thin?
           Pause.
KATE: Fuller than me. I think.
           Pause.
DEELEY: She was then?
KATE: I think so.
DEELEY: She may not be now.

(pp. 3–4)

Typical of traditional prologues, Pinter introduces a major motif—"then" vs. "now"; past vs. present. Untypical is the audience perspective. The object discussed in casual yet erotic terms ("Dark"; "fuller") is part of Kate's past experience but is visible to us in present time. Kate seems to create Anna through the language of memory (note two references to "think"), but at this point we are the only witnesses to this linguistic magic—like voyeurs we see what (from the perspective of the characters) should not be seen.

In the ensuing conversation, Deeley's probes and Kate' evasions parody the question-answer interrogations of realism and of earlier

Pinter. Like James of *The Collection*, Deeley likes to cross-examine, but not with James's detectivelike insistence. Instead, Deeley poses as amateur therapist (Pinter places him in the armchair, Kate on the couch), probing Kate's emotional blocks:

DEELEY: Can't you remember what you felt?

(p. 4)

Are you looking forward to seeing her?

(p. 7)

Coyly he introduces the theme of voyeurism: "I'll be watching you . . . To see if she's the same person" [ellipses mine] (pp. 7–8). He labels Anna Kate's "best friend" (p. 9) to heighten the drama of reunion, and when she corrects him with more precise wording, he jokingly twists her words to favor *his* image of the relationship.

KATE: She was my only friend.
DEELEY: Your best and only.
KATE: My one and only.
    Pause.
    If you have only one of something you can't say it's the best of anything.
DEELEY: Because you have nothing to compare it with?
KATE: Mmnn.
    Pause.
DEELEY *(Smiling):* She was incomparable.

(p. 5)

Laughing at this wriggling line of inquiry, the audience is prepared for the memory distortions that characterize every exchange in *Old Times.* When Deeley suggests that Anna "may be a vegetarian" (p. 8), Kate, moments later, changes the suggestion to an assertion: "You said she was a vegetarian" (p. 10). When Deeley apparently misses Kate's first reference to living with Anna, Kate mocks him with a claim to certainty:

DEELEY: You lived together?
KATE: Of course.
DEELEY: I didn't know that.
KATE: Didn't you?

(p. 12)

When Deely concludes "none of this matters," he may be recoiling from the disturbing connection between the "someone" Kate lived with and the woman who is visiting, but structurally the prologue "matters" a great deal. It establishes Deeley's comic posturing and the revisionary and deflationary impulse in both characters' speeches. It also identifies Kate's unique strategy: in the scene, as in the entire play, she seems victimized by a more articulate questioner until she quietly turns assertive.

The prologue, however, does not prepare us for Anna as she *"turns from the window, speaking."* After the spareness of Deeley and Kate's exchange, Anna's paean to youth pours out (like Lenny and Goldberg's monologues) with the momentum of a music-hall set piece.

> Queuing all night, the rain, do you remember? my goodness, the Albert Hall, Covent Garden, what did we eat? to look back, half the night, to do things we loved, we were young then of course, but what stamina, and to work in the morning . . . .
>
> (p. 13)

Like Goldberg, too, Anna drowns details in clichés and inflates a stereotype to absurd proportions. That she and Kate would meet for lunch is a harmless detail, but Anna buffs the image until it glows gaudily:

> . . . lunchtimes in Green Park, exchanging all our news, with our very own sandwiches, innocent girls, innocent secretaries.
>
> (p. 14)

Anna's verbal performance exerts a hegemonic pressure on the discourse of Deeley and Kate; she both asserts her authority over the past and reorganizes relationships in the present. Deeley answers her last question ("does it still exist?"), linking himself to Anna in present time; Kate answers her first question ("do you remember?"), linking herself to Anna in the past. In one speech, Anna has driven a wedge between the couple. She further destabilizes their relationship with a comic shift in diction. After her gushing reminiscence of the London past, she summarizes the present in a long-voweled operatic legato that damns Kate and Deeley's life with overpraise:

> No one who lived here would want to go far. I would not want to go far, I would be afraid of going far, lest when I returned the house would be gone.
>
> (p. 15)

As James *(The Collection)* mocks Bill's effete use of "scrumptious,"
Deeley mocks Anna's "lest." Kate does not compete; she contrib-
utes three simple facts that speak concretely to her life in the
present:

> Sometimes I walk to the sea. There aren't many people. It's a long
> beach.
>
> (p. 16)

But Anna returns the conversation to London, where "we were
girls together" (p. 16). With a slip of the tongue, she denigrates
Kate's role as wife (complimenting Deeley on his "casserole"), and
when Kate makes a last attempt to focus on the prsent ("Yes, I quite
like those kinds of things, doing it" [p. 17]), Anna again returns to
the past:

> We weren't terribly elaborate in cooking, didn't have the time, but
> every so often dished up an incredibly enormous stew, guzzled the lot,
> and then more often than not sat up half the night reading Yeats.
>
> (p. 18)

Anna's liberties with time and incident are pinpointed in her own
echoic commentary: "Yes. Every so often. More often than not."
Did they *usually* read Yeats *only* on those occasions of guzzling a
stew? The absurdity of the question reminds us of the temporal
slippage accompanying Anna's arrival. We are in one time-frame in
the prologue—before the casserole was eaten—in another after
Anna's entrance.

Nevertheless, Deeley anxiously follows Anna's lead, showing
interest in her delightful youth ("I wish I had known you both
then" [p. 16]) and in her present life ("I've been there [Sicily]"
[p. 18]). Soon they are discussing Kate, and the ensuing exchange
establishes their competitive interaction. Deeley claims that Kate
is spatially nonexistent (her face floats away), but Anna remembers
her as temporally unconscious (Kate thought Friday was Saturday).
Both insisting on their presence in Kate's past, Deeley and Anna
trade Gershwin-Kern love lyrics that celebrate or mourn a "true
love" apparently represented by Kate. Soon they settle into a
tensely comic duet, completing each other's verses, then singing
sequential lines—a mini-vaudeville.

The singing competition also rehearses the theme of perceptual
distortion. As prelude, Deeley mocks Anna's archaism "gaze," in-

terrupting the voyeuristic enjoyment of Kate that Anna describes and perhaps enacts. Yet many of the lyrics they sing to Kate reveal a gnawing desire *to* gaze: "The way you comb your hair"; "Oh but you're lovely, with your smile so warm." Deeley even changes the lyric of "Blue Moon" from "I saw" to "I *see* you standing alone" (p. 23). Toward the end of this routine, smoke gets in the eyes of the combatants and the image of the beloved is reduced to a "ghost" that "clings." Kate greets this romantic nostalgia with silence, comically taunting the singers for their zeal and perhaps for their desire.

Abruptly, after the *"silence"*—and until the next *"silence"*—Deeley ventures out boldly with comically aggressive narratives and speeches that assert *his* version of the past. The motif of meetings, so common in romantic songs, triggers an off-color monologue reminiscent of Lenny's front-cloth parodies. Like a practiced raconteur Deeley defers his punch line, stretching the story to include such titillating details as the seductive play of the lesbian usherettes. After hyperbolic praise of Robert Newton ("And I would commit murder for him, even now" [p. 25]), Deeley turns the spotlight on Kate, whom he introduces with murderous enthusiasm as a three-ring circus act:

> And there was only one other person in the cinema, one other person in the whole of the whole cinema, and there she is.
>
> (pp. 25–26)

Hostility seething behind banter, Deeley pays respect not to his wife-to-be but to a "true blue pick-up." As a final wrench to traditional sentiment, Deeley announces that Robert Newton (not love) brought them together and only Robert Newton (not death, as in a marriage ceremony) "can tear us apart" (p. 26).

The comic element in Deeley's narrative recalls Freud's analysis of the "smutty joke," a tendentious verbal act that seeks to expose the sexuality of the woman at whom it is aimed.[15] By linking Kate to the masturbating usherette (both she and Kate use the sound response "mmmnnn"), Deeley seems both to attack Kate's self-absorption and to reveal his inadequacy. Alluding to his own homosexual fantasies, Deeley admits that thinking about Robert Newton heightens the sexual appeal of Kate and midspeech draws a comic moral from his position in the cinema: "I was off centre and have remained so" (p. 26). Off-centeredness also refers to the skewed perception of a Pinter poser whose self-verification ("What happened to me was this") becomes a comic performance that demonstrates the unverifiability of all autobiographical statements.

Anna counters Deeley's comic narrative by remembering "some things" that "may never have happened" (p. 28), such as the sobbing man in the London apartment of twenty years ago. While Deeley constructs a narrative with extravagantly prurient details, Anna adds "realistic" touches. Like the man in the story, Deeley is sitting in an armchair; like Kate in the story, Kate sits on a bed (or sofa). In Deeley's story, women are lewd lesbians or pick-ups; Anna's male character sobs, is rejected, and finally settles for a humiliating position, lying across Kate's lap.

The passionate one-upmanship of these narratives and those that follow betrays a curious will to dominate. Kate, the pivotal character, is, in both stories, "still" and is kept still in present time; her interjections ("Are you talking about me?" [p. 19]; "You talk of me as if I were dead" [p. 30]), are either passed over or misunderstood. As the "classic female figure" (Deeley's words), Kate resembles "the other" in Roland Barthes' *A Lover's Discourse*, "a mere object, like a stuffed doll," whose wordly voice Anna and Deeley silence because it opposes the body they once tried to possess. As Barthes' amorous lover "enwraps[s] the other in words,"[16] Kate and Deeley swathe Kate in ludicrous clichés:

DEELEY: When she smiled . . . how can I describe it?
ANNA: Her eyes lit up.
DEELEY: I couldn't have put it better myself.

(pp. 30–31)

But they cannot deaden Kate's potency. Like Ruth in *The Homecoming*, Kate speaks a body language that brings verbal fantasy into action. Like the man who once looked down at Anna, Kate looks down at Anna with such sexual suggestiveness that Deeley drops his aloof mask: "*Stop that!*"

Far from stopping, Kate decisively enters the memory competition, deploying her sensuality in order to thrust Deeley into the odd man out position. Inquiring about Anna's sun-warmed terrace, she evokes her own trite romantic images, his time in Anna's territory, not in the London they all knew twenty years ago.

Do you drink orange juice on your terrace in the morning and bullshots at sunset, and look down at the sea?

(p. 38)

Strenuously attempting to intervene (to intercept the conversational ball), Deeley, like Edward in *A Slight Ache*, enlarges himself with comic exaggeration: "I had a great crew in Sicily . . . My name is Orson Welles [ellipses mine]." Despite his noisy assertions or perhaps because of them, Anna and Kate wait the length of a silence, then climax act 1 by fracturing the time-space continuum of the play: they enter the past, enacting a play-within-a-play, and leave Deeley behind as present-time witness.

In previous Pinter works, surface fracture is created by linguistic parody (the surreal shifts in act 2 of *The Homecoming*, the gamelike dialogue structure of *The Dumb Waiter*), verbal games that demonstrate the playwright's, not the characters', ingenuity. Closer to the inventiveness of *Old Times* is the play acting in *The Lover*, in which Richard and Sarah fracture the mundane surface of their daily lives with a sexual play world filled with special discourse and rehearsed movements. What is drastically new in the play acting of *Old Times* is Deeley's audience role, and the hidden messages conveyed by the performers. Enacting a night in their London apartment, Anna and Kate reveal an intimacy not evident in Deeley and Kate's relationship, in which the latter evades questions, resists manipulation. When Anna evokes an absurdly dangerous London ("men hiding behind trees and women with terrible voices" [p. 39]), Kate complies with her wish to stay indoors, coolly replacing husband with former roommate. Deeley becomes odd man out, a spectator on experience.

Act 2 moves to a setting typical of farce, the bedroom, where two divans and an armchair *"are disposed in precisely the same relation to each other as the furniture in the first act, but in reversed positions"* (p. 43). Look-alike rooms suggest a treadmill and anticipate the revolving set in *Betrayal*, with its seemingly inevitable progression from private room to family home to private room.

At the beginning we *"discern"* Anna, no longer at the window but sitting alone in the bedroom, symbolic proprietress of the intimate lives of Kate and Deeley. The scene also continues the past-present melding at the end of act 1; that is, Anna, sitting in the bedroom, waits for Kate to finish her bath. The London apartment of the past imposes itself on the converted farmhouse of the present—but not entirely, for Deeley's entrance returns us to the present. His strategy has changed. Like Anna in act 1, Deeley evokes the past *with* his opponent, manipulating her into his story as a means of gaining control.

Because he has become the outsider, Deeley plays the memory

game with greater intensity. He mocks Anna's solicitousness by serving tea and makes sadly funny innuendos about his sex life, listing all possible sleeping positions, "side by side" taking last place. He parodies Anna's romantic London of cafés, "almost private ones . . . where artists and writers and sometimes actors collected" (p. 14) by presenting The Wayfarers Tavern, with its ridiculous assortment of "poets, stunt men, jockeys, stand-up comedians" (p. 45). Anna merely hinted at Deeley's presence in the London apartment and at *Odd Man Out*, but Deeley names her specifically as the woman he picked up—in spite of Luke—at The Wayfarers and insists upon the clarity of his hindsight. At a party, Deeley claims that he gazed up Anna's skirt with her knowledge, thus mocking Anna's covert gazing at Kate. Moreover, Deeley borrows Anna's technique of couching the past in imagery from the present: he dresses his fictional Anna in black, like the Anna sitting before him, and insists on the likeness of the two:

> . . . nobody but I had a thigh-kissing view, nobody but you had the thighs which kissed. And here you are. Same woman. Same thighs.
>
> (p. 47)

Speaker and peeker, Deeley takes control of the relationship by reducing Anna to a vulgar seductress.

Similar to his story of the lesbian usherettes, Deeley's rendering of this voyeuristic tête-á-tête recalls the strategy of the smutty joke. According to Freud, smutty jokes, usually told for the pleasure of other men, arise from excited attempts at seduction and the shame or embarrassment they provoke in the woman is "only a reaction against the excitement, and, in a roundabout way . . . an admission of it."[17] Pinter comically exaggerates and inverts this model. Deeley's libidinal gaze meets not one but two pairs of thighs, the latter belonging to the friend (Kate?) who supposedly joins Anna on the sofa. Far from sharing his sexual aggressiveness with male friends, Deeley is content to gaze and drink until "a great multitude of men surrounded me, and demanded my opinion about death, or about China, or whatever it was (p. 47)". Fleeing their "stinking breath and broken teeth," Deeley loses his erotic vantage point, thus losing the women altogether. As comic as Deeley's images is the reply of the listening Anna, who admits to no sexual excitement, not even in a roundabout way. To Deeley's closing description of "the indentation of four buttocks" she comments: "I've rarely heard a sadder story." The theater audience, however, may rarely have heard a funnier one. Freud places great emphasis on the third-party audience to the tendentious joke. As Deeley and Anna, our civilized representatives on stage, rehearse a fantasy of social voyeurism, we draw pleasure from the violation of the repressive censor, the release of our own libidinal fantasies.

In the next dialogue Pinter raises the comic temperature. Deeley and Anna return to the present—Kate in the bath—and play a how-far-will-you-go game on the subject of Kate's bathing ritual. Actually the game might be titled "how-much-do-you-know"? When Deeley taunts Anna by describing Kate's sensuousness in the bath, Anna returns the taunt by implying that she is familiar with that sensuousness. Raising the stakes Deeley makes drying Kate the subject of inquiry. Anna needles him, challenging each new detail, until Deeley explodes with an image that stops further game playing.

> Listen, I'll tell you what. I'll do it. I'll do the whole lot. The towel and the powder. After all, I am her husband. But you can supervise the whole thing. And give me some hot tips while you're at it. That'll kill two birds with one stone.
> *Pause.*
> *(To himself.)* Christ.

(pp. 52–53)

Deeley's self-critical "Christ" marks his comic humiliation—comic because through posing he has humiliated himself. Drawing Anna into this verbal fondling of Kate's naked body, Deeley lays bare the power hierarchy of their relationship: Anna supervises the bath while Deeley merely assists. A swift tonal change registers Deeley's defeat. Wearily he attacks Anna's vanity (and implicitly his own) with the simple fact of time passing: "You must be about forty. . . . If I walked into The Wayfarers Tavern now . . . I wouldn't recognize you" (p. 53) [ellipses mine].

This moment of quiescent reflection is shattered by the entrance of Kate, smiling and sighing erotically ("Aahh"), from her bath. As Deeley and Anna join in a combative parody of Gershwin's "No They Can't Take That Away from Me," Pinter choreographs for maximum theatrical effect: "*Kate turns from the window to look at them,*" then *walks down towards them and stands, smiling.*" At the end of the song, Kate sits and thanks them. Now *she* raises the artificial register by assuming the tone of a talkshow interviewee, discussing what she likes about living in the country:

. . . The water's very soft here. Much softer than London. I always find the water very hard in London. That's one reason I like living in the country. Everything's softer. The water, the light, the shapes, the sounds. There aren't such edges here.

(p. 55)

Beneath her poised diction Kate may be subtly criticizing Anna (London's "edges"); she also replaces country living and Deeley with "somewhere very hot, where you can lie under a mosquito net and breathe quite slowly" (p. 55).

With language straining farther from reality, all three characters join in a reprise of play acting, and, in a highly comic reversal, the "odd man out" comes into the discussion of what male visitors Kate will entertain. Deeley then flips into present time ("Are you intending to visit anyone while you're in England?" [p. 64]), but just as quickly he and Anna return to the prison—or the sanctuary—of memories. It is as though Kate's autoerotic self-absorption, her resistance to "the look" or presence of others, forces Deeley and Anna to objectify her, this time as a Brontëean secretive type whose only passion, Anna implies, derives from voyeuristically imagining Anna's sexual exploits. Breaking into this layering of looking and listening, past and present, Deeley poses a question that sounds surprisingly like a climax to a realistic argument:

DEELEY: I mean I'd like to ask a question. Am I alone in beginning to find all this distasteful?

(p. 62)

No Pinter character attempts to sustain direct confrontation. In *A Slight Ache*, Edward wends his way through an exaggerated autobiography in order to tell the Matchseller to sit down. Mick attacks Davies by pretending to be disillusioned with Davies's interior-decorating skills. In *The Homecoming*, tribal hatreds translate into needles that probe, never passions that explode. Yet passions are thick at this point in *Old Times*. We are, after all, in the bedroom. Fed by Deeley and Anna's sexual innuendoes and by the presence of a freshly bathed Kate, comic pressure has built to a *scene à faire*.

Pinter remains true to his edicts: his characters tell him so much and no more. Deeley does not go on to confess his anger but rather to displace it in a fantasy of Mediterranean chic and a rehearsal of his own self-importance. Ironically, Kate expresses anger ("If you don't like it go" [p. 67]), and Anna shifts into the discourse of realism. Mistress of social rhetoric, she rationalizes her behavior during the evening.

> . . . All I wanted for her was her happiness. That is all I want for her still.
>
> (p. 65)

As Pinter well knows, the language of sentiment is insidious: Anna's clichés ring false but they resist contradiction. Anna, too, tells us so much and no more.

Anna's move into realism provokes panic in Deeley. Unable to compete with her calm confidence, he reworks his Wayfarers story, this time using Anna to reach Kate.

> . . . She thought she was you, said little, so little. Maybe she was you. Maybe it was you, having coffee with me, saying little, so little.
>
> (p. 65)

Deeley's comically improbable "maybes" undercut his new version of old times. As a perceiver he can no longer pretend objectivity about what he sees; both subject and object are too unstable. Anna, however, imposes stability. Violating all previous ambiguity, she posits a definite link between herself, Deeley, and Kate. *"Coldly"* she confirms that she was the woman in Deeley's story: "it was my skirt . . . I remember you well" [ellipses mine]. By confirming Deeley's story, Anna comes close to making fiction history, not simply for herself and Deeley, but for Kate.

Immediately Kate acts. Topping Anna's memory of Deeley are Kate's damning memories of both Anna and Deeley, which she verbalizes in two speeches that unite and undercut now-familiar motifs. Contradicting Anna's intimate moments of watching Kate, who "was quite unaware of my gaze" (p. 22), Kate claims, "You didn't know I was watching you" (p. 67). In contrast to Kate's near-obsessive cleanliness is Anna's dirty face—dirtied, significantly, by her own impassioned logorrhea, her "earnest inscriptions" (p. 68). Kate refers three times to "my room" thus denying the image of cozy roommates on which Anna has based all reminiscences. The dreamy unawareness Deeley and Anna attribute to Kate is contradicted by Kate's clear awareness of her "little tricks," just as her "little slow sly smile" (p. 68) mocks the romantic innocence of a Gershwin lyric. Kate's imagery has the fierceness of myth and ritual. Anna's death is decreed ("the time and season were appropriate" [p. 68]) and she dies "with proper decorum." As in Greek tragedy, Anna's murder occurs offstage; her suffering "happened elsewhere." Purging herself in "a lengthy bath," Kate retains an unholy fascination with the death object: "I . . . drew up a chair, sat naked beside you and watched you" [ellipses mine] (p. 68).

For Deeley, Kate's images are prosaic and as comically crude as Deeley's images for her. While he found their first sexual contact "agreeable," she calls it "grind[ing] noses" (p. 72). While he hoped she would be "sexually forthcoming," she intended to smear him with flowerpot dirt. Deeley hoped, "because he was a man," that he was different from Anna; Kate confirms he was not. Worst of all, she denies him the access of direct address, damning him in the third person as she talks to Anna.

Ultimately Kate nullifies both Deeley and Anna by completing a pattern of death motifs. When they smother her in romantic clichés, Kate complains, "You talk of me as if I were dead" and later amends to "as if I *am* dead" (p. 31). In retaliation she buries them with her own "talk" of the past and invades their fictions in present time. Deeley and Anna each fight by "seeing" the other humiliated in the past, but Kate's version of old times separates them into successive periods of her life, one as insignificant as the other.

However, Kate's memories do not conclude the play. Pinter suspends the quasi-naturalistic continuum in which we have been viewing events by freezing time, burying all signs of realism, in offering a mime that enacts Anna's memory of the past. Like *No Exit*, in which each character repeats his crime before the final curtain, Pinter's people enact their roles in the traumatic scene of their London past. At the end Pinter scorches them in a hellish bright light, imprisoning them somewhere between the frustrated desire of the present and the troubling memory of the past. At the end of *No Exit*, Garcin realizes that "Hell is—other people"[18]; we cannot escape the burden and pain of human contact. In *Old Times*, hell appears to be the obsession to repeat the past. Kate and Deeley resume their positions from the beginning of the play, but the presence of the sleeping Anna reminds them of pain not resolved, only buried. From this torture, there appears to be no exit.

Yet there is one exit: another word-world, another version of the past. The comedy of *Old Times* lies not only in the characters' sexual combat but also in their verbal resiliency. Competition shapes the dialogue but does not contain the play of language and desire; words float from speech to speech, recurring in revised or parodied form. The vagueness of Kate's "I quite like those kind of things" (p. 17) is mocked by Deeley when he describes her walking on the beach ("All that kind of thing" [p. 20]). Anna recalls Kate "flicking her hair" (p. 21); not to be outdone, Deeley recalls Kate "flicking her hair back" (p. 27). Kate's final speech has the smooth pace of practiced rhetoric, yet she begins by playing off Anna's "I remember" and continues with images that echo the fund of images already generated by Anna and Deeley. In the prologue Deeley cuts off discussion with "Anyway, none of this matters" (p. 13), and Kate, denigrating his proposals of "a wedding and a change of environment," also ends discussion with a cruel revision of his phrase: "Neither mattered" (p. 69).

That words can be echoed or stolen foregrounds their material power, not only to create experience but to construct masks. The verbal posing of Pinter's previous plays extends in *Old Times* to image making, another form of comic aggression. In his last long speech about The Wayfarers Tavern, Deeley leaps from British slang ("A bit squinky, quite honestly") to American slang ("We had a scene together. She freaked out" [p. 65]) with a rapidity that betrays growing panic but confirms his jet-set worldliness. In the same speech, Deeley decides to reestablish himself within male society, revising earlier grotesque images to create a connection:

> . . . We went to a party. Given by philosophers. *Not a bad bunch.* Edgeware road gang. *Nice lot.* Haven't seen any of them for years. *Old friends.* Always thinking. Spoke their thoughts. *These are the people I miss.*
>
> (p. 65)

My italicized phrases indicate Deeley's ladder of association, comic by its very precariousness. Promoting a masterful image of himself, Deeley skews clichés, yet these comic errors contain a certain logic. A visually oriented filmmaker, Deeley has his "eye," not his finger, on "a number of pulses." Threatened by Anna's prior attachment to Kate, Deeley commands authority over territory, wasting "space" instead of time (p. 63). Skewed clichés suggest a disintegrating control over language, hence declining strength. Yet when Kate tells Deeley to leave, he manages to hold his ground, however provisionally, with wordplay.

DEELEY: Go? Where can I go?
KATE: To China. Or Sicily.
DEELEY: I haven't got a speedboat. I haven't got a white dinner jacket.
KATE: China then.

DEELEY: You know what they'd do to me in China if they found me in a white dinner jacket. They'd bloodywell kill me. You know what they're like over there.

(p. 63–64)

Kate acts the straight man in this parodic music-hall duet, while Deeley plays out his fantastic predicament.

Anna, like Deeley, runs the linguistic gamut, from stilted drawing-room rhetoric to coy colloquialism. But there is nothing precarious about Anna's narratives; her verbal virtuosity reinforces her connection to the past. Words like "lest" and "gaze" arise from the delicate discourse of romance, but Anna girds her reminiscences with stressed phrases that parody romantic enthusiasm:

> . . . we sat hardly breathing with our coffee, heads bent, *so as not to* be seen, *so as not to* disturb, *so as not to* distract, *and listened and listened* to *all those words, all those* cafes, and *all those* people. [emphasis mine]

(p. 14)

These incantatory rhythms halt action in the present, breathe artificial life into memory. By the end of the speech, Anna's London past hovers hypnotically over the present.

Notwithstanding verbal creativity, language breaks down at the end of *Old Times*. In "*silence*" and "*long silence*" Pinter's characters act out, in skeletal form, an irretrievable scene of a complicated, unfinished story. Roland Barthes calls the image "peremptory [because] it always has the last word; no knowledge can contradict it . . . or refine it."[1] Contradiction and refinement are the tools of revision. Indeed, the dialectical play between past and present, the comic combat, and the pleasurable release of verbal and sexual energy arise from each character's impulse to contradict and refine the other's narratives. But the image has the last word; it cannot be played upon or revised. Our sense of loss at the end of *Old Times* is a result not only of the characters' predicament but also of the intractable nature of the stage image: it signifies a limbo, the end of the play. Pinter's next full-length work gives that limbo a name.

NO MAN'S LAND

Old Times probes the misty past; Pinter's *No Man's Land* (1974) hovers over less certain territory. Stamping stage image with metaphorical resonance, Pinter transforms a comfortable Hamstead room into a cell of inaction; the proprietor Hirst, a successful literary man, with his servant-protectors Briggs and Foster, enacts an "icy . . . silent" existence, resisting change. Into their world comes Spooner, a shabby poet seeking a liaison with Hirst, not because they share a specific past—though they may have—but because Spooner needs a sinecure in the present. Like the imposter Davies *(The Caretaker)*, Spooner requires shelter, and, like Davies, his comic posing and scheming launch the play's conflict. Like Davies, too, Spooner is rejected from Hirst's all-male household, but that rejection reaches beyond the imposter-exposure structure Pinter uses in earlier plays. Hirst's cell-home admits intrusion, conflict, even violence, but only temporarily. Action and words eventually exhaust themselves in the miasmal air of no man's land.

Acutely aware of the silence behind words, Pinter's four male characters are, to various degrees, verbally creative: Hirst is a famous poet-essayist, Spooner a master of terza rima, Foster a fledgling poet, and Briggs, a self-conscious raconteur, master of the colorful curse. Not surprisingly, this word-conscious cast is obsessed with literary tradition and production. As Spooner says: "All we have left is the English language. Can it be salvaged?" His name a reference to joking linguistic error, Spooner points to the salvaging operation Pinter performs in *No Man's Land*. Scoring the play's surface are the works of other word artists providing literary parody accessible to our ears. First-night critics heard and commented on echoes of Beckett and Eliot;[20] fragments of Emily Dickinson, Shakespeare, and Keats are also present. As with *Old Times*, Pinter lays bare the tools of creation, but in *No Man's Land* extratextual references are more personal, calling attention to Pinter's own historical moment in the production of literary and theatrical art. Evoking both comically and seriously Beckett's *Waiting for Godot* and *Endgame* and Eliot's *Four Quartets* and "The Love Song of J. Alfred Prufrock," Pinter acknowledges both the influence of two major modernist writers and his own sense of belatedness. In this writer-filled creation, the writing situation of Harold Pinter sounds an underlying theme.[21]

Waiting for Godot provides the central image of the Spooner-Hirst relationship. Beckett's Vladimir ponders the story of the two thieves, one saved, one damned; Pinter presents two men in their sixties, both educated at Oxford, both poets, yet one has succeeded while the other failed. Spooner ponders his fate:

I was one of the golden of my generation. Something happened. I don't know what it was.[22]

(p. 147)

Insisting on their underlying similarity, Spooner tells Hirst: "If I were wearing a suit such as your own you would see me in a different light" (p. 88), namely the rosy light of success. However, Hirst's success is tempered by his dependence on servants and painkillers, recalling Hamm's situation in *Endgame.* Both Hirst and Hamm sit in chairs facing front, both sleep and wake erratically, and both are concerned with ending: Hamm desires an end to life in the shelter; Hirst observes: "Today I shall come to a conclusion" (p. 144). The world outside Hamm's shelter is "corpsed," the light "sunk."[23] With "daylight . . . falling, rapidly" (p. 144), Hirst corpses himself behind thick curtains, and life on the interior slows to a Beckettian near zero.

Pinter's grounding in and parody of naturalism earmark his style, yet in *No Man's Land* he approaches Beckett's method of comically annihilating the fourth wall, making his characters conscious of speech as dialogue, room as scene. Typical of Beckett's surface fracture, Hamm informs Clov, "I'm warming up for my last soliloguy" (p. 78), and Clov tries to leave the shelter with the line, "This is what we call making an exit" (p. 81). In response to Clov's question, "What is there to keep me here?" Hamm pointedly replies: "The dialogue" (p. 58). In *No Man's Land*, Spooner fractures the conversational surface with an ironic barb that plays like a comic aside:

HIRST: Tonight . . . my friend . . . you find me in the last lap of a
           race . . . I had long forgotten to run.
SPOONER: A metaphor. Things are looking up.

(p. 94)

Less comically, Pinter deepens Foster's menace by linking him with the light booth.

FOSTER: Listen. You know what it's like when you're in a room with
         the lights on and then suddenly the light goes out? I'll show
         you. It's like this.

(p. 115)

"Room" and theater are made one: Foster extinguishes the light, Pinter calls for "*blackout.*" Such self-reflexive theatrical tricks draw

attention to the playwright as player, a role Pinter developed in
"the parody plays" (see Chapter 2). In those earlier works, however, Pinter tended to expose his game plan at the end, in tensely
ambiguous tableaux. In *No Man's Land,* Pinter, veering toward
Beckett, scatters literary allusions throughout the work, especially
in the dialogue between Spooner and Hirst: the playwright hovers
behind his characters pointing out chinks in the fourth wall.

Eliotic echoes contribute to the play's comedy and recall Pinter's
long association with Eliot's work. As early as his Bristol drama
speech, Pinter quoted from Eliot's "East Coker":

Each play was, for me a "different kind of failure."
And that fact, I suppose, sent me on to write the next one.[24]

When, in that same speech, Pinter speaks of the echo after silence,
he may be paraphrasing another line from *Four Quartets:* "Words,
after speech, reach / Into the silence."[25] Poet, essayist, and critic
like Hirst, Eliot may have inspired Hirst's line: "In my day nobody
changed. A man was. Only religion could alter him, and that at
least was a glorious misery" (p. 136). Eliot's Anglicanism created
glorious misery for himself, for his Harry *(The Family Reunion),*
and for Celia *(The Cocktail Party).* However, in the mouth of
Spooner, Pinter's poet râté and parasite, Eliot's texts are invoked
and exceeded with hyperbolic flourish. Identifying Hirst as "kindness itself, now and in England and in Hampstead and for all
eternity" (p. 79), Spooner equates the shrine at Little Gidding with
Hirst's sumptuous drawing room, his alcoholic toast with holy ceremony on consecrated grounds. Parodically sacrilegious, the line
nevertheless reveals the imposter's desperation to take part in the
feast he little deserves. For Spooner, shelter *would* be holy comfort, and Hirst may prove a ministering angel. Spooner lifts his
glass as he later bends his knee, in homage.

Echoes from "Prufrock" occur four times in Spooner's speech,
paraphrasing the opening lines ("[For] I have known them all already—known them all"[26]). Prufrock uses the present perfect to
distance himself from experience, then falls into present tense
within the stanza, involuntarily experiencing what he claims only
to recall. Each stanza ends with a rationalization for inaction: "[So
how] should I presume?" Pinter's Spooner echoes not only Prufrock's lines but also his techniques. Four times while alone on
stage, Spooner comments on the action in the present perfect,
then utters lines that speak to his immediate experience:

I have known this before. The exit through the door, by way of belly and floor.

(p. 96)

I have known this before. Morning. A locked door. A house of silence and strangers.

(p. 117)

I have known this before. The door unlocked. The entrance of a stranger. The offer of alms. The shark in the harbour.

(p. 118)

I have known this before. The voice unheard. A listener. The command from an upper floor.

(p. 126)

We laugh at these brief soliloquies not only because we recognize a famous modernist text but because of the interplay between two texts: Prufrock's quasi-comic alienation dramatized by Spooner whose drawing-room predicament in turn illuminates Prufrock's projection into that troubling social sphere of tea and ices, emotional crisis. And in this explicitly literary-textual moment, Spooner spontaneously produces his own text (Pinter underlining formal verbal performance more overtly here than in previous plays). Spooner's best literary performance—the third of the four listed above—generates a metaphor for the menacing Briggs: "the shark in the harbor," a Prufrockian and Pinterian demonstration of how language mediates in a terrifying situation.

Borrowing Prufrock's lines, Spooner also borrows his mock-heroics and ironic self-mockery, thus combining the *alazon's* boasting and the *eiron's* self-deprecating shrewdness. Unable to pose his "overwhelming question," Prufrock stalls for "a hundred visions and revisions," for time "to prepare a face to meet the faces that you meet." He admits that he is not a hero, a Prince Hamlet, but "an attendant Lord, one that will do"

> To swell a progress, start a scene or two,
> Advise the prince; no doubt, an easy tool,
> Deferential, glad to be of use,
> Politic, cautious, and meticulous;
> Full of high sentence, but a bit obtuse;
> At times, indeed, almost ridiculous—
> Almost, at times, the Fool.

(ll. 113–19)

Like Prufrock, Spooner dons an ironic mask to hide his terrors, but Spooner's self-mockery tilts toward aggression:

> . . . I shan't stay long. I never stay long, with others. They do not wish it. And that, for me, is a happy state of affairs. My only security, you see, my true comfort and solace, rests in the confirmation that I elicit from people of all kinds a common and constant level of indifference.
>
> (p. 79)

To these Wildean self-criticisms, Hirst finds no answer. By extravagantly protesting his weakness, Spooner soon dominates the conversation and, temporarily, the relationship. Similarly, in his long speech near the end of the play, Spooner offers his services with his version of Prufrockian modesty, a mixture of boasting and self-deprecation. Spooner's "good with tradespeople, hawkers, canvassers, nuns" (p. 146) recalls Prufrock's "politic" and "cautious." Spooner promises an "immaculate kitchen"; Prufrock, too, is "meticulous." Prufrock would attend Prince Hamlet; Spooner would attend Hirst, who—via Beckett's Hamm—may be associated with Hamlet. Spooner, like Prufrock, "swells a progress" with comically inflated rhetoric: "My sword shall be ready to dissever all manifest embodiments of malign forces that conspire to your ruin" (p. 147). Yet, as with Prufrock, Spooner's irony masks a need for acceptance.

The verbal parodies in *No Man's Land* echo Pinter's "parody plays" and Spooner's feints and failures recall his early posers. But *No Man's Land* goes further. Verbal gamesmanship carries the extra resonance of Pinter's favorite game, cricket. The four characters are named after cricketers (popular during Eliot's lifetime, dead heroes for the young Pinter); Spooner is the sole batsman among three bowlers. Like a cricket match, the play takes place in summer, and the leisurely pace and subtle verbal maneuvering in Pinter's play may be compared to cricket play. Hirst himself uses cricket as a means of dating his memories,

> Our last encounter—I remember it well. Pavilion at Lord's in '39, against the West Indies, Hutton and Compton batting superbly, Constantine bowling, war looming,
>
> (p. 127)

and Pinter celebrates his own sports enthusiasm with self-parody. These same cricketers appear in Pinter's tightly wrought prose eulogy titled resonantly, "Hutton and the Past."[27]

Pinter's nods to his own work, as well as to the work of Beckett,

Eliot, and others, feed the comedy of *No Man's Land.* In the opening moments of *No Man's Land,* references to Pinter's past themes and characters fall from Spooner's lips like items on a laundry list. Spooner's first topic of conversation is a critique of those who pretend strength but who possess "not strength but expertise" (p. 78). This description suits many Pinter posers (Goldberg, Edward, Lenny, the Man in *Monologue,* and Deeley) whose verbal facades wear thin despite their considerable defensive expertise. Of course, Spooner's rhetoric testifies to his own comic posing. If "the essential flabbiness" of earlier Pinter imposters was the key to their comedy, Spooner's vaunted ability to pierce that flabbiness is the key to his. Feeling "at peace" in Hirst's room, "safe from all danger" (p. 79), Spooner parodies the menace motif in Pinter's early "room" plays. As he calls attention to Hirst's reticence, "which appeals," he echoes the Pinter dictum of the strength in silence. On the other hand, Hirst's monosyllables heighten comic interaction by encouraging Spooner to fill the gaps with "gabble."

SPOONER: I often hang about Hampstead Heath myself, expecting nothing. I'm too old for any kind of expectation. Don't you agree?
HIRST: Yes.

(p. 80)

In this exchange, bowler Hirst almost outmaneuvers batter Spooner, but the latter replies without hesitation: "A pitfall and a snare, if there ever was one." This is relaxed play; neither wishes to force a crisis. Spooner's speeches about sex and sociality parody other Pinter themes:

> . . . when you can't keep the proper distance between yourself and others, when you can no longer maintain an objective relation to matter, the game's not worth the candle.

(p. 81)

Indeed, the game is lost by those earlier Pinter people who lose objectivity. For Edward (*A Slight Ache*) the "airs between me and my object" destroy equilibrium; for Davies (*The Caretaker*) the inability to distinguish kindness from irony destroys hopes for shelter.

As entertaining as Pinter's self-parody is the rhetorical slippage in Spooner's discourse, from overwrought rhetoric to colloquialism to nonsense without any indication of self-exposure.

. . . so forget it and remember that what is obligatory to keep in your vision is space, space in moonlight particularly, and lots of it.

(p. 81)

With this aggressive, impersonal illogicality, Spooner, like Goldberg *(The Birthday Party)*, succeeds in keeping his word-mask securely in place. Leaving matters of "experience" to "psychological interpreters, the wetdream world," Spooner insists on his poet's freedom to be "eternally present," echoing a younger Pinter who insisted that we attend not to verifying his characters' motives but to action in present time. However, Spooner also claims that "the present will not be distorted," a Pinterian untruth and blatantly contradicted by Spooner himself. Touting the present, he bounces into the past. Borrowing Deeley's tactic of recalling (and denigrating) Anna at The Wayfarer's Tavern, Spooner associates Hirst with an earlier acquaintance at Jack Straw's Castle. The comically incongruous metonymy with which he concludes his narrative—"his bald, tanned, unmoving table"—subtly dehumanizes both the acquaintance and, by implication, Hirst, although naturally this motive cannot be verified. Spooner debunks the entire experience by parodying the refrain of "will you still love me tomorrow?"

But will I wonder at you tomorrow, I wonder, as I still wonder at him today?

(p. 88)

Hirst replies: "I cannot say," and Spooner rejoins "It cannot be said"—or rather, in Pinter it can *only* be said, never verified, and Pinter's Spooner luxuriates in nonverifiable invention.

His next narrative invokes and falsifies his own past with an Edwardian daguerreotype-view of his country house ("windows open to the garden, my wife pouring long glasses of squash, with ice, on a summer evening"), complete with faded-rose diction ("what can ail? I mean who can gainsay us?" [p. 90]). Pinter's literary past is also invoked in this reminiscence. In 1969 he wrote the screenplay for *The Go-Between* based on G. B. Hartley's novel that features a narrator, a man in his sixties, who looks back on a summer in 1900 when he stayed with a wealthy family and carried messages between the daughter and her farmer lover.[28] The affair is discovered and the boy, forced to witness their love making, renounces sexual contact his entire adult life. (He may have inspired

Spooner's line about old men who die maiden.) Since by his class and youth, the narrator is a spectator, the novel is filled with snap-shotlike scenes of handsome young people in white gliding lei-surely across wide lawns, images of innocence that contrast with the lethal passion of the couple who ensnare the boy. The idea of falsity in elegant surroundings is echoed in the mixed imagery of Spooner's speech. Alluding to homosexuality and promiscuity, he admits that most of his young guests were not poets, though they presented a facade of innocence, singing ballads on the lawn on summer evenings. In the novel and screenplay, a cricket match crystalizes the theme of sexual hypocrisy, and Pinter parodies both works when Spooner pries for sexual secrets in cricket terminol-ogy—"Tell me . . . whether she was responsive to finger spin, whether you could bowl a shooter with her" [ellipses mine] (p. 92), a hilarious gambit of double entendre.

After their wives are mentioned, the comic volleying between Hirst and Spooner breaks down. Hirst throws his glass at his guest, and when Spooner proposes to supplant a dead marriage with friendship, Hirst utters a global "No"—no to the offer of compan-ionship, no to painful reminiscence, no, presumably, to game play-ing. His next lines encapsulate the play's title in halting ellipses, a poignant contrast to Spooner's bombast:

No man's land . . . does not move . . . or change . . . or grow old . . . remains . . . forever . . . icy . . . silent."

(p. 96)

Then he falls twice and, to the comic relief of the audiences view-ing the Richardson-Gielgud performance, crawls out on his hands and knees. The seriousness of Hirst's lines is undermined by Spooner's demonstration of poetic skill (the mocking doggerel: "You've lost your wife of hazel hue, you've lost her and what can you do" [p. 96]) and by pastiche Eliot. Despite its noncomic conno-tation, then, no man's land is here associated with comic gesture (falling and crawling) and verbal parody.

Comic gesture fraught with self-parody introduces the following scene between Spooner, Foster, and Briggs. Left alone on stage, Spooner "*looks at the room, walks about it, looking at each object closely*" as though he were a new proprietor or a practiced thief. When the door slams Spooner "*stiffens*," and Pinter presents us with archetypal Pinter menace: "A door can open at any moment and someone will come in."[29] Pinter emphasizes the belatedness of

the moment by giving us the length of a *"silence"* to compare the
Foster-Spooner *look* with that of Gus and Ben, Lenny and Teddy,
Mick and Davies. With self-parody, Pinter confronts and comically
revives the "stale dead terminology" of his own practice.[30] For
example, the interrogation by Foster and Briggs effectively replays
the comedy-of-menace style of the early plays. Under a heap of
autobiographical details and subtly skewed oppositions, Foster's
opening speech conceals threatening questions: "How are you?"
(p. 97), the social iteration to a friend or acquaintance, becomes a
pointed "Who are you?"—an abrupt question to a stranger. Labeling Spooner "Mr. Friend," "a bloody friend of everyone" (p. 38),
Briggs and Foster mock Spooner's supposed friendship with Hirst
and challenge his legitimacy in the house.

With Spooner's response, self-parody ends. Pinter's most articulate imposter, Spooner fabricates a "fish story" that blocks the pattern of interrogation; that is, he distracts his interrogators with a
complicated scene, details of which are hypnotically connected
through alliteration and off-rhymes.

> He *caught* a fish. He *lifted* it high. The waiter cheered and *applauded,*
> the two men, the waiter and the fisherman, *laughed.* A little girl,
> *passing, laughed.* Two *lovers,* passing, *kissed.* The fish was *lofted,* on the
> *rod.* [emphasis mine]
>
> (p. 101)

Having transformed incident into painter's image, Spooner suddenly poses his own question: "If you had seen the picture, and the
title, would the title have baffled you?" (p. 101). Parodies of quiz-
show contestants, Briggs and Foster turn to each other, baffled.
When Foster narrates his own story about a "complete stranger" (p.
42), Spooner cleverly refuses to see the inference. Foster's comment, "Double Dutch" (p. 105), testifies not only to the sleight-of-
hand in his own story but to Spooner's verbal trickery in his Am-
sterdam tale.

Hirst's reentry and apparent amnesia distract us from comic
combat. Yet the tension between Hirst's reverie of the past and
Spooner's attempt to regain recognition in the present hovers on
the brink of comedy. Hirst's nightmare of someone drowning in the
lake melds with the "changing light" of his photographs.

> What was it? Shadows. Brightness, through leaves . . .
> Who was drowning in my dream? [ellipses mine]
>
> (p. 108)

The images of drowning become felt sensations.

There's a flood running through me. I can't plug it.

(p. 108)

Attempting to plug the flood, Spooner interjects, "It was I drowning in your dream" and attaches himself to Hirst's history ("We both have fathered. We are of an age" [p. 109]). After Foster's comic tirade, in which he tries to oust Spooner from their world of "organdie" and "organization," Briggs adds the threat of physical violence. But Spooner is rewarded with recognition. Hauled from the room, Hirst manages to utter: "I know that man" (p. 114).

In act 2 Spooner's predicament grows desperate; his verbal forays are challenged and finally bested by the word maneuvers of Hirst, Foster, and Briggs. In this act, comic solos and duets expand the verbal spectrum while space shrinks. Hirst's no man's land forbids intimacy, friendship, or invasion of any emotion except that which "quickens," metaphorically, the still lives of his photograph album. The act ends by exploring metaphysics through metaphor, but it begins with an image of acute human distress. We see Spooner locked in Hirst's room (there is no sofa), shivering in the morning light. However, he has "known this before" (p. 60). When Briggs offers him the financial adviser's breakfast, Spooner, with comic disdain, refuses, then, equally disdainfully, accepts ("I abhor waste" [p. 118]). A breakfast of scrambled eggs and champagne is Spooner's regard for enduring the night; Briggs provides his entertainment.

Critics have been unimpressed with Briggs's long account of meeting Foster and his labyrinthine directions to Bolsover Street. Unlike Lenny's long speeches or Deeley's rambling autobiographical anecdotes, Briggs' speech seems to serve no dramatic purpose, nor does it conform to Pinter's usual geographical accuracy (Harold Hobson found Bolsover Street distinctly uncomplicated).[31] Yet Briggs's account is both comic and illuminating, consistent with Pinter's method in act 1. Parodying unverifiable narrators of past works (Lenny, Mick, Edward, Deeley), Briggs opens and closes his speech with the same disclaimers: "I should tell you he'll deny this account. His story will be different" (pp. 120–21). In other words, Briggs twice informs us that his monologue will reveal nothing true about himself, Foster, or, for that matter, the street. Pinter also uses the speech for internal parody. Bolsover Street (pronounced "balls over"),[32] inhabited by despairing, lost people with grey faces, becomes Briggs's image for purgatory and sterility. Sending his story to the *Times*, Briggs chooses a title that subtitles (and parodies) Pinter's *No Man's Land:* "Life at a Dead End" (p. 120).

Heightening the set-piece quality of the narrative, the speech bubbles up and dies with no apparent effect on Spooner. The latter puts food in his mouth while Briggs runs off at the mouth. Before and after his speech, Briggs plays the servant, pouring champagne. When Spooner makes a ludicrous escape attempt, trying to distract his captor by claiming a prior commitment to his poetry board, Briggs cleverly counters by producing two in-house poets, Foster and Hirst, and amour propre entangles Spooner into a recital of the mechanics of poetry submission. We sense his panic. After the telephone call, Spooner pointedly alludes to "Prufrock" and early Pinter.

> I have known this before. The voice unheard. A listener. The command from an upper floor.
>
> (p. 126)

Like Gus, the comic victim of *The Dumb Waiter*, Spooner senses a trap laid by unseen forces above.

Regardless of what he has known before, it is doubtful that even Spooner is prepared for Hirst's hearty booming entrance, Pinter's parody of old school-tie reminiscence. Pouring out coffee, Hirst confides that he seduced Spooner's wife over tea and crumpets (not to mention buttered scones, Wiltshire cream, and strawberries) but this was "once upon a time"—that is, a fiction. Apparently fictionalizing has rules. If Hirst claims that his adultery took place during teatime (as in *The Lover*), Spooner cannot disagree. Instead, he challenges Hirst to a remembrance that surpasses even *Old Times* in mocking the "impossibility of verification" theme. Topping Hirst's boasts of sexual prowess, Spooner endows his upper-class Oxfordian friends with outré sexual behavior, ranging from pederasty to incest. However, Hirst like Spooner recoils from criticism of his writing and retaliates by retreating to no man's land. Calling for whiskey from Briggs (whom he calls Denson), denouncing Spooner (whom he calls Charles Wetherby), Hirst resumes his chair and takes up his photograph album, signaling an end to combat and the beginning of the "last lap" of the play.

John Bush Jones argues that *No Man's Land* is structured by stasis;[33] certainly stasis characterizes Hirst's relationship to the past. Unlike Anna and Deeley, who boldly invent new texts for past events, Hirst clings to the stillness of photographs. The faces, jaws, backs of necks, "in their glass jars" (p. 137), possessing "all that emotion" resemble Keats's frozen figures on the Grecian urn. In Keats's ode, love is "For ever warm and still to be enjoyed, / For ever panting, and for ever young." Honoring his shrine of "true friends," Hirst sits "forever" in no man's land. Hirst's imperative, "Bow to it" (p. 137), echoes the authority of Keats's sylvan historian. Growing incantatory, Hirst blends biblical diction ("And so I say to you") with the Shakespearean repetition of "tender" in Polonius's advice to Ophelia (*Hamlet*, 1.3)—though Pinter's pun embraces yet another meaning: be tender of.

Hirst retains this elegiac distance while Spooner tries again to outmaneuver Hirst's keepers. When Briggs refuses to serve Hirst, Spooner leaps to do so. When Hirst insists on writing an essay instead of walking with Foster, Spooner offers to organize his files. Briggs labels Hirst's photographs "the blank dead" (p. 137), and Foster calls them "nameless" (p. 142), but Spooner promises to "put names to faces. A proper exhumation could take place" (pp. 141–42). When Hirst ventures: "Today I shall come to a conclusion," Spooner leaps before the younger men with "I'll help you" (p. 144).

This threat to the power hierarchy in the household produces shock waves, a comic concatenation of rhetorical postures. Foster bursts into a solo performance that rehearses his history with Hirst. Though he was probably procured by Briggs, Foster insists that his "work" gives him "dignity . . . service to a cause" and girds the connection with inane repetitions:

> I'm in touch with a very special intelligence. This intelligence I find nourishing. I have been nourished by it.
>
> (p. 147)

Briggs smashes through this pained discourse with a comical litany of obscenities directed at Spooner. But Spooner, parodying Marlowe's passionate shepherd, proposes: "Let me live with you and be your secretary" (p. 146). Taking his cue from Foster's "service to a cause," Spooner launches into a long aria that transforms Hirst into a feudal lord for whom he declares himself not only a fit secretary and companion, but also a chevalier ready to "accept death's challenge" (p. 147). Spooner, as he hinted in act 1, is "call[ing] up the calvary, throw[ing] everything forward out of the knowledge that when joy overfloweth there can be no holding of joy" (pp. 82–83). At this point, the maneuver works not to assert Spooner's freedom but his subservience. Yet as the list of offers grows in detail, as rhetoric becomes more florid, more impenetrable, Spooner's proffered subservience changes to palpable dominance. The others listen in stunned silence.

On the stage of *No Man's Land*, literary allusions culminate in a speech that describes the staging of a literary event: a poetry reading for Hirst. Spooner's salesmanship is characteristically excessive; as he enlarged a secretarial position to heroic proportions, he places Hirst's reading in "that rarest of categories: the unique" (p. 148). Spooner even plans a press photography session, envisioning perhaps new additions to Hirst's album. Unlike Kate's uncontradicted version of the past at the end of *Old Times*, Spooner's last speech proposes a scenario for the future and simultaneously tries to verify his connection to a poetry club. Hirst responds not once but twice. Before Spooner begins he asks, "Is there a big fly buzzing?" recalling Emily Dickinson's poem, "I heard a fly buzz when I died," in which a fly distracts from death's last unctions and becomes the ear-buzzing of the death throes. Like the poem's narrator, Hirst revolts against a disturbance to his serenity, but the abruptness of his question shocks us into laughter. After Spooner's long speech, Hirst again refuses. He carefully mimics Spooner's diction ("Let us content ourselves"), by proposing: "Let us change the subject . . . For the last time" (p. 149). Rejecting Spooner's scenario for professional collaboration, Hirst rejects Spooner himself. This time there is no laughter.

The final moments of *No Man's Land* move through rejection to stillness. Foster and Briggs attempt to bind Hirst to the subject of never changing the subject, but in fact Hirst does change the subject, twice. First, he acknowledges the irretrievability of the past by his inability to connect the birds he hears in the present to those he recalls in the past. Second, he removes Spooner entirely from his thoughts. As Kate denies Anna's influence by erasing her from her story, Hirst denies Spooner as the drowning man in his dream. Hirst seems grateful to Foster and Briggs for the "family life" they share because it provides him permanent citizenship in no man's land. Near the end of act 1, a short speech obscurely forecasts the final moments of the play:

> HIRST: What would I do without the two of you? I'd sit here forever, waiting for a stranger to fill up my glass. What would I do while I waited? Look through my album? Make plans for the future?
>
> (p. 107)

Spooner becomes the stranger who fills Hirst's glass, discusses his photograph album, and makes plans for the future. Spooner's error is in thinking that his suggestions will change the status quo in the household and the composition of Hirst's photograph album. Spooner would exhume the past, but Hirst wants to silence his "long ghosts" (p. 109). He quickens youthful memories only when he feels able to "Allow the love of the good ghost" (p. 137). Intolerant of these painful reminiscences, Hirst drinks, and intolerant of change, he dismisses Spooner. When Spooner reiterates Hirst's definition of no man's land, he formalizes phrases into a sentence-long epitaph. Hirst's conventional "I'll drink to that" resonates. Drink carries him to that oblivion and to release from memory and pain.

The slow fade of light on the last tableau complements the slow fade of language in the final moments of the play. In this talky work, it is appropriate that words themselves become the subject of discussion, focusing attention the power of language to build and destroy human relationships. When Hirst changes the subject "for the last time," Spooner's poetry reading becomes the "previous subject," which (Foster hastens to point out) is now "forgotten," "closed." In charge once again, Foster and Briggs present a united front, completing each other's sentences in singsong partnership:

BRIGGS: The trees—
FOSTER: Will never bud.
BRIGGS: Snow—
FOSTER: Will fall forever.

(p. 151)

Yet Hirst's repetitive line, "But what does that *mean*?" (p. 92), with its repeated stress, points to the volatility of definitions and labels. Although Spooner may be a "previous subject," he remains on stage in an ambiguous tableau, rejected but not expelled.

The ambiguity of the tableau is reinforced by verbal imagery connected to no man's land. Hirst's first monologue, uttered in fragmented language, evokes a twilight world between dreams and waking, darkness and dawn. Like Beth in *Landscape*, Hirst recalls intense experience in terms of light and shadow: "Shadows. Brightness . . . blinding shadows" (pp. 46–47). For both Beth and Hirst, visual obscurity becomes a metaphor for emotional confusion; the changing light on Hirst's photographs suggests not only the mistiness of the past but the changing perspectives of his own point of view. For both characters, painful experience triggers metaphor.

BETH: He felt my shadow. He looked up at me standing above him.

(p. 178)

HIRST: When I stood my shadow fell upon her. She looked up. Give me the bottle. Give me the bottle.
She looked up. I was staggered. I had never seen anything so beautiful. That's all poison. We can't be expected to live like that.

(p. 108)

Beth invokes the light-shadow memory for solace; Hirst prefers his shadowy memories stilled in photographs.

Verbal repetition, Pinter's characteristic rhetorical device, abets ambiguity, usually in comic contexts. The past relationship of Hirst and Spooner is always questionable, but Pinter mocks any motive hunting by dropping "clues" during their improbable memory contest at the beginning of act 2. Both Spooner and Hirst refer to Spooner's wife as Emily, and when Hirst gives a surname to Arabella, Spooner agrees to it. However, other repetitions cast doubt on a past connection. Exchanging each other's terms of affection ("very fond," "extremely fond," "frightfully fond") and terms of moral indignation ("scandalously," "unnaturally"), Hirst and Spooner emphasize game playing over sincerity, theatricality over communication.[34] Spooner plays the wronged husband, Hirst the wrongly accused rake; their roles are conventional and neither deviates. Pinter resolves this duet by extraneous means: Hirst calls for a drink and fades into reverie.

Yet if their mutual fictionalizing casts doubt on a past connection, Pinter plants other repetitions, suggesting a tandem or alter ego relationship. Opening the play Hirst pours drinks:

HIRST: As it is?
SPOONER: As it is, yes please, absolutely as it is.

(p. 77)

Later in the same scene, Spooner pours and the duet is replayed, parts reversed:

SPOONER: You'll take it as it is, as it comes?
HIRST: Oh, absolutely as it comes.

(p. 84)

Hirst teaches Spooner the lines describing no man's land, Spooner repeats them as recognition of his rejection, and Hirst salutes him. Spooner quotes and behaves like Prufrock, but Hirst also quotes Eliot's poem to praise his corpsed existence:

It's good to go to sleep in the late afternoon. After tea and toast.
(pp. 105–6)

Prufrock worries about the time for visions and revisions before toast and tea, but Hirst is beyond turmoil, "tucked up," isolated.

Repetition mocks serious themes. Spooner early identifies himself as a poet, drawing attention to verbal creativity. He chastises Hirst for not recognizing "truly accurate and therefore essentially poetic definition." When Briggs announces that Hirst, too, is a poet, Spooner is challenged; as Foster, too, is added to the ranks, he is frankly mocked. Similarly, repetition trivializes Hirst's dream imagery. His financial adviser also dreams—of eggs—and Spooner ludicrously previews Hirst's water dream with a reference to the "wetdream world." Echoes within an exchange—what Ruby Cohn calls "echo doublets"[35]—push mockery toward menace. Like Lenny, Foster discredits his antagonist by preempting details from his autobiography. However, Lenny merely supplants Ruth's Venice story with one of his own, while Foster spits Spooner's words back at him.

SPOONER: The landlord's a friend of mine. When he's shorthanded, I give him a helping hand.
(p. 99)

FOSTER: I know The Bull's Head. The landlord's a friend of mine. . . . I've known the landlord for years. [ellipses mine]
(p. 99)

Steady repetition, what Cohn aptly calls "pounders," attacks more aggressively.[36] Foster pounds the word "friend" and repeats his "old English name" eight times, mocking the English heritage Spooner claims to share with Hirst while at the same time indicating that Spooner has not identified himself.

A subtler comic pattern of repetition reinforces the sterility of no man's land. In this womanless household, repeated references to the masculine activities of cricket and war comically displace sexual desire. Spooner rehearses Von Kleist's retreat from the Caucasus with double-entendre references to witty withdrawal and overflow-

ing joy,[37] and, as noted previously, he twists cricket jargon to make
obscenely funny suggestions about Hirst's conjugal life. Hirst combines cricket and war in off-rhymes ("Constantine bowling, war
looming") as a prelude to sexual confession, and seconds later,
recounts his successful seduction of Emily Spooner. (He further
humiliates Spooner by topping the latter's navy service with his
own service in military intelligence, a branch requiring prestigious
connections.)[38]

Homosexuality creates tension in *Old Times;* in *No Man's Land,*
homosexual allusions, obscene and usually comic, abound.
Spooner salutes Hirst's impotence and admits that many of his own
young male guests were not poets. Briggs calls Foster a "poof," a
"ponce," a "vagabond cock"—all slang terms for homosexual—and
when he implies that he procured Foster for Hirst ("You came on
my recommendation" [p. 87]), Foster acknowledges that he finds
the work "fruitful." In act 1, Foster denies being a "cunt," meaning
fool, but in act 2, Briggs uses the label to mean both fool and
homosexual, making a near-explicit statement about the nature of
the family bond.

> FOSTER: Don't call me a cunt.
> HIRST: We three, never forget, are the oldest of friends.
> BRIGGS: That's why I called him a cunt.
> FOSTER (*to* BRIGGS): Stop talking.
>
> (p. 143)

Less brutally, Spooner remembers his "good companion" Hugo
(p. 63), and homosexual services may underlie his offer to be
Hirst's secretary: "I am a good companion" (p. 89).

Repeatedly, Pinter's males mock both women and marriage. The
typical Pinter females—grostesque mothers, adulterous wives, and
whores—appear respectively as Spooner's malevolent mother; his
adulterous wife; and Foster's Siamese whores (the promiscuous
Arabella Hinscott seems to fit the latter two categories). Perhaps
more degrading are the idealized portraits of women in Hirst's
photograph album:

> You'll be struck by the charm of the girls, their grace, the ease with
> which they sit, pour tea, loll.
>
> (p. 44)

Alive, however, women "poison" him; he feels strangled by a
woman's "muff" (slang for female genitals)[39] and remembers his

pastoral village garlanded not for matrimony but for those who "died maiden" (p. 92). When Spooner refers to the poetry reading with the feminine "her" (p. 149), equating an evening of intimate readings with female experience, Hirst emphatically refuses to "take part."

The repetitious commingling of obscenity, gaming, and sexual allusion, literary parody, and dream fragment contribute to the rich verbal music of *No Man's Land* and to the sudden tonal shifts of Pinter's comedy. Despite the overtones of ultimate silence, *No Man's Land* surpasses even *Old Times* as a celebration of the word, a comedy of language. Unlike the silent and ritualistic annihilation of Deeley in *Old Times,* Spooner's rejection is played off against Hirst's cynical drunken toast. Throughout the play, poets collide with bodyguards, poetry with profanity—collisions that stir the noncreative air, diffusing the gloom of no man's land.

In an interview in 1971, Harold Pinter, sounding like a younger Hirst, commented on creativity, sameness, and change:

> You're stuck as a writer. I'm stuck in my own tracks, whatever they are—for so long. Forever.[40]

Repetition is obstrusive in *No Man's Land,* because repetition is the writer's no man's land, his sense of being stuck. Pinter's "long ghosts"—his posers, raconteurs, shelter seekers, and hypocrites—along with the ghosts of other famous poets and playwrights, pass through Hirst's cell-room, chilling the atmosphere. Yet their collective echoes are absorbed into the comic texture of the play. Parody, including self-parody, declares war on the past, fighting repetition by making repetition comic. Though Pinter's long ghosts hover behind Spooner, Hirst, Foster, and Briggs, none of these four seems ready for icy silence. Comedy quickens, recharges their words, sparking life in *No Man's Land.*

BETRAYAL

Whereas *Old Times* and *No Man's Land* revive themes and characters of the Pinter canon, *Betrayal* (1978) seems to abandon them. Absent is the power struggle for territory or shelter. Gone are the menacing Goldbergs and Annas, the barely articulate Ruths and Berts, the crushingly verbal Lennys and Spooners. Like *Old Times* and *No Man's Land, Betrayal* explores the misty past, but its characters do not compose their comically unverifiable past histories; instead, they relive them. Pinter marches us back in time, verifying the betrayals of Robert, a book publisher, Emma his wife, and Jerry, Robert's best friend who sleeps with Emma for seven years. Nine scenes cover nine years (from 1977 to 1968); each scene is labeled by season and year, each scene change punctuated by one turn of a revolving set. Despite its innovation and its thin comedy, *Betrayal* retains elements of the self-parody of *Old Times* and *No Man's Land.* In muted colors, it echoes the loss and rejection of the "poser-loser" plays and the witty gamesmanship of the "parody plays." As we watch Jerry and Emma grow younger and happier, we make comparisons with our first view of them in a bar, older, communicating with difficulty. Yet the comic focus on sex and money, marriage and adultery, links *Betrayal* with *The Lover* and the comedy of manners tradition.

In *Old Times* and *No Man's Land,* Pinter uses and betrays his use of literary material. Echoes of Beckett, Eliot, and Sartre, of the flashback from film (the Anna-Kate scenes in *Old Times*), and the cricket metaphor (names and action in *No Man's Land*) all reflect Pinter's personal and theatrical activities. *Betrayal* shows comparable influences. In 1972–73, after *Old Times* and before *No Man's Land,* Pinter wrote the screenplay for Joseph Losey's production of *A la Recherche du Temps Perdu,* a work which was never realized. Rendering the rich fabric of Proust's work, Pinter offers "momentary images . . . concise visual segments."[41] Similarly, in *Betrayal,* Pinter distills the complex tapestry of three characters' lives into discrete, economical segments. In the Proust screenplay, Pinter overlays the major themes of the indestructability of art and the disillusionment of experience. In his stage play, the theme of betrayal is also multitextured. Emma and Jerry betray Robert, but Robert betrays Jerry in concealing that he knows about the affair, and Emma betrays Jerry by concealing Robert's knowledge. The screenplay moves backward and forward in time, recreating Proustian memory. *Betrayal* is also ordered nonchronologically. The first two scenes take place in 1977 and follow sequentially. Then the play jogs back in time, passing through the end of Jerry and Emma's affair in 1975, through their happy days in 1971, ending on a scene in 1968, at the beginning of their affair, when a drunk Jerry makes his first declaration of love to Emma in Robert and Emma's bedroom. The middle three scenes follow chronologically, in order to clarify the crucial betrayals. In his introduction to the published screenplay, Pinter notes Proust's "remarkable conception":

> When Marcel, in "Le Temps Retrouvé," says that he is now able to start his work, he has already written it. We have just read it.[42]

When we come to the end of *Betrayal,* we are at the beginning of the affair that launches the betrayals we have just witnessed. Like Proust's Marcel (and his readers), we are the ones who put together the story.

Two of Pinter's directing projects, Joyce's *Exiles* (1970), and Simon Gray's *Otherwise Engaged* (1975), may have influenced the themes and action of *Betrayal.* Pinter's association with Gray dates back at least to *Butley,* which Pinter directed for the theater (1970) and for film (1974). Gray dedicates *Otherwise Engaged* to Pinter and Pinter dedicates *Betrayal* to Gray. Both *Otherwise Engaged* and *Betrayal* concern marriage and betrayal among contemporary London literati. Like Pinter's Robert Downs, Gray's Simon Hench is a bored book publisher who plays squash. Robert's oldest friend Jerry sells books and Simon's old friend Jeff criticizes them. Both Robert and Simon betray their wives and their wives betray them, creating paternity problems. Most significantly, in Gray and Pinter's plays, male friendship weathers the strain of betrayal and female interference. Despite Davina's malicious lies, Simon and Jeff are reconciled, sharing a final pristine moment listening to Wagner's *Parsifal.* Despite mutual betrayals, Robert and Jerry reaffirm their friendship and common tastes, each cherishing Yeats. Moreover, Pinter echoes Gray in the treatment of betrayals. Simon knows about his wife's infidelity but does not mention it, preferring to accept her efforts to please him as subtle revenge. Similarly, Robert takes revenge on Jerry by refusing to reveal his knowledge of the affair. The quasi-incestuous interlocking adulteries in *Betrayal* may have occurred to Pinter in response to Simon Hench's self-imposed restrictions:

> I make a point, you see, of not sleeping with friends, or the wives of friends, or acquaintances even. No one in our circle. Relationships can be awkward enough—[43]

Such awkwardness nurtures the conflict and the comedy of *Betrayal.*

Joyce's *Exiles* explores the philosophical dimension of marital betrayal, but, as in the Gray and Pinter works, the moment of revelation—which the cuckold manipulates—is spotlighted theatrically. *Exiles* also concerns literary men: Richard Rowan, a writer, and his wife Bertha return to Ireland after nine years of exile and renew contact with Richard's oldest friend Robert, a journalist. Robert, we learn, is trying to seduce Bertha; he arrives with "overblown" roses, kisses her, and arranges a secret assignation. Richard enters, Robert leaves soon after, and immediately Bertha gives Richard minute details of Robert's growing attachment, informing him of what we have just witnessed. For Joyce, the Richard-Robert relationship (like Pinter's Robert-Jerry relationship) overshadows the wife's adultery. Richard sympathizes with Robert's passion and passionately tells him so:

RICHARD: I told you that when I saw your eyes this afternoon I felt sad. Your humility and confusion, I felt, united you to me in brotherhood. (*He turns half round towards him.*) At that moment I felt our whole life together in the past, and I longed to put my arm around your neck.[44]

The hint of repressed homosexuality is raised explicitly in Joyce's endnotes to the play:

The bodily possession of Bertha by Robert, repeated often, would certainly bring into almost carnal contact the two men. Do they desire this? (p. 123)

Robert's sneering remarks to Emma after discovering her affair with Jerry, answer Joyce's query about male intimacy:

ROBERT: I've always liked Jerry. To be honest, I've always liked him rather more than I've liked you. Maybe I should have had an affair with him myself.[45]

(p. 225)

The exile of nine years that separates Robert and Richard in *Exiles* is echoed in the nine-year relationship of Jerry and Robert. In discussing the play, Pinter significantly neglects to mention Emma. "*Betrayal*," he says, "is about a nine-year relationship between two men who are best friends."[46]

Joyce's Richard and Pinter's Robert are not dissimilar, but Joyce's overweight Robert and Pinter's hypochondriacal Jerry share obvious traits. Each falls headlong in love with the wife of his best friend—falls in love, too, with romantic hyperbole.

ROBERT: Let me feel your lips touch mine.
BERTHA: And then you will be satisfied?

ROBERT (*murmurs*): Your lips, Bertha!
BERTHA *closes her eyes and kisses him quickly*):
There. (*Puts her hands on his shoulders.*)
Why don't you say: thanks?
ROBERT (*sighs*): My life is finished—over.
BERTHA: O, don't speak like that now, Robert.
ROBERT: Over, over. I want to end it and have done with it.
BERTHA (*concerned but lightly*): You silly fellow!
ROBERT (*presses her to him*): To end it all—death. To fall from a great
    high cliff, down, right down to the sea.

(p. 35)

JERRY: Look at the way you're looking at me. I can't wait for you, I'm
    bowled over, I'm totally knocked out, you dazzle me, you
    jewel, my jewel, I can't ever sleep again, no, listen, it's the
    truth, I won't walk, I'll be a cripple, I'll descend, I'll dimin-
    ish, into total paralysis, my life is in your hands, that's what
    you're banishing me to, a state of catatonia. . . .

(p. 266)

Death and catatonia—such romantic self-immolation provokes laughter in both plays. Bertha's commonsensical remarks, Emma's commonsensical silence mock their suitors' flourish while Joyce and Pinter expose the human silliness in these life-altering events.

    Betrayal is further linked to Pinter's earlier thematic concerns. In *The Collection, The Lover,* and *The Homecoming*, adultery is the major subject, and in nine other plays marital betrayal figures in the behavior of the characters. Burt's violence in *The Room*, for example, is triggered by the discovery of another man alone with his wife; in *A Slight Ache*, Edward, like Robert in *Betrayal*, finds himself in the farcical position of all cuckolded husbands—on the wrong side of the bedroom door. In spirit, *Betrayal* most closely resembles *The Lover* because of that play's relation to the comedy of manners tradition. However, *The Lover* presents a fantasy adultery; *Betrayal* exposes a real one. With its story unfolding in nine panels, *Betrayal* resembles a Hogarthian "Rake's Progress" in reverse, a mocking indictment of marriage à la mode. Yet the gamesmanship of manners comedy and of Pinter's "parody plays" is tempered in *Betrayal*. As Jerry's pose of strength (based on the illusion of a secret affair) evaporates, *Betrayal* illustrates the making of a loser.

    Posing and losing are themes sounded in scene 1 of *Betrayal*. Emma and Jerry circle around the subjects of health, jobs, children, avoiding intimacy with skillful conversational feints. Then Jerry clarifies the manners appropriate to their meeting: "You remember the form. I ask about your husband, you ask about my wife" (p. 161). Gradually they arrive at an incident that recurs in conversation throughout the play: Jerry, surrounded by both families, threw Emma's daughter into the air. Soon Jerry attempts an endearment, and Emma recounts a nostalgic return to the flat where they used to meet. Like the couple in *Night* (1969), Jerry and Emma try to piece together their past. But past comments on present. With his deft feel for the psychology of subtext, Pinter charts the precise moment when the focus shifts: recalling their affair recalls its end, and Jerry abruptly inquires about Emma's new liaison with Casey, a writer whom Jerry discovered and Robert publishes. Like a Restoration gallant, Jerry denies being jealous but shows real admiration for Robert's gamesmanship—his ability to disguise his infidelities from Jerry. Insisting that he and Emma were equally "brilliant" at deception, Jerry allies himself with earlier Pinter imposters, such as Edward *(A Slight Ache)* and Stanley *(The Birthday Party)*. The circumstances of his discovery are more mundane than those in earlier plays, but for Jerry they are no less menacing.

In scene 2, betrayals multiply, and the comic barometer mounts. As in *Old Times* and *No Man's Land*, the effort to determine who said what to whom when undermines sentimentality, and Jerry's melodramatic apology is all the more ludicrous because it comes four years late. Jerry wants Robert to—in Joyce's words—"use against [Jerry] the weapons which social conventions and morals put in the hands of a husband" (p. 113). However, jealous husbands are traditionally comic butts, and Robert, like Joyce's Richard, refuses that role. Instead, Robert's affection for Jerry, at a four-year remove, overrides the cuckold's wrath: "I hope she looked after you all right" (p. 187). If Robert mourns anything, it is that Jerry's love affair with Emma put an end to their squash game.

Mention of squash foregrounds the game-playing aspect of these good-natured mutual treacheries. In particular, Casey's affair illustrates the win-lose trade-off in adultery, offering a cruder version of the Robet-Emma-Jerry betrayals. Casey betrays Robert (and implicitly Jerry) by sleeping with Emma. Yet both Jerry and Robert "do very well out of Casey" as agent and publisher of his work. Sexual loss is balanced by financial gain; such is the way of the world. After their discussion of Casey, Jerry stops apologizing for his own betrayal.

The playwright's gamesmanship in scene 3 amplifies the metaphors already established. Carrying surface fracture further than in any previous play, Pinter alters the naturalistic sequence of events, presenting the end of Jerry and Emma's affair two years earlier. This scene is comic for the way in which Jerry and Emma confront each other by avoiding confrontation. Rather than hurl insults, Emma icily refuses cash for the furniture they bought. Instead of criticizing Emma, Jerry reiterates his affection for Robert.

> JERRY: . . . I might remind you that your husband is my oldest friend.
> EMMA: What do you mean by that?
> JERRY: I don't *mean* anything by it.
> EMMA: But what are you trying to say by saying that?
> JERRY: Jesus. I'm not *trying* to say anything. I've said precisely what I wanted to say.
> EMMA: I see.
> *Pause.*
>
> (pp. 194–95)

With his celebrated accurate "ear," Pinter satirizes the new language of the 1970s—a psychoanalytic version of witty repartee. Emma and Jerry dramatize the wisdom of Simon Hench's remark in *Otherwise Engaged:* "In my experience the worst thing you can do to an important problem is discuss it" (p. 52).

Pinter's scene shift leaves little time for discussion, but even those with short memories should recall that in 1974, the time of scene 4, Jerry is sleeping with Emma and Robert knows about it. Having oriented his audience to backward movement, Pinter packs this three-character confrontation (the only one in the play) with amusing and accessible dramatic ironies. On Robert's territory, Jerry drinks Robert's liquor; in a flat across London he makes him a cuckold. Knowing that Jerry considers himself "brilliant" in disguising his affair, we provide an ironic subtext for even the most harmless dialogue:

> JERRY: . . . how is your sleep these days?
> ROBERT: What?
> JERRY: Do you still have bad nights? With Ned, I mean?
> ROBERT: Oh, I see. Well, no. No, it's getting better.
>
> (p. 202)

Curbing his hostility, Robert joins Jerry in a clever parody of the medical professionals and their views about "boy babies" and "girl babies." Irrelevant questions in Pinter dialogue usually serve to intimidate (as in Lenny, Foster, and Anna's speeches). In this exchange Jerry parries a false assertion with questions of his own (mimicking Robert's "Why do you think that is?" [p. 204]) and provides an appropriately ludicrous explanation for the fact that boy babies cry more than girl babies: "Do you think it might have something to do with the difference between the sexes?" (p. 205).

Joking deflects their own anxieties. Unable to discuss their personal lives, they establish—as males—a pose of nonchalance, thus becoming teammates in a game that excludes Emma. Her suggestion that she watch a squash game is trounced by Robert's inspired verbal performance—a comic invective of repetitious assertions and lists.

> Well, to be brutally honest, we wouldn't actually want a woman around, would we, Jerry? I mean a game of squash isn't simply a game of squash, it's rather more than that. You see, first there's the game. And then there's the shower. And then there's the pint. And then there's lunch. After all, you've been at it. You've had your battle. What you want is your pint and your lunch. You really don't want a woman buying you lunch. You don't actually want a woman within a mile of the place, any of the places, really. You don't want her in the squash court, you don't want her in the shower, or the pub, or the restaurant. You see, at lunch you want to talk about squash, or cricket, or books, or even women, with your friend, and be able to warm to your theme without fear of improper interruption. That's what it's all about.
>
> (pp. 209–10)

A game of squash is more than a game of squash: it functions as a Restoration masquerade in which emotions can be vented in a publicly acceptable way; a way for men to do battle and to love without self-consciousness.[47] Were Emma to watch, the battle would become a competition, a distasteful image Pinter worked through in *The Basement* when Jane holds up her scarf to start Law and Stott on a race. Law, who is attracted to Jane, wants to run, while Scott, a younger version of Robert, refuses to participate. (Stott also notes that Law's squash playing has grown less "deceptive.") Robert may want to fight Jerry, but he also wants to share an intimacy—the game, the shower, the lunch, the talk. Emma's presence on the squash courts, Robert hints, would be as "improper" as his presence in her flat. Since Robert's two squash partners become Emma's lovers, it is not surprising that Robert feels hostile. Afternoons spent with *her* in the flat deny *him* pleasure on the courts.

The closing image of the scene recalls Joyce's endnotes on *Exiles*. Intimacy in sports satisfies Robert's desire for "carnal contact" (p. 123). Robert proposes a game of squash, and aroused by this gesture toward Jerry, he embraces Emma. Similarly, Richard and Sarah *(The Lover)* spice their sex life by inventing a lover, Max, and in *Otherwise Engaged* Simon suggests that his wife's love making has improved with guilt. Does Jerry provide the same sexual titillation for Robert and Emma? Leaving questions unanswered about his principals, Pinter allows us to be Cassandras about Casey. We learn that Casey has left his wife and moved to a room near Robert and Emma's house. Three years later, instead of battling Robert on the squash courts, Casey will cuckold him with Emma.

Scenes 5, 6, and 7 follow chronologically, exposing crucial betrayals. The Venice hotel scene between Robert and Emma echoes what is by now a pattern of indirection. Robert poses the topic of betrayal by discussing the novel Emma is reading; then he launches into a condemnation of the Venetian American Express. As Foster *(No Man's Land)* hammers the word "friend" into the shape of "stranger," Robert draws a more insidious equation between stranger and husband:

> I mean, just because my name is Downs and your name is Downs doesn't mean that we're the Mr. and Mrs. Downs that they, in their laughing Mediterranean way, assume we are. We could be, and in fact are vastly more likely to be, total strangers.
>
> (p. 218)

In *The Homecoming*, Ruth comments on the breakup of her marriage with the same comparison. Her line, "Eddie, don't become a stranger," implies that he has already become a stranger. Robert continues to torture Emma, reminding her that Venice and Torcello were scenes of their honeymoon; he in turn is tortured by learning that for half of his married life to date, he has been sharing Emma with Jerry. The juxtaposition of "love" and "lovers" adds to Robert's pain; Jerry will not send "love" to Robert while he is Emma's lover.

Emma suffers other agonies: knowing the affair has been discovered, she listens to Jerry's anxiety about the affair being discovered. The image that haunts Jerry—his throwing Robert's daughter in the air while both families watch—suggests both his sexual intimacy with Emma (her daughter resembles her) and his terror at its discovery. Significantly, at this point, he views the incident as a violation of Robert's trust; four years later (in scene 1) he views it as a *token* of Robert's trust.

Not surprisingly, Emma finds it easier to conceal than to reveal Robert's discovery. However, Robert's scene with Jerry, though we know the factual outcome, piques our interest. Typically, Pinter undercuts melodrama, defusing tension with comedy—in this case an Italian waiter. Twice Jerry asks about Venice; twice the waiter prevents a response by arriving to take their order and by answering the question himself. Yet there is a confrontation, indirect as usual. Unable to accuse Jerry of betraying him with Emma, Robert accuses them both of loving what he hates, "modern prose literature" (p. 250), and the commercial activity of producing it. In contrast, Robert describes the private, personal experience of reading Yeats on Torcello.

The contrast has implications for Pinter's own view of human experience. Early in his career, Pinter discussed the importance of the private being in relation to the world:

> We all, I think . . . have sexual relationships or go to political meetings or discuss ideas, but when we get back to our rooms and are faced with a bed and we are either alone or with someone else, then . . . I don't think we go on long about ideas . . I mean, there comes a point, surely, when this living in *the* world must be tied up with living in *your own* world.[48]

Almost twenty years later, Pinter is suggesting that our own world is harder to locate. Like the novelists Casey and Spinks, Robert, Emma and Jerry pass from private rooms to family homes to private rooms, their composite set a metaphor for London, as the enclosed Restoration stage was a metaphor for the closed society of the royal court. In the business of producing modern prose literature, Robert and Jerry, like Restoration courtiers, support artists whose fictions mirror and parody their lives. Emma, for example, reads Spinks's novel about betrayal while she betrays Robert with Jerry, the agent who sold Spinks's novel.

Robert's rebellion in the name of privacy is short-lived. Jerry reduces the value of the Torcello experience by reminding Robert that his angst is common in modern life—it is, in fact, likely to appear in works of modern prose literature. Symbolically rejoining their world, Robert praises Casey, Emma, and their family life together. Yet he exacts a price for acquiescence, for in Pinter's world view, victims are also victimizers. Robert betrays even as he is betrayed, punishing Emma's adultery with his own well-concealed infidelities, repaying Jerry's secrecy by keeping his own counsel. Robert's distress darkens the mood, but a farcical tit-for-tat revenge pattern emerges nonetheless. At the end, when Robert invites Jerry to visit Emma, we understand and appreciate his irony.

Scene 8, depicting the rosy world of undiscovered adultery, invokes and extends the parodic adulteries of *The Lover*. As in Restoration comedy, Richard and Sarah locate their fantasies in a public park, that fragment of a city world that permits release from civilized behavior. Despite the excitement of their games and their invented Max, Richard grows bored with their eternal teatime, having "as the constant image of his lust a milk jug and a teapot." In *Betrayal* Pinter goes further, not merely parodying adultery but exposing it as domestic. We now have a real lover and a special flat rented for afternoon lust, and even the leisure to walk through a real park and gaze at the river. Nevertheless there is still the milk jug and the teapot. In scene 5, Emma calls the flat a "home," to which she adds a tablecloth. In scene 8, she displays a new apron and cooks Jerry a stew. She even hints that since she is pregnant three years into the affair, Jerry might change his status from lover to husband. Though the child is Robert's, Emma could transfer responsibility to Jerry; apparently one man will do as well as another.

The image of female rapacity is not new in Pinter (think of Flora and Ruth, Diana in *Tea Party*). In *Betrayal*, however, Pinter justifies Emma's impulse with a cumulative double image. Jerry and Robert are not only best friends, they are almost the same man. One went to Oxford, the other to Cambridge; both were poetry editors; both married and had two children; both cheat on their wives; both buy and sell literary talent; both like Yeats, and both, for seven years, sleep with the same woman. If Spooner and Hirst are alter egos, Jerry and Robert are mirror images of each other. However, Jerry perceives only the uniqueness of his situation, refusing to think that Robert and even Judith might also be unfaithful in other private rooms, while he meets Emma.

Blindness, the metaphysical affliction of all Pinter posers, is dramatized in Jerry's drunkenness in scene 9. Seducing Emma in the conjugal bedroom, Jerry rehearses the lusty acrobatics of Restoration rakes and the sentiments of Etherege's Dorimant: "there is no charm so infallibly makes me fall in love with a woman as my knowing a friend loves her."[49] However, Jerry's sexual competitiveness is surprisingly brutal:

> I should have had you, in your white, before the wedding. I should have blackened you, in your white wedding dress, blackened you in your bridal dress, before ushering you into your wedding, as your best man.
>
> (p. 265)

Blackening Emma recalls the sex-in-the-rubbish-dump images in *The Homecoming, The Lover,* and *Night,* but they are more complex in *Betrayal.* Does Jerry make love to Emma in the same battling, loving spirit as Robert proposing a game of squash? Whatever the answer, Pinter frees Jerry from the tedium of soul searching. Jerry is blinded by drink, excitement, maybe even love. Thus he views adultery simplistically, in terms of black and white.

As with Robert's Torcello experience, Jerry insists that his love is special, original. Like Congreve's Mirabell and Millamant who make vehement distinctions between the corrupt manners of the world and the world of private feeling, Jerry claims that "Everyone knows. The world knows. It knows. But they'll never know, they're in a different world" (p. 266). Jerry is also a professional image maker, and images cloud his perception. He watches himself make love to Emma ("Look at the way you look at me . . . Look at the way you're looking at me" [p. 266]), and as he warms to his theme ("I won't walk, I'll be a cripple, I'll descend, I'll diminish into total paralysis" [p. 266]), he resembles not only Joyce's impassioned Robert, but Lady Wishfort on her couch, affecting "a sort of dyingness."[50] Jerry is the Prince of Catatonia, a hero of fiction, and it is possible that images of black and white occur because he sees himself immortalized on the printed page, in the novels of Spinks and Casey. In Pinter's *Betrayal,* however, he is merely poser turned loser: in contrast to a fictional romantic hero, Jerry is presented at the beginning of the play, aging and hung over.

Inviting comparisons, Pinter ties his past-present technique not only to comedy of manners but to the conventional memento mori implicit in his Hogarthian panels. Time distorts human relationships as the discontinuity of the scenes in *Betrayal* undermines the characters' illusions that success in stratagems and love affairs will continue indefinitely. Jerry's delusions, which we view from different perspectives, personalize this tale of adultery. Yet the revolving panels also depersonalize. Like *The Collection*, with its two residences in view, the stage world of *Betrayal* is deliberately artificial; characters move mechanically, like specimens, tagged for our scrutiny by season and year.

Though Pinter's time technique dehumanizes the characters, it seduces audience interest. The movement from present to past makes us secondary authors, completing the scenario with details we accumulate. As Peter Hall remarked, we "put more and more into each scene"[5]—not only because we know the outcome of the actions we witness but because these sophisticated types, living through their marital fractures in the 1970s, are as familiar to us as the wits and witwoulds were to audiences of the Restoration theater. Like the novelists of *Betrayal*, Pinter is our successful literary man, providing images of our own reflection.

Exploring images of contemporary life, Pinter reduces his verbal range. Language in *Betrayal* is economical, almost transparent; we identify characters not by how they speak, as in former plays, but by what they say. Yet linguistic rhythms and repetitions weave subtle emotional patterns. For example, Jerry and Emma's language of closure becomes a halting duet.

> EMMA: The fact is that in the old days we used our imagination and
> we'd take a night and make an arrangement and go to an hotel.
> JERRY: Yes. We did.
> *Pause.*

(p. 195)

Emma's singsong phrases connected by conjunctions, and the "take-make" rhyme are answered affirmatively by Jerry's "yes," then undercut by his past-tense "we did." Jerry continues in a four-stress line:

> JERRY: But that was . . . in the main . . . before we got this flat.
> EMMA: We haven't spent many nights . . . in this flat.
> JERRY: No.
> *Pause.*

(pp. 53–54)

Like Eliot in his verse plays, Pinter mocks and revives dead rhetoric: "in the main" slows the line and postpones the pain of ending, while "flat," prominent in both Jerry and Emma's lines, does double duty—naming their abandoned sanctuary and the condition of love gone stale.

Rhythm and repetition create poetic echoes in a dialogue about poets.

ROBERT: Have you read any good books lately?
JERRY: I've been reading Yeats.
ROBERT: Ah. Yeats. Yes.
         Pause.
JERRY: You read Yeats on Torcello once.
ROBERT: On Torcello?
JERRY: Don't you remember? Years ago. You went over to Torcello in
         the dawn, alone. And read Yeats.
ROBERT: So I did. I told you that, yes.
         Pause.
         Yes.
         Pause.
         Where are you going this summer, you and the family?
JERRY: The Lake District.

                                                      (pp. 189–90)

Jerry's "Yeats" and "years" are linked by assonance to Robert's "yes," suggesting a connection between their stories and affinities. Robert's repetitive "I did . . . I told" indicates his impulse to communicate, while Jerry's half-rhymed "dawn/alone" suggests his belated sympathy for Robert's isolation and his own feelings of solitude. Significantly, Robert's Torcello experience is the one fact that Jerry, without prodding, remembers. Choosing the Lake District, traditional retreat of English poets, as a vacation spot for his family, Jerry knits that isolation into the larger fabric of his life.

Isolation, frequent and terrifying in early menace plays, still plaguing Deeley in *Old Times* and Hirst in *No Man's Land,* is redefined in *Betrayal.* Robert, Emma, and Jerry move freely in the world, sharing a common language, common desires that their mutual betrayals confirm. Comedy arises in the verbal and gestural adjustments each character makes to the code of social behavior. As in former Pinter plays, personal motives are unverifiable. However, *Betrayal* links private anxiety with worldly experience— menace with manners. We are isolated not only by what we fear, but how we live.

4

Comic Words in *Other Places*

Reviewing Pinter's plays from *The Basement* through *No Man's Land,* one critic remarked that while Pinter's themes remain constant, his methods have changed.[1] The same may be said for his comedy. From the first, Pinter has exploited traditional comic elements—exposure of the imposter, witty game playing, theatrical and linguistic parody—but certain methods have changed. Comic physical gesture—the farcical assembly line in *The Dumb Waiter,* the bag gag in *The Caretaker,* the passionate mugging in *The Lover,* the clownish fight in *The Homecoming*—have been supplanted by intensified verbal gestures—the singing contest in *Old Times,* Spooner's aria on servitude in *No Man's Land,* Jerry's self-reflecting love song in *Betrayal.* Language, however, has always been the core of Pinter's comic achievement.[2] Across the canon, hectoring repetition, serial lists, rambling anecdotes, phatic inanities, jargon parodies produce a comically shocking, baffling smoke screen that blocks our attempts either to verify character motive or to rationalize play action.

What we do know is that words in Pinter's plays have a comic *and* a controlling power. An educated word (Mick's "penchant") a technical word (Ben's "ballcock"), or an exotic foreign label (Edward's "Wachenheimer Fuchsmantel Reisling Beeren Auselese") confers superiority on the user. Pinter relishes technical or arcane language for its own sake—as in the "hemi unibal spherical rod end" in "Trouble in the Works" and "phytonomy" in *The Hothouse*—but more comic is the fact that such words function as a primitive force, silencing or intimidating a listener. Pinter's interrogation routines hold stage victims in thrall even as the audience responds to comically disjunct form and content: Goldberg's threatening questions contain ridiculous references; Foster's menacing inquiries are concealed in a flow of badinage. Dominance and subservience, which Pinter once called a "repeated theme in my plays,"[3] is transacted through a language riddled with incongruity, a language that informs and simultaneously mocks its informing function.

Two recent miniplays, *Victoria Station* and *Family Voices* (collected with *A Kind of Alaska* under the title *Other Places*), offer an index of Pinter's verbal comedy while opening up new dimensions to the problem of unverifiability. In both plays, characters inhabit distinct stage regions and make no physical contact; hence Pinter eliminates territorial battles and focuses on the world that language limns for each speaker. In *Victoria Station,* a cab company controller and his driver negotiate or refuse to negotiate a conversational situation normally governed by strict rules: Controller orders and Driver obeys. In their first exchanges, however, Driver, like Mr. Kidd in *The Room,* subtly mars communication:

> CONTROLLER: Is that 274?
> DRIVER: That's me.
> CONTROLLER: Where are you?
> DRIVER: What?[4]

When Driver asks Controller "Who are you?" (p. 46), he calls into question Controller's position of authority. Like Mr. Kidd, too, Driver confuses the spatial coordinates of his interlocutor's world, refusing to know the whereabouts or even the existence of Victoria Station. The comic structure of these first exchanges, a conflict of language worlds, persists until the end of the play. Controller (like Ben in *The Dumb Waiter*) pursues the rules of the old game, abusing Driver as though he were capable, if coerced enough, of proceeding to Victoria Station. Although the dominance-subservience issue (who controls whom) recalls typical Pinterian combat, Driver's comic feints touch on the epistomological problem of how we know what we know and how we manage to refer to it:

> DRIVER: [I am sitting] By the side of a park.
> CONTROLLER: By the side of a park?
> DRIVER: Yes.
> CONTROLLER: What park.
> DRIVER: A dark park.
> CONTROLLER: Why is it dark?
> DRIVER: That's not an easy question.
>   *Pause.*

(p. 51)

Having destabilized Controller, Driver suddenly reverses his position, feigning sincerity: he has "honestly" lost track of his actions, is the only one who merits Controller's "trust." Just as quickly he mocks those claims by producing a wife, a daughter ("I think that's what she is"), and, most dramatically a passenger, first referred to as "he" then "she" then as "true love"—"I'm going to marry her in this car" (p. 61). Controller, now voyeuristically captivated, deserts his position of authority to search for Driver and his mysterious "P.O.B"—(passenger on board).

However, Controller does not renounce power easily; as Driver grows more obscure, Controller boils over in invective reminiscent of Max's tirades in *The Homecoming*. Menacingly, Controller promises to attend Driver's Golden Wedding: "I'll bring along some of the boys to drink to your health, won't I? Yes, I'll bring along some of the boys" (pp. 60–61) Like Duff, he displaces his rage with a detailed listing of the parts of a Ford Cortina, exploding with "If I did have a jack in the boot I'd stick it right up your arse," a fine example of condensation in which jack in the boot becomes a kicking jack boot as well as, hypothetically, an instrument for disemboweling. Controller loses control of his invective: "I'm going to tie you up bollock naked to a butcher's table and flog you to death all the way to Crystal Place" (p. 54)—a violent, slapstick image bordering on the surreal.

With its invective, feints, and obscurities, *Victoria Station* revives in miniature the comic potential of the problem of unverifiability. Language alone creates the "shared common ground" of "reality" but can also produce the "quicksand" of subjective, unverifiable experience. In Pinter's previous works, characters give or withhold verification as a power move in game playing. In *Victoria Station,* the world itself resists verification. When Controller insists, "I'm just talking into this machine, trying to make some sense out of our lives" (p. 50), he soon strays into a self-mocking sally about his God-given function, but the statement is suggestive for all verbal acts: in speaking we seek to become controllers, we *make sense* of experience. In Pinter's world, however, that "sense" is constantly and comically revised by another's speaking. The attempt to pin down, verify, control experience becomes a mechanical obsession (CONTROLLER: "You're beginning to obsess me. I think I'm going to die" [p. 58]), a deathlike rigidity meriting in Pinter, as in Bergson, a cruel, comic comeuppance. For Controller not only abandons his position of authority, he foolishly assumes that Driver's "I'll be here" means that he can be found at an exact location, a discoverable, verifiable "here."

Victoria Station is a small but energetic representation of many of Pinter's most successful comic verbal devices; *Family Voices*, less comic, more convoluted, combines these devices in new ways. *Family Voices* seems to be Pinter's wry version of the Freudian family romance:[5] the son-protagonist "writes" home to his mother and refers to his father but lives among or invents a surreal family of grotesques who not only parody his "real" family but also permit him to play out his sexual fantasies and fears. What is comic in the play derives from the son's naïve and futile attempts to verify the connections in the Withers family, as well as from the echoic commentary by the Pinter family of characters who emerge, like the trauma of family history, repeatedly in his works. Both a character's self-revealing posturing and Pinter's self-regarding verbal and theatrical gestures are familiar elements in his comic spectrum. What is different in this play is Pinter's recasting of what I have called the exuberant verbal performance, the long solo speech with its combination of clichéd and arcane discourse, its surprising tonal shifts, repetitions, and odd metonymies. About the content of such speeches nothing can be verified except that the speech itself is aggressive and confrontative. Strutting out their intellects, Pinter's Mick, Harry, Lenny, Anna, and Deeley challenge their listeners and simultaneously imply that their challenge should not be met. In *Family Voices*, however, characters are trapped in individual worlds so that aggressive speeches, such as that made when the mother passes from anguish to anger, fizzle midair. Further distancing the characters is Pinter's unusual device: character dialogue consists of spoken correspondence, although Pinter establishes early on that no letter is received. The voices communicate, spark off one another only in the mind of the audience.

What do we hear? Primarily the combined bafflement and pretentiousness of the son's discourse, his attempted objectivity that is comically undermined by cliché and equivocation: "The weather is up and down, but surprisingly warm, on the whole, more often than not."[6] More comic are the repetitions of erotic fantasy. Invited to Lady Withers's room for tea, the son is seated next to Jane, and as her toes work into his thighs he becomes obsessed with buns, those masticated slowly by the women, those "perched" surrealistically "on cakestands, all over the room," but most of all by "my own bun," which is "rock solid" then "juggled" by Jane's skillful toes (p. 73). Lying in his bath, the son passively enjoys the scrutiny of the policeman Riley who admires his "wellknit yet slender frame" (p. 75). However, Riley's comically perverse images ("It's breathtaking, the discipline I'm called upon to exert" [p. 79]) point to the son's excitation and anxiety about homosexual encounter.

In *Family Voices* as in *The Homecoming*, everything refers back to the mother; Pinter subtly connects the son's unresolved Oedipal conflicts to his mother's sensuous description of shampooing her son and to her unacknowledged possessiveness: "[I] looked into your eyes, and saw you look into mine, knowing that you wanted no-one else, no-one at all" (p. 76). The mother's behavior is hilariously parodied by drunken Mrs. Withers who also makes significant eye contact with the son:

> Then she looked at me and said: You are my little pet. I've always wanted a little pet but I've never had one and now I've got one.
>
> (p. 72)

Similarly, the clichéd but threatening speech of the dead father is mocked by Mr. Withers's rambling, obscene logorrhea ("the macaroni tatters, the dumplings in jam mayonnaise" [p. 78]), as the terrifying image of the father's glassy grave is grotesquely complemented by Mr. Wither's awesome look: "It was like looking into a pit of molten lava, mother. One look was enough for me" (p. 78). Through internal echo and parody, Pinter suggests that the Witherses are the demonic double of the son's family, his projection of his own familial dreams and fears. Skewed perception and double vision have also haunted Pinter's earliest posers, reminding us of the double life the characters of *Family Voices* share with other Pinter voices. Old Mrs. Withers is a crude version of the comically possessive Meg in *The Birthday Party*; Lady Withers and Jane recall Pinter's sexually promiscuous and inscrutable women, particularly Ruth of *The Homecoming*. Riley, first named in *The Room*, has at least a double ancestry in Briggs and McCann, and the father's sinister "A last little kiss from Dad" (p. 81) recalls Max's combative "cuddle and kiss."

Despite these Pinterian echoes and resonances, *Family Voices* and *Victoria Station* celebrate the comic power of Pinter's dramatic language.[7] Like previous Pinter works, both plays rehearse the old theme of failure of communication, and both reject the impoverishment of that theme by offering new word-worlds, new versions of the verbal smoke screen. Having little in common, both plays bear the Pinter signature—a comic language of feints, circumlocutions, bombast, and banality, a language that throughout the Pinter oeuvre captivates our attention but refuses to issue verifiable facts or to confirm simple truths. Between his characters' fear and emptiness and their comic verbal excess lies a territory that, to paraphrase Pinter, is worthy of exploration and that this study has attempted to explore. It is the territory of Pinter's comic play, an unstable ground that mocks our craving for stability, a traditional terrain in which traditional assumptions will not apply.

Notes

INTRODUCTION

1. I am paraphrasing Eric Bentley's partial definition of comedy in *Life of the Drama* (New York: Atheneum, 1974), 309. Bentley's phrase touches on different aspects of comedy: errors can refer to the entanglements of plot or to the limitations of character—the lack of self-knowledge that Plato, in *Philebus,* names as the spur to ridiculous behavior.

2. See for example, "Two People in a Room," *New Yorker,* 25 February 1967, 36 (interview with Pinter): Harold Pinter. "Writing for Myself," in *Complete Works: Two* (New York: Grove Press, 1977), 9–12 (based on a conversation with Richard Findlater, 1961); Mel Gussow, "A Conversation (Pause) with Harold Pinter," *New York Times Magazine,* 5 December 1971, 126.

3. See Martin Esslin, *Pinter, A Study of His Plays,* expanded edition (New York: W. W. Norton, 1976), 37–38.

4. The Bristol Drama Festival speech, first published as "Between the lines" in *The Sunday Times* (London) (4 March 1962), 25, was revised and reprinted as "Writing for the Theatre," in *Evergreen Review* (August–September 1964): 80–83 and in *Complete Works: One* (New York: Grove Press, 1977), 9–16. All references are to the latter version.

5. Ibid., 11.

6. Ibid., 12.

7. See Harold Pinter, "A Letter to Peter Wood," in *Drama* (Winter 1981), p. 4. The full citation reads: Meaning begins in the words, in the action, continues in your head and ends nowhere. There is no end to meaning. Meaning which is resolved, parcelled, labelled and ready for export is dead, impertinent—and meaningless."

8. For a review of "superiority" and "incongruity" theories, see Willard Smith, *The Nature of Comedy* (Boston: Gorham Press, 1976), 29–68.

9. This statement marks the difference between my study and Bernard Dukore's *Where Laughter Stops: Pinter's Tragicomedy* (Columbia: University of Missouri Press, 1976). Dukore makes a rigid distinction between the funny and the unfunny; each play analysis identifies the moment "where laughter stops."

10. Henri Bergson, *Laughter,* in *Comedy,* ed. Wylie Sypher (New York: Doubleday, 1956), 84ff. For an excellent discussion of this work and Freud's *Jokes and Their Relation to the Unconscious,* see George McFadden, *Discovering the Comic* (Princeton: Princeton University Press, 1982).

11. Sigmund Freud, *Jokes and Their Relation to the Unconscious,* trans. James Strachey (New York: W. W. Norton, 1960), 100ff.

12. See Pinter's *Mac* in *Complete Works: Three* (New York: Grove Press, 1978), 13.

13. Cf. Guido Almansi and Simon Henderson, *Harold Pinter* (London: Methuen, 1983), a book published after my study was completed. Almansi and Henderson argue that strategy and game playing are the only motivators of Pinter's characters.

CHAPTER 1. POSERS AND LOSERS

1. Lawrence M. Bensky, "Harold Pinter: An Interview," in *Pinter*, ed. Arthur Ganz (Englewood Cliffs, N.J.: Prentice-Hall, 1972), 31.

2. Pinter interviewed by John Sherwood, B.B.C. European Service, 3 March 1960, cited in Martin Esslin, *Pinter, A Study of His Plays*, expanded edition (New York: W. W. Norton, 1976), 38.

3. Cited in Esslin, *Pinter, A Study*, 40.

4. Pinter interviewed by Sherwood, cited in ibid., 35–36.

5. See Henri Bergson's discussion of comic characterization in *Laughter*, in *Comedy*, ed. Wylie Sypher (New York: Doubleday 1956), 146ff.

6. Francis M. Cornford, *The Origin of Attic Comedy* (Cambridge: Cambridge University Press, 1934), 140ff.

7. Daniel C. Boughner, *The Braggart in Renaissance Comedy* (Minneapolis: University of Minnesota Press, 1954), 5. See also Boughner's discussion of the morality Vice with regard to Pinter's Goldberg, 145–178.

8. In *Time*, 10 November 1961; cited in Steven H. Gale, *butter's going up* (Durham: Duke University Press. 1977), 24.

9. Bensky, "An Interview," 20.

10. In my chapter, *A Slight Ache* follows *The Room* because the nature of exposure in these plays differs qualitatively from the unmaskings in either *The Birthday Party* or *The Caretaker*.

11. Harold Pinter, "Writing for the Theatre," in *Complete Works: One* (New York: Grove Press, 1977), 12.

12. See George McFadden, *Discovering the Comic* (Princeton: Princeton University Press, 1982), 11.

13. Cited in Esslin, *Pinter, A Study*, 17.

14. See J. T. Boulton, "Harold Pinter: *The Caretaker* and Other Plays," *Modern Drama* 6, no. 2 (September 1963): 131–140.

15. See Arnold P. Hinchlife, *Harold Pinter* (New York: Twayne, 1967), 46.

16. Martin Esslin's comment is typical: "by an accumulation of . . . basically realistic detail, Pinter succeeds in building up an atmosphere of menace, of Kafka-esque uncertainty" (*Pinter, A Study,* 62).

17. Ibid., 61.

18. Lois Gordon, *Stratagems to Uncover Nakedness* (Columbia: University of Missouri Press, 1969), 13.

19. Austin Quigley, *The Pinter Problem* (Princeton: Princeton University Press, 1975), 78.

20. Harold Pinter, *The Room*, in *Complete Works: One* (New York: Grove Press, 1977). All references are to this edition.

21. "Absentmindedness," referred to throughout *Laughter*, is fundamental to Bergson's conception of comic character and comic language; See pp. 127–90.

22. J. R. Brown, "Dialogue in Pinter and Others," *Critical Quarterly* 7, no. 3 (Autumn 1965): 228.

23. See Leslie Smith, "Pinter the Player," *Modern Drama* 22, no. 4 (December 1979): 353.

24. Frank Vosper, *Love from a Stranger*, adapted from Agatha Christie's story (New York: Samuel French, 1936), 72.

25. Pinter interviewed by Sherwood; cited in Esslin, *Pinter, A Study*, 38.

26. Pinter, "Writing for the Theatre," 12.

27. See Bergson on the "reciprocal interference of series" especially his variation: "One series of events belonging to the past and another belonging to the present," in *Laughter,* 125.

28. Cited in Gordon, *Strategems,* 19.

29. Harold Pinter, *A Slight Ache,* in *Complete Works: One* (New York: Grove Press, 1977). All page references are to this edition.

30. Pinter, "Writing for the Theatre," 14.

31. "The Examination" and "Problem," in Harold Pinter, *Poems and Prose, 1948–1977* (New York: Grove, 1978).

32. Pinter was apparently convinced of the dramatic appeal of his earlier story. He read "The Examination" for the B.B.C. Third Programme in 1961, the same series that produced *A Slight Ache* in 1959. See "Chronology of a Career," in Martin Esslin, *Pinter, A Study,* 21, 26.

33. Pinter, "Writing for the Theatre," 14.

34. See Freud's discussion of aggression released through tendentious jokes in *Jokes and Their Relation to the Unconscious,* trans. James Strachey (New York: W. W. Norton, 1960), 101ff.

35. See Sykes, *Harold Pinter,* 95.

36. Hayman, *Harold Pinter* 46.

37. Sykes, *Harold Pinter,* 50.

38. Pinter, "Writing for the Theatre," 11.

39. See Ruby Cohn, "The World of Harold Pinter," in *Printer,* ed. Ganz, 87–89.

40. See Martin Esslin, *The Theatre of the Absurd,* rev. ed. (New York: Doubleday, 1969), 237; Gordon, *Stratagems,* 27.

41. Esslin, *Pinter, A Study,* 83.

42. Alrene Sykes, *Harold Pinter* (St. Lucia: University of Queensland Press, 1970), 18.

43. Cf. Bernard Spivack, *Shakespeare and the Allegory of Evil* (New York: Columbia University Press, 1958), 194. Spivack finds the Vice, "with his deceit and laughter . . . incipient in the figure of Worldly Goods."

44. Ibid., 141–42.

45. Ibid., 154.

46. Ibid., 155. See also Robert Potter, *The English Morality Play* (London: Routledge, 1975), 35ff. Potter disagrees with the use of "allegorical" to describe the Vice. However, in regard to the Vice as "tempter," Spivack and Potter's views coincide.

47. L. W. Cushman, *The Devil and the Vice in the English Dramatic Literature before Shakespeare* (Halle: Max Niemeyer, 1900), 63.

48. Spivack, *Allegory of Evil,* 163.

49. Ibid., 188–93.

50. See Robert Potter's provocative analysis of the Vice in Jonson's *Volpone,* in *The English Morality Play,* 144ff. See also A. P. Rossiter, *English Drama from Early Times to the Elizabethans* (New York: Barnes and Noble, 1950), 144ff.

51. Mr. S., *Gammer Gurton's Needle,* in *Elizabethan and Stuart Plays,* ed. Baskervill, Heltzel, and Nethercot (New York: Holt, Rinehart, 1934), 50. All page references are to this edition.

52. Spivack, *Allegory of Evil,* 16.

53. William Shakespeare, *Othello* (London: Penguin 1958), 151. All page references are to this edition.

54. Rossiter, *English Drama,* 99.

55. See Harold Pinter's *Mac,* in *Complete Works: Three* (New York: Grove Press, 1978), 13.

56. See Spivack, *Allegory of Evil*, 52: "the Vice's very existence resulted from the homiletic concept of a *root* evil."

57. Cushman, *The Devil and the Vice*, 118.

58. Harold Pinter, *The Birthday Party*, in *Complete Works: One* (New York: Grove Press, 1977). All page references are to this edition.

59. Bergson, *Laughter*, 128.

60. Cf. John Russell Brown, *Theatre Language* (New York: Taplinger, 1972), 22. Brown detects a power play between Meg and Petey in the opening dialogue: "Her questions, statements, and action all establish that she is calling the tune; she wishes to make him acknowledge her presence and his dependence." I disagree that this subtext is evident in the dialogue; it could as easily be argued that Petey is deliberately withholding information.

61. Cushman, *The Devil and the Vice*, 118.

62. Though conformity of dress is a motif throughout Kafka's *The Trial*, Josef K's executioners are the most extreme example. Both are dressed in black, both "pallid and plump, with top-hats that were apparently uncollapsible." Like Goldberg and McCann, these two act and talk with the coordination of a music-hall duo. See Franz Kafka, *The Trial* (1925; reprint, New York: Penguin Edition, 1965), 245–51. Pinter may have also recalled Hemingway's thugs in "The Killers."

63. Cushman, *The Devil and the Vice*, 108–9.

64. See ibid., 102ff. Among the Vice's verbal tricks are puns, distortions, and double entendres.

65. See Steven Gale's analysis of the symbolism of Goldberg and McCann in *butter's going up*, 55–59. See also Sykes *Harold Pinter*, 19–21.

66. See Cushman, *The Devil and the Vice*, 68: "after 1560, at the time when the serious role of the Vice had fallen into the background and the farcical role was more and more on the increase, the term Vice came to be simply a synonym for buffoon." Most medieval drama critics quote Puttenham from his *Arte of English Poesie* (1589), when he refers to "Carols and rounds and such light or lascivious poems, which are commonly more commodiously uttered by those buffoons or Vices in plays than by any other person," in *The Arte of English Poesie*, ed. Gladys Willcock and Alice Walker (Cambridge: The University Press 1936), 84.

67. Harold Pinter, "A Letter to Peter Wood," *Drama* (Winter 1981): 4.

68. Cited in Cushman, *The Devil and the Vice*, 139.

69. Esslin, *Pinter, A Study*, 82.

70. See Cushman, *The Devil and the Vice*, 73. "In the later Moralities, the figure of the Good practically disappears and the allegorical man is replaced by typical characters from various classes in real life, clowns and ruffians."

71. In Pinter's production of *The Birthday Party* in the Aldwych Theatre Summer Repertoire (1964), "Stanley was stronger as a character, bandying words with the strangers, torturing Meg with the haunting idea of her being carted away in a wheelbarrow, a fear she still retains at the end of the play" (Hinchliffe, *Harold Pinter*, 63).

72. See Samuel Beckett, *Watt* (New York: Grove Press, 1959), 46–47.

73. Harold Pinter, *The Caretaker*, in *Complete Works: Two* (New York: Grove Press, 1977). All page references are to this edition.

74. Pinter was pleased with the film version of the play because it extended the feeling of the physical world:

What I'm very pleased about myself is that in the film as opposed to the play, we see a real house and real snow outside, dirty snow and the streets. . . . In the play, when people were confronted with just a set, a room and a door, they often assumed it was all taking place in limbo, in a vacuum, and the world outside hardly existed.

B.B.C. Transcript, *New Comment,* cited in Hinchliffe, *Harold Pinter,* 99.

75. Interview with Harold Pinter, B.B.C. Home Service, 28 October 1960.

76. See John Towson, *Clowns* (New York: Hawthorn Books, 1976), 282–305.

77. Cornford, *Origin of Attic Comedy,* 140.

78. See Northrop Frye, *The Anatomy of Criticism* (Toronto: University of Toronto Press, 1957), 172; Madelaine Doran, *Endeavors of Art* (Madison: University of Wisconsin Press, 1964), 230.

79. Cited in Esslin, *Pinter, A Study,* 40.

80. Sigmund Freud, *Jokes and Their Relation to the Unconscious,* trans. James Strachey (New York: W. W. Norton), 90–119ff.

81. Bensky, "An Interview," 28.

82. Bergson, "Laughter," 143.

83. Gale and Dukore endorse the conventional view. Gale regards the smile as a signal of a renewed relationship and future change: "Now that Aston's faith in his brother is reestablished, he has the strength to begin work on his shed" (*butter's going up,* 89). For Dukore, "the smile reveals friendly communication between the brothers, an essentially comic note"; see his *Where Laughter Stops: Pinter's Tragicomedy,* 26.

84. Cited in Charles Marowitz, "Theatre Abroad," *Village Voice,* 1 September 1960.

85. Harold Pinter, "Letter to the Editor," *The Sunday Times* (London), 14 August 1960. He was responding to Leonard Russell's open letter to Harold Pinter in *The Times,* August 1960, expressing distress at audience laughter during a performance of *The Caretaker.*

86. See Bergson, *Laughter,* 146ff.

CHAPTER 2. THE PARODY PLAYS

1. Eric Bentley, *Theatre of War* (New York: Viking, 1960), 100.

2. Andrew Kennedy, *Six Dramatists in Search of a Language* (Cambridge: Cambridge University Press, 1975), 1–37, 165–91. See also Kennedy, *Dramatic Dialogue* (London: Cambridge University Press, 1975), 220–27ff.

3. Lawrence M. Bensky, "Harold Pinter: An Interview," in *Pinter,* ed. Arthur Ganz (Englewood Cliffs, N.J.: Prentice-Hall 1972), 25.

4. "Two People in a Room," *New Yorker,* 25 February 1967, 36 (interview with Pinter.)

5. Bensky, "An Interview," 21.

6. Harold Pinter, "Writing for Myself," in *Harold Pinter, Complete Works: Two* (New York: Grove Press, 1977), 9.

7. Leslie Smith, "Pinter the Player," *Modern Drama* 22, no. 4 (December 1979): 353. Two incidents from J. B. Priestley's *Mr. Kettle and Mrs. Moon* in which Pinter twice acted in 1956 are adapted for *The Birthday Party* (1957).

8. Peter Davison, "Contemporary Drama and Popular Dramatic Forms," in *Aspects of Drama and the Theatre* (Sydney: Sydney University Press, 1965), 143–97.

9. Harold Pinter, television interview, 1968; cited in *A Casebook on Harold Pinter's* The Homecoming, ed. John Lahr (New York: Grove Press, 1971).

10. Pinter, "Writing for Myself," 9.

11. Lahr, *A Casebook,* 11.

12. Pinter, "Writing for the Theatre," in *Harold Pinter, Complete Works: One* (New York: Grove Press, 1977), 10.

13. Bentley, *Theatre of War* 100.

14. Ibid., 9, 11. Following Bentley, I use the term "parody" and not "burlesque" to stress the literary critical aspect of Pinter's comedy. John Jump (*Burlesque* [London: Methuen

1972] treats parody as a subcategory of burlesque; parody becomes a stylistic imitation of a work or an author's style with "a less worthy subject" (p. 2). Jump allows that parody in *Ulysses* has little to do with a less worthy subject but, rather, serves "to carry forward serious themes" (p. 34). Jump refers the reader to Dwight Macdonald's essay "Some Notes on Parody," appended to *Parodies: An Anthology from Chaucer to Beerbohm—and After* (New York: Random House 1960), but in that essay Macdonald divorces parody from burlesque; the latter "imitates the style of the original" with "ludicrous" content, while parody is "a form of literary criticism" (557–59). The farcical broadness that accompanies burlesque makes the term unsuitable to describe Pinter's style.

15. Harold Bloom, *The Anxiety of Influence* (New York: Oxford University Press, 1973), 5.

16. Boris Tomashevsky, "Thematics," in *Russian Formalist Criticism*, trans. Lee T. Lemon and Marion J. Reis (Lincoln: University of Nebraska Press, 1965), 84.

17. Bertel Pedersen, *The Theory and Practice of Parody in the Modern Novel: Mann, Joyce, and Nabokov* (Ann Arbor: University Microfilms, 1975), 21ff.

18. Kennedy, *Six Dramatists in Search of a Language*, 64. Kennedy uses the phrase in reference to Shaw, but it applies to Pinter's manner of exposing the " 'absurd' potentiality" in any given speech style, 167.

19. Margaret A. Rose, *Parody/Meta-fiction* (London: Croom Helm, 1979), 147.

20. Pinter, "Writing for the Theatre," 13. The Bristol Drama Festival Speech, first published as "Between the Lines" in *The Sunday Times* (4 March 1962) is reprinted under this title in *Complete Works: One* (New York: Grove Press, 1977), 9–16.

21. For a description of play as rule-bound behavior see Johan Huizinga, *Homo Ludens* (Boston: Beacon Press, 1950), 1–27, and Roger Caillois, *Man, Play, Games* (New York: Free Press of Glencoe, Crowell-Collier, 1961), 3–14. See also my analyses of *The Dumb Waiter* and *The Lover*.

22. Mel Gussow, "A Conversation (Pause) with Harold Pinter," *New York Times Magazine*, 5 December 1971, 43. This interview begins with a discussion of *Old Times*, during which Pinter admits having seen *Odd Man Out*.

23. Harold Pinter, *The Dumb Waiter*, in *Complete Works: One* (New York: Grove Press, 1977). All page references are to this edition.

24. Roger Manvell, ed., *Three British Screen Plays* (London: Methuen, 1950), 119.

25. Ibid., 121. The differences between the script Manvell prints and the film dialogue are negligible.

26. William Gillette, *Sherlock Holmes, A Play* (New York: Doubleday, 1935), 111.

27. Ibid., 112–13.

28. See Simon Trussler, *The Plays of Harold Pinter* (London: Victor Gollancz, 1973), 54; Charles Carpenter, "The Absurdity of Dread: Pinter's *The Dumb Waiter*," *Modern Drama* 16 (December 1973): 279–85; Ruby Cohn, "The Absurdly Absurd: Avatars of Godot," *Comparative Literature Studies* 2 (1965): 233–40.

29. Samuel Beckett, *Waiting for Godot* (New York: Grove Press, 1954), 61.

30. See Peter Davison, "Contemporary Drama and Popular Dramatic Forms," in *Aspects of Drama and the Theatre* (Sydney: Sydney University Press, 1965), 143–97.

31. For details about Stan Laurel's life and career, see John McCabe, *The Comedy of Stan Laurel* (New York: Doubleday, 1974).

32. See Johan Huizinga, *Homo Ludens* (Boston: Beacon Press, 1950), 13. Also: "All play moves and has its being within a playground marked off beforehand . . . [these] are temporary worlds within the ordinary world, dedicated to the performance of an act apart" (10). The obvious artificiality of these "temporary worlds" disturbs Gus. Perhaps this is the "something" he wants to verify with Wilson.

33. See John H. Towson, *Clowns* (New York: Hawthorn Books, 1976), 206ff. We may associate Ben, who keeps himself immaculate, with the tradition of the "whiteface" clown, and Gus, the comic victim, with the *auguste* or *stupidus*. Gus may be an incarnation of the traditional English rustic (in British slang, a "birk"). In Elizabethan drama, the rustic combines with the court fool; both were "licensed critics of the action" (62).

34. McCabe, *Stan Laurel*, 87–93.

35. John Russell Brown, *Theatre Language* (London: Taplinger, 1972), 33ff.

36. See Theodore Huff, *Charlie Chaplin* (London: Cassell, 1952), 77–78.

37. Henri Bergson, *Laughter*, in *Comedy*, ed. Wylie Sypher (New York: Doubleday, 1956), 79.

38. Eric Bentley, *The Life of the Drama* (New York: Atheneum, 1974), 247.

39. See Arthur Conan Doyle, "The Adventure of the Final Problem" in *The Adventures of Sherlock Holmes* (New York: Avenal Books, 1976), 315–26.

40. Davison, "Contemporary Drama," 192.

41. Leslie Smith, "Pinter the Player," *Modern Drama* 22, no. 4 (December 1979): 353.

42. Quoted in Lois Gordon, *Stratagems to Uncover Nakedness* (Columbia: University of Missouri Press, 1969), 52.

43. Robert B. Heilman, "Tragedy and Melodrama: Speculations on Generic Form," *Texas Quarterly* 3, no. 2 (Summer 1960): 48ff. See also Heilman's book, *Tragedy and Melodrama: Versions of Experience* (Seattle: University of Washington Press, 1968); and Michael Booth, *English Melodrama* (London: Herbert Jenkins, 1965), 118ff.

44. Arthur W. Pinero, *The Second Mrs. Tanqueray*, in *Sixteen Famous British Plays*, ed. Cerf and Cartmell (New York: Modern Library, 1942), 64. All page references are to this edition.

45. Henry A. Jones, *The Lie* (New York: George H. Doran, 1915), 110.

46. Madelaine Edmondson and David Rounds, *The Soaps: Daytime Serials of Radio and TV* (New York: Stein and Day, 1973), 249–50.

47. Derek Granger quoted in David Robinson, "Coronation Street," *New Society*, 25 February 1965, 24.

48. Pinter, "Writing for the Theatre," 11.

49. Harold Pinter, *The Collection* in *Complete Works: Two* (New York: Grove Press, 1977). All page references are to this edition.

50. See Booth, *English Melodrama*, 199.

51. Ibid., 38.

52. See Alrene Sykes, *Harold Pinter*, 105.

53. Martin Esslin, *Pinter, A Study of His Plays*, expanded edition (New York: W. W. Norton, 1976), p. 129.

54. Trussler, *Plays of Harold Pinter*, 111.

55. John Vanbrugh, *The Provoked Wife*, Regents Restoration Drama Series, ed. Curt A. Zimansky (Lincoln: University of Nebraska Press, 1969), 95.

56. Cf. L. A. Beaurline and Fredson Bowers, eds., *John Dryden: Four Comedies* (Chicago: University of Chicago Press, 1967), 16–20.

57. *The Country Wife* treats adultery openly and comically, but Wycherley begs the moral question by emphasizing Margery's country bumpkin naïveté.

58. Somerset Maugham, *The Constant Wife*, in *Representative Modern British Plays*, ed. Robert Warnock (Glenview, Ill: Scott, Foresman, 1953), 499. All page references are to this edition.

59. Harold Pinter, *The Lover*, in *Complete Works: Two* (New York: Grove Press, 1977). All page references are to this edition.

60. See Beaurline and Bowers, *John Dryden: Four Comedies*, 19.

61. William Wycherley, *The Country Wife*, Regent's Restoration Drama Series, ed. Thomas Fujimura (Lincoln: University of Nebraska Press, 1965), 43. All page references are to this edition.

62. See Johan Huizinga, *Homo Ludens* (Boston: Beacon Press, 1950), 1–27, and Roger Caillois, *Man, Play, Games* (New York: Free Press of Glencoe, Crowell-Collier, 1961), 3–10.

63. Jacques Ehrmann, "Homo Ludens Revisited," in *Game, Play, Literature*, ed. Jacques Ehrmann (Boston: Beacon Press, 1968), 42.

64. See Freud on the sexual hostility of the tendentious joke, in *Jokes*, pp. 94–102.

65. Noel Coward, *Blithe Spirit*, in *Representative Modern British Plays*, 522.

66. Oscar Wilde, *The Importance of Being Earnest* (New York: Doubleday), 484.

67. Kennedy, *Six Dramatists in Search of a Language*, 32.

68. Pinter "Writing for Myself," 10.

69. Arthur Koestler discusses the pleasure of "seeing the joke," especially in witty dialogue, in *The Act of Creation* (London: Hutchinson, 1976), 89.

70. John Russell Taylor, *Anger and After* (London: Methuen, 1962), 274.

71. T. S. Eliot, *The Family Reunion* (London: Faber and Faber, 1939), 15.

72. Peter Shaffer, *Five Finger Exercise* (New York: Harcourt, Brace, 1958), 23.

73. Eliot, *The Family Reunion*, 70.

74. Harold Pinter, *The Homecoming*, in *Complete Works: Three* (New York: Grove Press, 1978). All page references are to this edition.

75. Kathleen Halton, "Pinter," *Vogue*, 1 October 1967, 245.

76. R. F. Storch, "Harold Pinter's Happy Families," *Massachusetts Review* 8 (August 1967): 704.

77. See John Russell Taylor, "Pinter's Game of Happy Families," in *A Casebook on Harold Pinter's* The Homecoming, ed. John Lahr (New York: Grove Press), 65.

78. Halton, "Pinter," 195.

79. Pinter, "Writing for the Theatre," 14.

80. Paul Rogers cited in *A Casebook*, 165.

81. Brown, *Theatre Language*, 75–78.

82. From *Cocoanuts*, in Joe Adamson, *Groucho, Harpo, Chico and Sometimes Zeppo* (New York: Simon and Schuster, 1973), 96.

83. Towson, *Clowns*, 276.

84. Kennedy, *Six Dramatists*, 185.

85. See Freud, *Jokes*, p. 189.

86. See Esslin, *Pinter, A Study*, 151–52. See also Augusta Walker, "Why the Lady Does It," in *A Casebook*, 117–21.

87. Henry Hewes, "Probing Pinter's Play," *Saturday Review* 50 (8 April 1967): 58.

88. Bert O. States, "Pinter's *Homecoming*: The Shock of Nonrecognition," in *Pinter*, ed. Ganz, 151ff.

89. Pinter, "Writing for the Theatre," 11.

90. Austin Quigley, *The Pinter Problem* (Princeton: Princeton University Press, 1975), 225.

91. See Esslin, *Pinter, A Study*, 240–41. He discusses the tragic overtones of this colloquial expression.

CHAPTER 3. PLAYING ON THE PAST

1. Michael Dean, "Late Night Line-Up," *Listener*, 6 March 1969, 312.

2. See Barbara Kreps, "Time and Harold Pinter's Possible Realities: Art as Life and Vice Versa," *Modern Drama* 22, no. 1 (March 1979): 52ff.

3. Harold Pinter, *Landscape*, in *Complete Works: Three* (New York: Grove Press, 1978). All page references are to this edition.

4. Working out her method for *The Moths* (which became *The Waves*), Woolf hit on the idea of "a mind thinking," and a nameless "she" who could "think backwards and forwards." In general, she insisted, "there must be great freedom from reality." See *A Writer's Diary* (New York: Harcourt, Brace, Jovanovich, 1954), 140–41.

5. Mel Gussow, "A Conversation (Pause) With Harold Pinter," *New York Times Magazine*, 5 December 1971, 43.

6. See Freud's discussion of the pleasure of the third party to the tendentious joke in *Jokes*.

7. Roland Barthes, *The Pleasure of the Text*, trans. Richard Miller (New York: Hill and Wang, 1975), p. 23. For Barthes, pleasure arises from an "excess of the text, to what in it exceeds any (social) function and any (structural) functioning" (p. 19). Deeley, Anna, and Kate's speeches, like so many verbal performances in previous Pinter works (Goldberg's, Mick's, Lenny's), seem to work on this principle of excess.

8. Harold Pinter, *Poems and Prose, 1949–1977* (New York: Grove Press, 1978), 39.

9. Sartre says: "I am fixing the people whom I *see* into objects; I am in relation to them as the Other is in relation to me," in *Being and Nothingness*, trans. Hazel E. Barnes (New York: Pocket Books 1956), 356.

10. Dorothy McCall, *The Theatre of Jean-Paul Sartre* (New York: Columbia University Press, 1969), 113–31.

11. Sartre, *Being and Nothingness*, 356.

12. Harold Pinter, *Old Times*, in *Complete Works: Four* (New York: Grove Press, 1981). All page references are to this edition.

13. The crucial scene takes place in Lukey's studio. See *Three British Screenplays*, ed. Roger Manvell (London: Methuen, 1950), 193–97.

14. Gussow, "A Conversation," 132.

15. Freud, *Jokes*, 97–98.

16. Roland Barthes, *A Lover's Discourse, Fragments*, trans. Richard Howard (New York: Hill and Wang, 1978), p. 73.

17. Freud, *Jokes*, 97.

18. Jean-Paul Sartre, *No Exit*, in *No Exit and Three Other Plays* (New York: Vintage Books, 1948), 47.

19. Barthes, *A Lover's Discourse*, p. 132.

20. See, for example, Sheridan Morley, "Twice Knightly," *Punch* 268 (30 April 1975): 773; Benedict Nightingale, "Inaction Replay," *New Statesman* 89 (2 May 1975): 601; Irving Wardle, "In a Land of Dreams and Actuality," *The Times* (London), 24 April 1975, 10.

21. Cf. Noel King, "Pinter's Progress," *Modern Drama* 23, no. 3 (September 1980): 251ff.

22. Harold Pinter, *No Man's Land*, in *Complete Works: Four* (New York: Grove Press, 1981). All page references are to this edition.

23. Samuel Beckett, *Endgame* (New York: Grove Press, 1958), 30. All page references are to this edition.

24. Pinter, "Writing for the Theatre," 13. The phrase, "a different kind of failure" is from T. S. Eliot, *Four Quartets* (New York: Harcourt Brace, 1943), 30.

25. T. S. Eliot, *Four Quartets*, 19.

26. T. S. Eliot, "The Love Song of J. Alfred Prufrock," in *Selected Poems* (New York: Harbrace, 1964), 13. All page references are to this edition.

27. Pinter, *Prose and Poems, 1949–1977*, 87–90.

28. See also Martin Esslin, *Pinter, A Study of His Plays*, exp. ed. (New York: W. W. Norton, 1976), 199, and King, "Pinter's Progress," 247–48.

29. Cited in Esslin, *Pinter, A Study*, 38.

30. See King, "Pinter's Progress," 251. I disagree that Pinter *"forestalls* any movement into self-parody."

31. Harold Hobson, "Unanswered Questions," *The Sunday Times* (London), 4 May 1975, 39.

32. Ruby Cohn notes this pun in "Words Working Overtime: *Endgame* and *No Man's Land,*" *Yearbook of English Studies* 9 (1979): 198.

33. John Bush Jones, "Stasis as Structure in Pinter's *No Man's Land,*" *Modern Drama* 19, no. 3 (September 1976): 291ff.

34. See Andrew Kennedy, "Natural, Mannered, and Parodic Dialogue," *Yearbook of English Studies* 9 (1979): 28–54.

35. Cohn, "Words Working Overtime," 199.

36. Ibid., 197.

37. *Complete Works: Four* omits part of this speech. For the complete version see *No Man's Land* (New York: Grove Press, 1975), 20–21.

38. The silence following Hirst's disclosure may not only mean that he has topped Spooner; it could also be a tacit acknowlegment between former British military men of the fact that those connected with military intelligence were forbidden—even after many years—to discuss their duties. Military intelligence attracted literary men, like Graham Greene, because they knew languages.

39. Kristin Morrison notes this reference in *Canters and Chronicles* (Chicago: University of Chicago Press, 1983), p. 209.

40. Gussow, "A Conversation (Pause) with Harold Pinter," 126.

41. Enoch Brater, "Time and Memory in Pinter's Proust Screenplay," *Comparative Drama* 13, no. 2 (Summer 1979): 122.

42. Harold Pinter, *The Proust Screenplay* (New York: Grove Press, 1977), x.

43. Simon Gray, *Otherwise Engaged,* in *Otherwise Engaged and Other Plays* (London: Penguin Books, 1975), 37. All page references are to this edition.

44. James Joyce, *Exiles* (New York: Viking Press, 1951), 69. All page references are to this edition.

45. Harold Pinter, *Betrayal* (New York: Grove Press, 1979). All page references are to this edition.

46. Mel Gussow, "Harold Pinter: 'I Started with Two People in a Pub,'" *The New York Times* (Sunday), 30 December 1979, 7.

47. See Beaurline and Bowers's discussion of the Restoration masquerade in their introduction to *John Dryden: Four Comedies* (Chicago: University of Chicago Press, 1967), 1–2.

48. Cited in Esslin, *Pinter, A Study,* 34.

49. George Etherege, *The Man of Mode,* Regents Restoration Drama Series, ed. W. B. Carnochan (Lincoln: University of Nebraska Press, 1966), 64.

50. William Congreve, *The Way of the World,* Regents Restoration Drama Series, ed. Kathleen M. Lynch (Lincoln: University of Nebraska Press, 1965), 58.

51. Interview with Dick Cavett, WNET New York, 21 December 1979. Peter Hall directed both the London and New York productions of *Betrayal.*

CHAPTER 4. COMIC WORDS IN *OTHER PLACES*

1. Barbara Kreps, "Time and Harold Pinter's Possible Realities: Art as Life, and Vice Versa," *Modern Drama* 22, no. 1 (March 1979): 48–49.

2. For other studies of Pinter's language see Martin Esslin, "Language and Silence," in

Pinter, A Study of His Plays, expanded edition (New York: W. W. Norton, 1976), 210–41. John Russell Brown, "Pinter, Words and Silence," in *Theatre Language* (London: Taplinger, 1972), 15–53; Andrew Kennedy, "Pinter," in *Six Dramatists in Search of a Language* (Cambridge: Cambridge University Press, 1975), 166–91.

3. Lawrence M. Bensky, "Harold Pinter: An Interview," in *Pinter,* ed. Arthur Ganz (Englewood Cliffs, N.J.: Prentice-Hall, 1972), 29.

4. Harold Pinter, *Victoria Station,* in *Other Places* (New York: Grove Press, 1983), 45. All references are to this edition.

5. See Sigmund Freud, *The Standard Edition of the Complete Psychological Works* (London: Hogarth Press, 1953), vol. 1, pp. 244, 253, 265.

6. Harold Pinter, *Family Voices,* in *Other Places* (New York: Grove Press, 1983), p. 67. All references are to this edition.

7. See Fred Miller Robinson, *The Comedy of Language* (Amherst: University of Massachusetts Press, 1980), 1–27. Robinson's description of the ability of language to "extend its field of operations," promoting the double awareness of pleasure and irony, is appropriate for Pinter's comic language, although Robinson's emphasis on the joy of creation seems perhaps too optimistic for the tone Pinter's work.

Select Bibliography

PLAYS BY HAROLD PINTER

Betrayal. New York: Grove Press, 1978.

The Birthday Party *and* The Room: *Two Plays by Harold Pinter,* New York: Grove Press, 1961.

The Caretaker *and* The Dumb Waiter: *Two Plays by Harold Pinter.* New York: Grove Press, 1961.

The Collection *and* The Lover. London: Methuen, 1963. (This includes the short story, "The Examination.")

Family Voices. London: Faber and Faber, 1981.

The Homecoming. New York: Grove Press, 1966.

The Hothouse. London: Methuen, 1979.

Landscape *and* Silence. London: Methuen, 1969. (This includes the dramatic sketch, *Night.*)

The Lover, Tea Party, The Basement: *Two Plays and a Film Script by Harold Pinter.* New York: Grove Press, 1967.

Monologue. London: Covent Garden Press, 1973.

A Night Out, Night School, Revue Sketches: *Early Plays by Harold Pinter.* New York: Grove Press, 1967. (The Revue sketches include "Trouble in the Works," "The Black and White," "Request Stop," "Last to Go," and "Applicant.")

No Man's Land. London: Methuen, 1975.

Old Times. New York: Grove Press, 1971.

Other Places. New York: Grove Press, 1983.

Poems and Prose, 1948–1977. New York: Grove Press, 1978.

A Slight Ache *and Other Plays.* London: Methuen, 1969. (This includes *A Slight Ache, A Night Out,* and *The Dwarfs.*)

Tea Party *and Other Plays.* London: Methuen, 1967. (This includes *Tea Party, The Basement,* and *Night School.*)

Three Plays by Harold Pinter. New York: Grove Press, 1962. (This includes *A Slight Ache, The Collection,* and *The Dwarfs.*)

Complete Works: One. New York: Grove Press, 1977. Includes reprints of *The Birthday Party, The Room, The Dumb Waiter, A Slight Ache, A Night Out,* "The Black and White" (prose version), "The Examination," and "Writing for the Theatre."

Complete Works: Two. New York: Grove Press, 1977. Includes reprints of *The Caretaker, Night School, The Dwarfs, The Collection, The Lover,* "Trouble in the Works," "The Black and White" (revue sketch), "Request Stop," "Last to go," "Special Offer," and "Writing for Myself."

Complete Works: Three. New York: Grove Press, 1978. Includes reprints of *The Homecoming, Landscape, Silence, The Basement, Night,* "That's All," "That's Your Trouble," "Interview," "Applicant," "Dialogue for Three," "Tea Party" (short story), *Tea Party,* and *Mac.*

Complete Works: Four. New York: Grove Press, 1981. Includes reprints of *Old Times, No Man's Land, Betrayal, Monologue, Family Voices.*

WORKS CITED AND OTHER USEFUL SECONDARY SOURCES

Adamson, Joe. *Groucho, Harpo, Chico and Sometimes Zeppo.* New York: Simon and Schuster, 1973.

Almansi, Guido. "Harold Pinter's Idiom of Lies." In *Contemporary English Drama, Stratford-Upon-Avon Studies 19,* edited by C. W. E. Bigsley, 79–84. London: Edward Arnold, 1981.

Almansi, Guido, and Simon Henderson. *Harold Pinter.* London: Methuen, 1983.

Baker, William, and Ely Tabachnick. *Harold Pinter.* Edinburgh: Oliver and Boyd, 1973.

Barber, C. L. *Shakespeare's Festive Comedy.* Princeton: Princeton University Press, 1959.

Barthes, Roland. *A Lover's Discourse, Fragments.* Translated by Richard Howard. New York: Farrar, Strauss and Giroux, 1978.

———. *The Pleasure of the Text.* Translated by Richard Miller. New York: Farrar, Strauss and Giroux, 1975.

Beaurline, L. A., and Fredson Bowers, eds., General Introduction to *John Dryden: Four Comedies.* Chicago: University of Chicago Press, 1967.

Beckett, Samuel. *Endgame.* New York: Grove Press, 1958.

———. *Waiting for Godot.* New York: Grove Press, 1954.

———. *Watt.* New York: Grove Press, 1959.

Bentley, Eric. *Life of the Drama.* New York: Atheneum, 1964.

————. *Theatre of War.* New York: Viking Press, 1960.

Bergson, Henri. *Laughter.* In *Comedy,* edited by Wylie Sypher. New York: Doubleday, 1956.

Berne, Eric. *Games People Play.* New York: Ballantine Books, 1964.

Blau, Herbert. *The Impossible Theatre: A Manifesto.* New York: Macmillan, 1964.

Bloom, Harold. *The Anxiety of Influence.* New York: Oxford University Press, 1973.

Bock, Hedwig. "Harold Pinter: The Room as Symbol." In *Essays on Contemporary British Drama,* edited by Hedwig Bock and Albert Wertheim, 171–84. Munich: Max Hueber Verlag, 1981.

Booth, Michael. *English Melodrama.* London: Herbert Jenkins, 1965.

Booth, Wayne C. *A Rhetoric of Irony.* Chicago: University of Chicago Press, 1974.

Boughner, D. C. *The Braggart in Renaissance Comedy.* Minneapolis: University of Minnesota Press, 1954.

Boulton, James T. "Harold Pinter: *The Caretaker* and Other Plays." *Modern Drama* 6 (September 1963): 131–40.

Bovie, Palmer. "Seduction: The Amphitryon Theme from Plautus to Pinter." *Minnesota Review* 7, no. 3–4, (1967): 304–13.

Brater, Enoch. "Cinematic Fidelity and the Forms of Pinter's *Betrayal*." *Modern Drama* 24 (December 1981): 503–13.

————. "Time and Memory in Pinter's Screenplay." *Comparative Drama* 13, no. 2 (Summer 1979): 121–26.

Braunmuller, Albert R. "Harold Pinter: The Metamorphosis of Memory." In *Essays on Contemporary British Drama,* edited by Hedwig Bock and Albert Wertheim, 155–70. Munich: Max Hueber Verlag, 1981.

Brown, John R. "Dialogue in Pinter and Others." *Critical Quarterly* 7 (Autumn 1965): 225–43.

————. "Mr. Pinter's Shakespeare." *Critical Quarterly* 5 (Autumn 1963): 251–65.

————. *Theatre Language.* London: Lane, 1972.

————, ed., *Modern British Dramatists.* Englewood Cliffs, N.J.: Prentice-Hall, 1968.

Bryden, Ronald. "Pinter's New Pacemaker." *The Observer* (London), June 1971.

————. "A Stink of Pinter." *New Statesman,* 11 June 1965, 928.

Burghardt, Lorraine Hall. "Game Playing in Three by Pinter." *Modern Drama* 17 (1974): 363–75.

Burkman, Katherine. *The Dramatic World of Harold Pinter: Its Basis in Ritual.* Columbus: Ohio State University Press, 1971.

Caillois, Roger. *Man, Play, and Games.* Translated by Meyer Barash. New York: Free Press of Glencoe, 1961.

Callen, A. "Comedy and Passion in the Plays of Harold Pinter." *Forum for Modern Language Studies* 4 (July 1968): 299–305.

Carpenter, "The Absurdity of Dread: Pinter's *The Dumb Waiter.*" *Modern Drama* 16 (December 1973): 279–85.

Charney, Maurice. *Comedy High and Low: An Introduction to the Experience of Comedy.* New York: Oxford University Press, 1978.

Cohn, Ruby. "The Absurdity Absurd: Avatars of Godot." *Comparative Literature Studies* 2 (1965): 233–40.

———. *Currents in Contemporary Drama.* Bloomington: Indiana University Press, 1969.

———. "Words Working Overtime: *Endgame and No Man's Land.*" *Yearbook of English Studies* 9 (1979): 181–203.

———. "The World of Harold Pinter." In *Pinter: A Collection of Essays,* ed. Arthur Ganz. Englewood Cliffs, N.J.: Prentice-Hall, 1972.

Colby, Douglas. *As the Curtain Rises: On Contemporary British Drama, 1966–1976.* Rutherford, N.J.: Fairleigh Dickinson University Press, 1978.

Cook, Albert. *The Dark Voyage and the Golden Mean.* Cambridge: Harvard University Press, 1949.

Cooper, Lane. *An Aristotelean Theory of Comedy.* Ithaca: Cornell University Press, 1935.

Cornford, F. M. *The Origin of Attic Comedy.* Edited by Theodore H. Gastner. Gloucester, Mass.: P. Smith, 1968.

Corrigan, Robert W. *Comedy: Meaning and Form.* Scranton, Penn.: Chandler Publishing, 1965.

Coward, Noel. *Blithe Spirit* in *Representative Modern Plays: British,* edited by Robert Warnock. (Glenview, Ill: Scott, Foresman, 1953), 515–603.

Cushman, L. W. *The Devil and the Vice in the English Dramatic Literature before Shakespeare.* Halle: Max Niemeyer, 1900.

Davison, Peter. "Contemporary Drama and Popular Dramatic Forms." In *Aspects of Drama and the Theatre,* 143–97. Sydney: Sydney University Press, 1965.

Dawick, John. "'Punctuation' and Patterning in *The Homecoming.*" *Modern Drama* 14 (May 1971): 37–46.

Dean, Michael. "Late Night Line-Up." *Listener,* 6 March 1969. An Interview.

Dennis, Nigel. "Pintermania." *New York Review of Books,* 17 December 1970, 21–22.

Diamond, Elin. "Parody Play in Pinter." *Modern Drama* 25, no. 4 (December 1982): 477–88.

———. "Pinter's *Betrayal* and the Comedy of Manners." *Modern Drama* 23, no. 3 (September 1980): 238–45.

Dobree, Bonamy. *Restoration Comedy.* Oxford: Oxford University Press, 1924.

Donaldson, Ian. *The World Upside Down.* Oxford: Clarendon Press, 1970.

Doran, Madelaine. *Endeavors of Art.* Madison: University of Wisconsin Press, 1964.

Dugan, Gerald Robert. *British Black Comedy: 1955–1970. Dissertation Abstracts* 38 (1978): 6404A–D4B.

Dukore, Bernard F. "The Pinter Collection." *Educational Theatre Journal* 26 (March 1974): 81–85.

———. *Where Laughter Stops: Pinter's Tragicomedy.* Columbia: University of Missouri Press, 1976.

Eastman, Max. *The Enjoyment of Laughter.* New York: Simon and Schuster, 1936.

Edmondson, Madelaine, David Rounds. *The Soaps: Daytime Serials of Radio and TV.* New York: Stein and Day, 1973.

Ehrmann, Jacques, ed. *Game, Play, Literature.* Boston: Beacon Press, 1968.

Eigo, James. "Pinter's *Landscape.*" *Modern Drama* 16 (September 1973): 179–83.

Eliot, T. S. *The Family Reunion.* London: Faber and Faber, 1939.

———. *Four Quartets.* New York: Harcourt Brace, 1943.

———. "The Love Song of J. Alfred Prufrock." In *Selected Poems.* New York: Harbrace, 1964.

English, Alan C. "A Descriptive Analysis of Harold Pinter's Use of Comic Elements in His Stage Plays." *Dissertation Abstracts* 30 (1970): 4597A–98A.

Esslin, Martin. *Pinter: A Study of His Plays.* London: Methuen, 1976.

———. "Pinter Translated. On International Non-Communication." *Encounter* 30 (March 1968): 45–47.

———. *The Theatre of the Absurd.* Rev. ed. New York: Doubleday, 1969.

Etherege, George. *The Man of Mode.* Regents Restoration Drama Series, edited by W. B. Carnochan Lincoln: University of Nebraska Press, 1966.

Feibleman, James. *In Praise of Comedy.* New York: Russell and Russell, 1962.

Freud, Sigmund. *Civilization and Its Discontents.* Translated by James Strachey. New York: W. W. Norton, 1960.

——. *Jokes and Their Relation to the Unconscious.* Translated by James Strachey. New York: W. W. Norton, 1960.

Frye, Northrop. *Anatomy of Criticism: Four Essays.* Princeton: Princeton University Press, 1957.

——. *A Natural Perspective: The Development of Shakespearean Comedy and Romance.* New York: Columbia University Press, 1965.

Fujimura, Thomas H. *The Restoration Comedy of Wit.* Princeton: Princeton University Press, 1952.

Gabbard, Lucina Paquet. *The Dream Structure of Pinter's Plays: A Psychoanalytic Approach.* Rutherford, N.J.: Fairleigh Dickinson University Press, 1976.

Gale, Steven. *butter's going up.* Durham: Duke University Press, 1977.

Ganz, Arthur. *Realms of the Self.* New York: New York University Press, 1980.

Ganz, Arthur F., ed. *Pinter: A Collection of Critical Essays.* Englewood Cliffs, N.J.: Prentice-Hall, 1972.

Gordon, Lois G. *Strategems to Uncover Nakedness.* Columbia: Univ. of Missouri Press, 1969.

Gray, Simon. *Otherwise Engaged.* In *Otherwise Engaged and Other Plays.* London: Penguin, 1975.

Grotjahn, Martin. *Beyond Laughter.* New York: McGraw-Hill, 1966.

Gurewitch, M. *Comedy: The Irrational Vision.* Ithaca: Cornell University Press, 1975.

Hayman, Ronald. *Harold Pinter.* New York: Frederick Unger, 1973.

Hirst, David L. *Comedy of Manners.* London: Methuen, 1979.

Hobson, Harold. "Unanswered Questions." *The Sunday Times* (London), 4 May 1975.

Hollis, James R. *The Poetics of Silence.* Carbondale: Southern Illinois University Press, 1970.

Hoy, Cyrus. *The Hyacinth Room.* New York: Knopf, 1964.

Huff, Theodore. *Charlie Chaplin.* London: Cassell, 1952.

Hughes, Alan. "Myth and Memory in Pinter's *Old Times.*" *Modern Drama* 17 (December 1974): 467–76.

Huizinga, Johan. *Homo Ludens.* Boston: Beacon Press, 1950.

Jones, Henry Arthur. *The Lie.* New York: George H. Doran, 1915.

Jones, John Bush. "Stasis as Structure in Pinter's *No Man's Land.*" *Modern Drama* 19 (September 1976): 291–304.

Joyce, James. *Exiles.* New York: Viking Press, 1951.

Jump, John. *Burlesque.* London: Methuen, 1972.

Kant, Emmanuel. *Critique of Aesthetic Judgment.* Translated by J. C. Meredith. Oxford: Clarendon Press, 1911.

Kaufman, Michael W. "Actions That a Man Might Play: Pinter's *The Birthday Party.*" *Modern Drama* 16 (September 1973): 167–78.

Kaul, A. N. *The Action of English Comedy.* New Haven: Yale University Press, 1970.

Kennedy, Andrew. *Dramatic Dialogue.* Cambridge: Cambridge University Press, 1983.

————. "Natural, Mannered, and Parodic Dialogue." *Yearbook of English Studies* 9 (1979): 22–54.

————. *Six Dramatists in Search of a Language.* Cambridge: Cambridge University Press, 1975.

Kern, Edith. *The Absolute Comic.* New York: Columbia University Press, 1980.

Kernan, Alan. *The Cankered Muse.* New Haven: Yale University Press, 1950.

Kerr, Walter. *Harold Pinter.* New York: Columbia University Press, 1967.

————. *Tragedy and Comedy.* New York: Simon and Schuster, 1967.

King, Noel. "Pinter's Progress." *Modern Drama* 23, no. 3 (September 1980): 246–57.

Kitchin, George. *Burlesque and Parody.* Edinburgh: Oliver and Boyd, 1931.

Kitchin, Laurence. *Drama in the Sixties.* London: Faber and Faber, 1966.

————. *Mid-Century Drama.* 2d ed. London: Faber and Faber, 1966.

Knight, G. Wilson. "The Kitchen Sink." *Encounter* 21 (December 1963): 48–54.

Knights, L. C. "Notes on Comedy." In *The Importance of Scrutiny,* edited by Eric Bentley. New York: New York University Press, 1964.

Lahr, John. *A Casebook on Harold Pinter's* The Homecoming. New York: Grove Press, 1970.

————. "The Language of Silence." *Evergreen Review* 13 (March 1969): 53–55, 82–90.

————. "Pinter the Spaceman." *Evergreen Review* 12 (June 1968): 49–52, 87–90.

Langer, Susanne. *Feeling and Form.* New York: Scribners, 1953.

Lauter, Paul. *Theories of Comedy.* Garden City, N.Y.: Anchor Books, 1964.

Lemon, Lee T., and Marion J. Reis. *Russian Formalist Criticism.* Lincoln: University of Nebraska Press, 1965.

Levin, Harry, ed. *Veins of Humor.* Cambridge: Harvard University Press, 1972.

Leyburn, Ellen D. "Comedy and Tragedy Transposed." *Yale Review* 53 (Summer 1964): 553–62.

Manvell, Roger, ed. *Three British Screenplays.* London: Methuen, 1950.

Marowitz, Charles. "'Pinterism' is Maximum Tension through Minimum Information." *New York Times,* 1 October 1967, sec. 6, 36–37, 89–90, 92, 94–96.

Martineau, Stephen. "Pinter's *Old Times:* The Memory Game." *Modern Drama* 16 (December 1973): 287–97.

Master S. *Gammer Gurton's Needle in Elizabethan and Stuart Plays.* Edited by Baskerville, Heltzel, and Nethercot. New York: Holt, Rinehart, 1934.

Maugham, Somerset. *The Constant Wife.* In *Representative Modern British Plays,* edited by Robert Warnock. Glenview, Ill.: Scott, Foresman, 1953.

McCabe, John. *The Comedy of Stan Laurel.* New York: Doubleday, 1974.

McCall, Dorothy. *The Theatre of Jean-Paul Sartre.* New York: Columbia University Press, 1969.

McCollom, William C. *The Divine Average: A View of Comedy.* Cleveland: Case Western Reserve University Press, 1971.

McFadden, George. *Discovering the Comic.* Princeton: Princeton University Press, 1982.

Merchant, M. *Comedy.* London: Methuen, 1972.

Meredith, George. "An Essay on Comedy." In *Comedy.* Edited by Wylie Sypher. New York: Doubleday, 1956.

Moore, John B. *The Comic and the Realistic in English Drama.* Chicago: University of Chicago Press, 1925.

Morrison, Kristin. *Canters and Chronicles.* Chicago: University of Chicago Press, 1983.

———. "Pinter and the New Irony." *Quarterly Journal of Speech* 55 (December 1969): 388–93.

Muecke, Douglas C. *The Compass of Irony.* London: Methuen, 1969.

Muir, Kenneth. *The Comedy of Manners.* London: Hutchinson University Library, 1970.

Munro, D. *Argument of Laughter.* Melbourne: Melbourne University Press, 1951.

Nicoll, Allardyce. *English Drama: A Modern Viewpoint.* New York: Barnes and Noble, 1968.

———. *Theatre and Dramatic Theory.* New York: Barnes and Noble, 1962.

Olson, Elder. *Theory and Comedy.* Bloomington: Indiana University Press, 1968.

Palmer, John L. *Comedy.* London: M. Secker, 1914.

Parrott, Reverend Bob W. *Ontology of Humor.* New York: Philosophical Library, 1982.

Pedersen, Bertel. *The Theory and Practice of Parody in the Modern Novel: Mann, Joyce, and Nabokov.* Ann Arbor: Xerox University Microfilms, 1975.

Pinero, Arthur Wing. *The Second Mrs. Tanqueray.* In *Sixteen Famous British Plays,* edited by Bennett Cerf and Van H. Cartmell. New York: Modern Library, 1942.

Potter, Robert. *The English Morality Play.* London: Routledge, 1975.

Potts, L. J. *Comedy.* New York: Hutchinson University Library, 1948.

Quigley, Austin. *The Pinter Problem.* Princeton: Princeton University Press, 1975.

Robinson, David. "Coronation Street." *New Statesman,* 25 February 1965.

Robinson, Fred Miller. *The Comedy of Language.* Amherst: University of Masachusetts Press, 1980.

Rodway, Alan. *English Comedy, Its Role and Nature from Chaucer to the Present Day.* Berkeley and Los Angeles: University of California Press, 1975.

Rose, Margaret A. *Parody/Meta-Fiction.* London: Croom Helm, 1979.

Rossiter, A. P. *English Drama from Early Times to the Elizabethans.* New York: Barnes and Noble, 1950.

Sartre, Jean-Paul. *Being and Nothingness.* Translated by Hazel E. Barnes. New York: Pocket Books, 1956.

Shaffer, Peter. *Five Finger Exercise.* New York: Harcourt Brace, 1958.

Smith, Leslie. "Pinter the Player." *Modern Drama* 22, no. 4 (December 1979): 349–63.

Smith, Willard. *The Nature of Comedy.* Folcroft, Pa.: Folcroft Press, 1930.

Sontag, Susan. *Against Interpretation.* New York: Dell, 1966.

Sorell, Walter. *Facets of Comedy.* New York: Grosset and Dunlap, 1972.

Spivack, Bernard. *Shakespeare and the Allegory of Evil.* New York: Columbia University Press, 1958.

States, Bert O. *Irony and Drama.* Ithaca: Cornell University Press, 1971.

———. "Pinter's *Homecoming:* The Shock of Nonrecognition." *Hudson Review* 21 (Autumn 1968): 474–86.

Stevenson, David Lloyd. *The Love-Game Comedy.* New York: Columbia University Press, 1946.

Storch, R. F. "Harold Pinter's Happy Families." *Massachusetts Review* 8 (Autumn 1967): 703–12.

Styan, J. L. *The Dark Comedy.* Cambridge: Cambridge University Press, 1968.

Sykes, Alrene. *Harold Pinter.* St. Lucia: Queensland University Press, 1970.

Sypher, Wylie, ed. *Comedy.* New York: Doubleday, 1956.

Taylor, John Russell. *Anger and After.* London: Methuen, 1962.

———. *The Rise and Fall of the Well-Made Play.* New York: Hill and Wang, 1967.

Thompson, Alan R. *The Dry Mock.* Berkeley and Los Angeles: University of California Press, 1948.

Towson, John. *Clowns.* New York: Hawthorn, 1976.

Trussler, Simon. *The Plays of Harold Pinter.* London: Victor Gollancz, 1973.

Tynan, Kenneth. *Curtains,* New York, 1961.

Vanbrugh, John. *The Provoked Wife.* Restoration Drama Series, edited by Curt A. Zimansky. Lincoln: University of Nebraska Press, 1969.

Van Laan, Thomas F. "*The Dumb Waiter* and Pinter's Play with the Audience." *Modern Drama* 24 (December 1981): 494–502.

Vannier, Jean. "Theatre of Language." *Tulane Drama Review* 7, no. 3 (Spring 1963), 180–186.

Vosper, Frank. *Love from a Stranger.* New York: Samuel French, 1936.

Walker, Augusta. "Messages from Pinter." *Modern Drama* 10 (May 1967): 1–10.

Wardle, Irving. "Comedy of Menace." *Encore* 5 (September–October 1958): 28–33.

———, "Old Times." *The Times* (London), 3 June 1971.

———. ed. *The Enclore Reader.* London: Methuen, 1965.

Wellwarth, George E. *The Theatre of Protest and Paradox.* New York: New York University Press, 1964.

Welsford, Enid. *The Fool.* Gloucester, Mass.: P. Smith, 1966.

Wilde, Oscar. *The Importance of Being Ernest.* New York: Doubleday, 1958.

Williams, Raymond. *Drama from Ibsen to Brecht.* London: Chatto and Windus, 1968.

Wray, P. "Pinter's Dialogue: The Play on Words." *Modern Drama* 13 (February 1971): 418–22.

Wycherley, William. *The Country Wife.* Restoration Drama Series, edited by Thomas Fujimura. Lincoln: University of Nebraska Press, 1965.

Index

239